Lady Mary Shepherd

Selected Writings

Edited and introduced
by Deborah Boyle

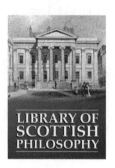

LIBRARY OF
SCOTTISH
PHILOSOPHY

IMPRINT ACADEMIC

Published in the UK by Imprint Academic
PO Box 200, Exeter EX5 5YX, UK

Distributed in the USA by
Ingram Book Company,
One Ingram Blvd., La Vergne, TN 37086, USA

ISBN 9781845409890

A CIP catalogue record for this book is available from the
British Library and US Library of Congress

Full series details:

www.imprint-academic.com/losp

Contents

Contents

Series Editor's Note

The principal purpose of volumes in the *Library of Scottish Philosophy* is not to provide scholars with accurate editions, but to make the writings of Scottish philosophers accessible to a new generation of modern readers in an attractively produced and competitively priced format. In accordance with this purpose, certain changes have been made to the original texts:

- Spelling and punctuation have been modernized.
- In some cases the selections have been given new titles.
- Some original footnotes and references have not been included.
- Some extracts have been shortened from their original length.
- Quotations from Greek have been transliterated, and passages in languages other than English translated, or omitted altogether.

This is the nineteenth volume in the series. It is importantly different from others for three reasons. First, Lady Mary Shepherd is the only woman philosopher represented in the *Library of Scottish Philosophy*, and as a woman, a rarity in the history of philosophy quite generally. Secondly, unlike all the other philosophers in the series, whose writings are well known and available in scholarly editions, this selection makes the writings it contains effectively available for the first time. Thirdly, the selection reveals a distinctively novel voice in the Scottish philosophical tradition. Shepherd truly is a discovery.

Her discovery is owed to the enthusiasm and industry of Deborah Boyle. Without Boyle's valuable work, it seems likely that Shepherd's contributions to Scottish philosophy would have continued to lie neglected. One hope for this volume as the last in the series is that the *Library of Scottish Philosophy* has opened up a completely new area for research and study.

Gordon Graham,
Princeton, June 2018

Deborah Boyle

Introduction

1. Lady Mary Shepherd's Life and Works

Lady Mary Shepherd's writings reveal an astute and lively intellect. Her two philosophical treatises engage with the views of Hume, Berkeley, Reid, Stewart, and others, but they also present an original and carefully argued philosophical system of her own. Unfortunately, her work faded into obscurity after her death, although she seems to have been highly regarded in her day. According to a memoir written by Shepherd's daughter Mary Elizabeth Shepherd Brandreth, geologist Charles Lyell called Shepherd an 'unanswerable logician, in whose argument it was impossible to find loophole or flaw', and William Whewell used one of her books as a textbook at Cambridge.[1] Shepherd's work is discussed and praised in Robert Blakey's nineteenth-century history of philosophy,[2] and Blakey recalled being greatly impressed, when he met her, by the 'subtility of her mind'.[3] This collection of selections from Shepherd's writings is intended to bring her work back into focus for students and scholars.

Mary Shepherd, née Primrose, was born at Barnbougle Castle, outside Edinburgh, in 1777. She was the second of six children of Mary Vincent and Neil Primrose, 3rd Earl of

[1] Mary Elizabeth Shepherd Brandreth, *Some Family and Friendly Recollections of Seventy Years* (Westerham: C. Hooker, 1886), p. 29.
[2] Robert Blakey, *History of the Philosophy of the Mind*, Vol. 4 (London: Saunders, 1848), p. 40.
[3] Robert Blakey, *Memoirs of Dr. Robert Blakey*, ed. Rev. Henry Miller (London: Trübner & Co., 1879), p. 159.

Rosebery;[4] she and her sisters were educated by a tutor at home, learning Latin, geography, mathematics, and history.[5] Her religious upbringing was most likely Presbyterian, for Brandreth reports that the Primroses' tutor taught them Presbyterian doctrine, and historian Jennifer McRobert notes that Mary's father, as a Scottish nobleman, would have been expected to support the local Presbyterian parish.[6] The family also spent time in London; it was probably there that Mary met barrister Henry John Shepherd, whom she married in 1808 at the relatively late age of 30. They had three children. According to Brandreth, her parents 'gathered in those days both the scientific and the literary sides of the learned world, into easy and intimate intercourse', with their social circle including Lyell, Whewell, Charles Babbage, Mary Somerville, Sydney Smith, Thomas Malthus, and David Ricardo.[7] Shepherd was also an acquaintance of Samuel Taylor Coleridge, who in 1833 wrote two draft poems about her, although they were not complimentary; in one, he describes her as 'a desperate Scholar, / Like the Heavens, DEEP BLUE',[8] linking her with the intellectual women of the Enlightenment who were pejoratively called 'Bluestockings'.

Brandreth mentions that her mother wrote 'metaphysical disquisitions' about Hume and Priestley before she was married.[9] Margaret Atherton suggests that these writings are Shepherd's 1824 *Essay Upon the Relation of Cause and Effect* and

---

4   The *Oxford Dictionary of National Biography* lists Shepherd as the second of five children, but Jennifer McRobert notes that the Primroses had a sixth child who died in infancy. See Mary Anne Perkins, 'Shepherd (née Primrose), Lady Mary (1777–1847), philosopher', *Oxford Dictionary of National Biography* (2004), www.oxforddnb.com; Jennifer McRobert, 'Mary Shepherd and the Causal Relation' (2002; rev. 2014), p. 9, http://philpapers.org/rec/MCRMSA.

5   Brandreth, p. 26.

6   McRobert, p. 23.

7   Brandreth, pp. 41–2.

8   Kathleen Coburn and Anthony John Harding, eds., *The Notebooks of Samuel Taylor Coleridge, Vol. 5: 1827–1834, Part 2* (Princeton: Princeton University Press, 2002), 6828 Q.72.

9   Brandreth, pp. 28–9.

1827 *Essays on the Perception of an External Universe.*[10] Intriguingly, however, Shepherd's daughter contrasts the 'manuscript metaphysical essays' with the books, which she says 'were written some years later'.[11] Indeed, while the 1824 book does engage with Hume, the 1827 book has only a foot-note referring to Priestley, suggesting that there might have been a separate, earlier essay that engaged more extensively with Priestley. If so, however, it is as yet unknown.[12]

Shepherd's 1824 book, *An Essay Upon the Relation of Cause and Effect,* argues that causal principles can be known by reason to be necessary truths. In particular, she argues that we can know through reason alone both that nothing can come to exist without a cause other than itself (which I will refer to as the Causal Principle) and that like causes necessarily have like effects (the Causal Likeness Principle). Her primary target in this book is Hume, although she also addresses the views of Thomas Brown, who had written about Hume's causal theory in his 1805, 1806, and 1818 essays on causation, and William Lawrence, who had quoted extensively from Brown in his 1819 *Lectures on Physiology, Zoology, and the Natural History of Man.*

---

[10] Margaret Atherton, 'Shepherd, Mary (née Primrose: 1777-1847)', in *The Continuum Encyclopedia of British Philosophy,* Vol. 4, ed. A.C. Grayling, Naomi Goulder, and Andrew Pyle (Bristol: Thoemmes Continuum, 2006), pp. 2901–03.

[11] Brandreth, p. 29.

[12] Jennifer McRobert notes that the *Dictionary of National Biography* and a typewritten insert in Cambridge University's copy of Shepherd's 1827 book hint that Shepherd also wrote the 1819 *Enquiry respecting the Relation of Cause and Effect: in which the Theories of Professors Brown, and Mr. Hume, are Examined; with a Statement of Such Observations as are Calculated to Shew the Inconsistency of these Theories; and from which a New Theory is Deduced, More Consonant to Facts and Experience. Also a New Theory of the Earth, Deduced from Geological Observations* (Edinburgh: James Ballantyne, 1819) (Jennifer McRobert, 'Introduction', *Philosophical Works of Lady Mary Shepherd,* Vol. 1 [Bristol: Thoemmes Press, 2000], pp. vii-viii). However, Shepherd never refers to such a book, while in her 1827 book she does frequently refer in footnotes to her 1824 book. Nor do her other works evince any interest in geology. Atherton's view is that 'in the absence of strong external evidence to the contrary, it seems best not to accept this attribution to Shepherd' (Atherton, p. 2902), and I concur.

As is clear from the title of her 1827 book, *Essays on the Perception of an External Universe, and Other Subjects Connected with the Doctrine of Causation*, Shepherd considered it to be an extension of the earlier project on causation. Taking the 1824 essay to have established both the Causal Principle and the Causal Likeness Principle, she appeals to those principles in the first, long essay (comprising nearly half the book) to argue that we can know through reason that an external world of con- tinually-existing objects must exist independently of us, as the causes of our sensations. Along the way, she raises objections to Thomas Reid's account of primary and secondary qualities, Berkeley's use of the word 'idea' and his comments on dreams, and Hume's appeal to 'vivacity', but these are incidental remarks; her real goal is to argue for her own account of how we know that there is an external world. Her footnotes in this essay draw further connections between her views and those of Berkeley, Hume, and Reid, as well as of Dugald Stewart, Locke, Kant, James Mill, Joseph Priestley, and the French philosophers Étienne Bonnot de Condillac, Antoine Destutt de Tracy, and Joseph Marie de Gérando.

Along with the long essay on our knowledge of an external world, *Essays on the Perception of an External Universe* includes fourteen shorter essays, most of which take up and expand on issues mentioned only briefly in the longer essay and in the book on causation. She examines Berkeley's idealism; criticizes Stewart and Reid on their accounts of the perception of colour and extension; discusses the role of sense organs in her account of our perception of the external world; explains how her theory distinguishes between veridical perceptions and non- veridical perceptions such as dreams; elaborates on a compari- son she made in the 1824 book between reasoning about the course of nature and mathematical reasoning; discusses the nature of mind and mind–body interaction; and addresses issues of religion, including our knowledge of God, the reasonableness of belief in reports of miracles, and the preserva- tion of personal identity in the afterlife. In the final essay, she addresses some puzzles about vision.

A year after publishing *Essays on the Perception of an External Universe, and Other Subjects Connected with the Doctrine of Causation*, Shepherd returned to the issue of vision, publishing a longer piece, 'On the Causes of Single and Erect Vision', in the scientific journal *The Philosophical Magazine and Annals of Philosophy;* this essay was reprinted the following month in two consecutive issues of the popular English weekly magazine *The Kaleidoscope; or, Literary and Scientific Mirror*. 1828 also saw the publication of Shepherd's short essay on the writings of retired naval officer and amateur philosopher John Fearn, along with his much longer (and quite condescending) reply. Shepherd did not let Fearn have the last word; in 1832 she published her essay 'Lady Mary Shepherd's Metaphysics', in which she replied to Fearn's reply. She also indicated there that she had not written her original essay on Fearn for publication, noting that she was 'much surprised' to see the exchange with Fearn in print, and that her surprise 'was accompanied by some little anxiety, from the recollection of the haste and incorrectness with which I had written a paper, really not intended for the public eye'.[13] She undertakes in her 'Metaphysics' to show that Fearn's remarks were 'unphilosophical' and 'inconsistent with each other' (LMSM 697), and, in doing so, provides a clear and concise summary of her own views on extension, sensation, ideas, and causation. Shepherd published nothing more after 1832, and died in 1847 in London.

2. Causation

Shepherd's writings engage with the views of an impressive range of thinkers, but one of her primary targets is David Hume and his account of causation in terms of constant conjunctions of events and habitual inferences. In her 1824 *Essay Upon the Relation of Cause and Effect*, Shepherd argues that causal principles can be known by reason to be necessary truths. While Hume had first presented his account of causation some eighty years before Shepherd's essay, it was still the subject of considerable discussion. In her Preface (not included in this volume), Shepherd alludes to the 'Leslie affair', a controversy from 1805 in which Sir John Leslie had nearly lost an appointment to the Chair of Mathematics at Edinburgh University because of his endorsement of Hume's causal theory. Leslie's

---

13 Mary Shepherd, 'Lady Mary Shepherd's Metaphysics', *Fraser's Magazine for Town and Country* 5, no. 30 (1832), p. 697. Hereafter cited as LMSM, followed by original page number and page reference for this volume.

1804 *An Experimental Inquiry into the Nature and Propagation of Heat* was, as the title suggests, an account of various experiments Leslie had conducted to investigate how heat and cold are absorbed and transmitted, and thus to develop a theory of what heat and cold are; his appointment to the university was challenged not because of his views on heat, but because of a footnote in which he praised Hume's discussion of necessary connection in the *Enquiry Concerning Human Understanding*.[14] The debate over how to interpret Hume's account of causation played out in the Edinburgh newspapers and led to several publications on the topic, including Dugald Stewart's defence of Leslie[15] and Thomas Brown's 1805 pamphlet, *Observations on the Nature and Tendency of the Doctrine of Mr. Hume, Concerning the Relation of Cause and Effect*, which was published in expanded versions in 1806 and 1818.[16] Humean causation was very much a live topic when Shepherd stepped into the debate in 1824.

Shepherd devotes the opening chapter (omitted in this volume) to quoting passages from Hume's *Treatise on Human Nature* and *Enquiry Concerning Human Understanding* pertaining to three claims for which Hume argues: first, that we cannot prove that causes and effects are necessarily connected; second, that our causal inferences are due to custom rather than reason; and, third, that causation should be understood in terms of constant conjunctions and causal inferences. Shepherd then devotes the second chapter to arguing against what she takes to be Hume's positions, and to establishing her own accounts of causation and causal inference.

---

[14]   For discussion of the broader implications of the Leslie affair, see Charles Bradford Bow, 'In Defence of the Scottish Enlightenment: Dugald Stewart's Role in the 1805 John Leslie Affair', *The Scottish Historical Review* 92, 1, no. 233 (April 2013), pp. 123–46.

[15]   Dugald Stewart, *A Short Statement of some Important Facts, relative to the late election of a mathematical professor in the University of Edinburgh* (Edinburgh, 1805).

[16]   Thomas Brown, *Observations on the Nature and Tendency of the Doctrine of Mr. Hume, Concerning the Relation of Cause and Effect* (Edinburgh: Mundell and Son, 1805 and 1806); Thomas Brown, *Inquiry into the Relation of Cause and Effect* (Edinburgh: Archibald Constable, 1818).

every effect has a cause

Shepherd reads Hume's claim that it is 'neither intuitively nor demonstrably certain' that *'whatever begins to exist, must have a cause of existence'*[17] as entailing the claim that 'beings can begin their existences themselves'. It is to that claim that Shepherd directs her arguments in the second chapter, arguing that it can be demonstratively proven that nothing can bring itself into existence; it is therefore *'Reason,* and not *Custom,* which guides our minds in forming the notions of necessary connexion, of belief and of expectation.'[18] She holds that the causal principle (CP) *'that no idea, or quality, can* BEGIN *its* own existence' is the 'primeval truth' that is the 'key to every difficulty that concerns the sources of our belief or knowledge'.[19] Suppose, she says, that some object *can* come into existence without a cause. This object which allegedly has no cause itself 'START[S] FORTH into existence, and make[s] the first breach on the wide non-entity around' (ERCE 35; 33). This 'starting forth', or coming into existence, is an *action,* and an action is a *quality* of an object; but the object that supposedly has the quality of coming into existence cannot have that quality until *after* it has come into existence (EPEU 290; 216–17). Thus to deny the Causal Principle requires asserting both that an object does not exist and that it does exist; so, she says, 'we must conclude *that there is no object which begins to exist, but must owe its existence to some cause'* (ERCE 36; 33).

Shepherd deploys CP to argue, against Hume, that we can rationally prove the Causal Likeness Principle (CLP) that like causes must necessarily have like effects. We know CLP

---

[17] David Hume, *A Treatise of Human Nature,* ed. David Fate Norton and Mary J. Norton (Oxford: Oxford University Press, 2000), 1.3.3.1–2 (p. 56).

[18] Mary Shepherd, *An Essay upon the Relation of Cause and Effect, controverting the Doctrine of Mr. Hume, concerning the Nature of that Relation; with Observations upon the Opinions of Dr. Brown and Mr. Lawrence, connected with the same subject* (London: Printed for T. Hookham, 1824), p. 42; see pp. 36 in this volume. Hereafter cited as ERCE, with original page numbers followed by page references to this volume.

[19] Mary Shepherd, *Essays on the Perception of an External Universe, and Other Subjects Connected with the Doctrine of Causation* (London: John Hatchard and Son, 1827), p. 138n; see p. 150 n53 in this volume. Hereafter cited as EPEU, with original page numbers followed by page references to this volume.

through what she calls 'reasoning upon experiment' (ERCE 45; 37). Imagine a scenario in which all circumstances over a short period of time remain unchanged, except for one event; for example, imagine that in an otherwise unchanged room over the course of a minute, an observer puts a piece of wood into a fire, whereupon the wood turns to ash. An observer who knows CP thereby knows that the burning of the wood — which Shepherd would call a 'new quality', or a 'difference' — cannot have arisen without a cause. And since (by hypothesis) all circumstances remained the same other than the piece of wood being put into the fire, the observer can infer that putting the wood in the fire *necessarily caused* it to burn. In knowing that there is a necessary connection between the two events, the observer can *know* that every subsequent relevantly similar case of putting wood into fire will have the same effect (ERCE 47–9 and 70–71; 38–9 and 49).

If causes and effects are necessarily connected, then, Shepherd argues, they are never really separable. Thus, contrary to what Hume had maintained, Shepherd holds that an event being antecedent to another is irrelevant to whether or not it is a cause of that event (ERCE 49 and 67; 39 and 47). In fact, as Martha Brandt Bolton points out, Shepherd's view is that an event that precedes another in time *cannot* be a proximate cause of the second. Suppose Y normally follows X. Since X and the appearance of Y are (to use Bolton's terms) 'temporally discrete', it is possible for there to be a case where X occurs, but where something else intervenes before Y occurs, thereby preventing Y from occurring. In this case, there is no necessary connection between X and Y. And, if there is no necessary connection, then X cannot be the cause of Y.[20] Thus, according to Shepherd, effects do not *follow* their causes; causes and effects are synchronous, and it is misleading to express a causal relationship between A and B as 'A followed by B'. We should say, rather, that 'A x B = C', where that means that when two items A and B 'mix' or conjoin, item C arises (ERCE 141; 78).

[20]   Martha Bolton, 'Causality and Causal Induction: The Necessitarian Theory of Lady Mary Shepherd', in *Causation and Modern Philosophy*, ed. Keith Allen and Tom Stoneham (New York: Routledge, 2011), p. 244.

This volume contains (as **Selection A**) most of Shepherd's *Essay on the Relation of Cause and Effect*. I have omitted the Advertisement, the Preface, and the 'Introductory Chapter'. The brief Advertisement is Shepherd's self-deprecating assessment of the book as 'little more than marginal observations' on the works of Hume, Thomas Brown, and William Lawrence. The Preface merely gives a brief overview of Shepherd's project, while the Introductory Chapter consists mainly of quotations from Hume's *Treatise* and *Enquiry Concerning Human Understanding* regarding his doctrine of causation. I have also omitted certain sections of the fourth, fifth, and sixth chapters where Shepherd focuses more on rebutting particular claims by Thomas Brown and William Lawrence regarding causation than on elucidating her own views.

This section also includes (as **Selection B**) selections from Essays 6 and 7 from *Essays on the Perception of an External Universe*. In Essay 6, Shepherd applies her account of causation to her account of the relationship between mind and the external world; in Essay 7, she argues that we understand the Causal Principle and the Causal Likeness Principle due to 'latent reasoning', in opposition to philosophers like Thomas Reid and Thomas Brown, who thought that causal principles are among the 'first principles' of human thought[21] or 'intuitive beliefs'.[22]

---

[21] Reid writes that it is a 'first principle' '[t]hat whatever begins to exist, must have a cause which produced it' (Thomas Reid, *Essays on the Intellectual Powers of Man: A Critical Edition*, ed. Derek R. Brookes [University Park: Pennsylvania State University Press, 2002], 1.2 [p. 45] and 6.6 [p. 497]. Hereafter cited as *Essays*, followed by essay and chapter numbers, with page numbers). Regarding CLP, he says it is among the 'first principles of natural philosophy' that 'similar effects proceed from the same or similar causes' (*Essays* 1.2 [p. 40]). Humans in general have a 'natural, original, and unaccountable propensity to believe, that the connections which we have observed in time past, will continue in time to come' (Thomas Reid, *An Inquiry Into the Human Mind on the Principles of Common Sense*, ed. Derek R. Brookes [University Park: Pennsylvania State University Press, 1997], 2.9 [p. 41]. Hereafter cited as *Inquiry*, followed by chapter and section numbers, with page numbers).

[22] Brown, *Inquiry*, p. 246.

3. Knowledge of an External World

The first, long essay of Shepherd's 1827 book, *Essays on the Perception of an External Universe,* argues that we can know by reason that an external universe exists independently of us. Skeptical concerns about our knowledge of an external world have a long history, but Shepherd was concerned in particular with Hume's claim that our belief in an external world is a 'fiction' created by the imagination (EPEU 1–2; 96); with Thomas Reid's suggestion that external-world skepticism can be rejected because we have a 'natural instinct' to believe that such a world exists (EPEU 5); and with Berkeley's thesis that *'nothing material could exist unfelt'* (EPEU 25; 105).

While the book's title speaks of our 'perception' of an external universe, Shepherd actually prefers the word 'sensation' to 'perception'. Every conscious mental state is, for Shepherd, a sensation: 'in reality, every thought, notion, idea, feeling, and perception, which distinguishes a sentient nature from unconscious existence, may be considered generally as sensation' (EPEU 7; 98). To call a thought a 'sensation', then, does not indicate that sense organs were used in its production; even conclusions that we reach through reason are a variety of sensation. Reason is 'the *observation of the relation of our simple sensations'* (EPEU 19; 103). Thus whenever a thinker compares sensations, draws inferences from sensations, or otherwise relates sensations together, the thinker is using reason—but the thoughts that result from such processes are themselves a variety of sensation.

Shepherd's argument for the existence of an external world occurs in three steps. First she argues that we can know by reason that something *continuous* must exist, in contrast to our interrupted sensations; then she argues that these continuous objects can be known to be *external to,* and not part of, the sensing mind; and finally she argues that these external continuous objects must be *independent of* the existence of the sensing mind. Shepherd maintains that knowledge that external objects exist is achieved through 'latent reasoning silently generated in the minds of all men, from infancy' (EPEU 14; 101). 'Children, peasants, and brutes' implicitly grasp the conclusions of such reasoning even though they 'cannot analyse them' and do not 'argue formally on the subject' (EPEU 171 and 315–16; 159 and 87).

According to Shepherd, then, the external world exists continuously, independently of and external to our sensations and mind; it is a partial cause of our sensations when it 'mixes' or 'coalesces' with our sense organs and the mind. Nonetheless, Shepherd holds that our sensations do not *copy* features of the external world. Since a sensation is the effect of some external object 'mixing' with the sense organs and mind, the sensation is a *new* quality arising from this mixture, a quality that did not exist before the mixture. If the sensation were *just like* the external object that is one of its causes, then the interaction of the external object with the sense organs and mind would not result in any *new* modification (EPEU 184–5; 165). Indeed, she says that 'the doctrine that the ideas of things resemble the qualities of their causes' has absurd consequences: a sensory perception of wind would itself be a 'windy idea' and a sensory perception of 'the rough ear of a lap-dog, would itself be the rough ear of a lap-dog' (LMSM 698; 201). However, while sensations are not copies of the external objects that cause them, Shepherd holds that they do indicate to us certain features of external objects: we can infer that the *relations* among external objects are the same as the correlative relationships among our sensations of them. That is,

> [t]he perceived qualities are as a *landscape*, sent from an unseen country by which we may know it; as *algebraic signs*, by which we can compute and know the proportions of their qualities; as a *language,* which must be translated, before it can explain the actions of nature. (EPEU 261; 196)

In her essay 'Lady Mary Shepherd's Metaphysics', Shepherd elaborates on the relationship between our sensations and the external causes of those sensations and ingeniously develops the analogy with algebra. She suggests we can represent the external causes of our ideas by algebraic variables, and the ideas themselves by the squares of those variables. For example, the external cause of a sensation of a colour could be represented with the variable c, while the sensation of the colour would be represented as c^2 (LMSM 703; 206–7). This analogy captures two key features of Shepherd's views: first, that there are relationships between external objects and our ideas;

second, that the essence of an external object is entirely different from the essence of the sensation it causes, just as 9 is an entirely different number from its square root, 3.

The section 'Knowledge of an External World' contains nearly the complete text of Shepherd's first, long essay from *Essays on the Perception of an External Universe* (**Selection C**); Essays 1–4 from the second part of *Essays on the Perception of an External Universe* (**Selection D**); and passages from 'Lady Mary Shepherd's Metaphysics' where she elucidates her own philosophical theory, with her criticisms of specific claims by John Fearn and Dugald Stewart omitted (**Selection E**).

4. Mathematical and Physical Induction

Shepherd holds that we know the Causal Principle (CP) and the Causal Likeness Principle (CLP) through reason, although she does not characterize this knowledge as *a priori* or innate, perhaps because she holds that some sensations are needed in order to know CP and CLP. In theory, she thinks, even just two sensations would be enough for a thinker to come to know CP and CLP, for the thinker would realize that for a change to occur, for the second sensation to come into existence, it must have some cause. This is because (by Shepherd's reasoning, discussed above in 'Causation') it would violate the principle of non-contradiction for a sensation to possess the quality of coming-into-existence without already existing in order to perform that action. This is why Shepherd holds that even 'fetal consciousness' (EPEU 379; 245) is sufficient to provide the materials for knowing CP. The succession of sensations had by a fetus

> would be observed as a change of that being which was already in existence: — the action of *beginning* any existence would therefore appear as a quality of *self*, or the *accident* of a continuing existence; and it would be a manifest contradiction, to predicate of such a quality its self-existence. Thus, *to begin of itself*, would appear to every child under the faintest and most indistinct form of latent conception, to be a contradiction. (EPEU xiii; 94)

Although Shepherd does not say so, she seems to be assuming that knowledge of the principle of non-contradiction is in some sense even more fundamental than knowledge of CP. A fetus could know CP if it were able to reason explicitly on its succession of sensations, and could explicitly perceive the truth of the principle of non-contradiction. Until such explicit knowledge occurs, Shepherd maintains that the knowledge is 'latent'.

Other knowledge that Shepherd maintains can be known through the rational consideration of relationships inherent in our thoughts are the Causal Likeness Principle (CLP), the existence of the external world, and (if we reason using the first of the two approaches described in section 5, below) the existence of God. The arguments establishing these truths are what Shepherd, following Locke and Hume, calls 'demonstrations'; their conclusions are necessarily true and thus absolutely certain.

But Shepherd does not downplay the importance of empirical observation in her account of knowledge. Our knowledge that some *particular* cause will produce some particular effect is acquired by a method Shepherd calls 'experimental reasoning', which requires both observation and demonstration (ERCE 108; 66). That is, once we have observed some event in nature, and once we know with demonstrative certainty that if the same cause recurs in identical circumstances, then the same effect will occur, then we can know that that same particular cause will have the same particular effect in the future. But learning about how causes and effects operate in the real world requires careful, close, empirical observations. The difficulty is in being sure that the circumstances facing us at a given moment are exactly the same as some past situation, since our powers of observation are finite. We cannot know with complete certainty that a loaf of bread (one of Shepherd's examples, itself drawn from Hume's second *Enquiry*) that looks identical to one eaten previously really is qualitatively identical. Shepherd argues that we judge whether two items are similar (and thus will have similar effects) by judging whether they themselves were caused in similar ways. Thus, we need to consider whether the loaf of bread now before us came from the same bakery as the one we ate previously, whether the same ingredients were used in their formation, whether the temperature at which they were baked was the same, and so on. 'Nevertheless,' Shepherd writes, 'the proposition founded on these trials, is but a probability, although a high one' (ERCE 119; 70); that is, our causal inferences about particular items and events fall short of 'demonstration', because our powers of observation are limited. In the ideal case, if we really could know that an item before us is identical to one we have previously considered, then we could know with demonstrative certainty that its effects will be the same as those of the already-experienced item.

So, as Shepherd makes clear in **Selection F**, induction in the ideal case is analogous to mathematical knowledge. But while philosophers such as Descartes held that the epitome of demonstrative knowledge is mathematical knowledge—so that we should aspire to produce metaphysical proofs with conclusions as certain as those as of geometry—Shepherd sees causal reasoning as the model for mathematical knowledge. She writes:

> the science of mathematics is truly but one branch of physics: for that all the conclusions its method of induction demonstrates, depend for their truth upon the implied proposition, 'That like cause must have like effect'; a proposition which being the only foundation for the truths of physical science, and which gives validity to the result of any experiment whatever, ranks mathematics as a *species* under the same *genus*. (EPEU 278–9; 213)

Just as geometrical relationships can be established by reasoning based on diagrams (EPEU 285; 214), causal relationships can (at least in theory, if not always in actual practice) be established by one 'experimentum crucis'.

Indeed, Shepherd says we should think of a mixture of causes as already containing their effect: 'C [the effect] *is* INCLUDED *in the* MIXTURE OF THE OBJECTS called CAUSE' (ERCE 141; 78). Shepherd means us to take seriously the suggestion that a causal relationship can be represented by an *equation*, as 'A x B = C'. A and B are, literally, factors, entities that produce something else when multiplied together, and the very combining of those factors *is* the effect, just as 'the results of all arithmetical combinations are *included* in their statements' (ERCE 142; 79).

5. Religion

Shepherd stresses that the underlying motivation for her philosophical project is religious. Hume's doctrines on causation, she writes, 'lead directly to a scepticism of an atheistical tendency' (ERCE 4). She pursues the implications of her philosophical system for two theological issues: whether or not we have good reason to believe in reported miracles, and the basis of belief in God.

Shepherd considers belief in miracles in Essay 8 of *Essays Upon the Perception of an External World* (**Selection G**). Shepherd's target, unsurprisingly, is Hume, whose argument in *Enquiry* 10 that it is unreasonable to believe others' testimony regarding alleged miracles had already been subjected to various critiques.[23] On some points she agrees with Hume; she agrees that we should trust the testimony of others 'in all cases where we cannot distinctly perceive any motive to falsehood; and in like manner that we proportion our jealousy of the truth of their assertions, according as we may suppose them influenced by any circumstance of self-interest', and she agrees that we should look carefully for self-interested motives when people report *'marvellous events'* (EPEU 328; 220). As she writes, quite consistently with Hume's views,

> the testimony of those who assert miracles to have taken place
> in order to establish some favourite dogma of their own, with-
> out the sacrifice of any interest in consequence, is liable to the
> strongest suspicion of being the result of self-interest and fraud.
> (EPEU 339–40; 223–4)

Indeed, the best evidence that people are telling the truth in giving such reports is that they would actually have something to *fear* from doing so (EPEU 337; 222–3).

What, then, are her objections to Hume? Her most fundamental objection is that Hume incorrectly defines miracles as 'violations of the laws of nature' (EPEU 329; 220). Her critique is based in her theory of causation: it is a necessary truth that similar causes result in similar effects, and, because this is necessarily true, it is impossible for it to be violated (EPEU 334–

---

[23]   For texts from 1749 to 1883 that engage with Hume's account of miracles, see James Fieser, 'A Bibliography of Hume's Writings and Early Responses' (Thoemmes Press, 2003), http://www.rrbltd.co.uk/bibliographies.php.

5). Not even God can make a cause that is truly exactly identical to another cause result in different effects:

> for nature otherwise to change, and to vary either her '*Effects*', or '*Secret powers*', without varying the causes or prevening circumstances whose junction formed the objects, whence these result;—is so obviously impossible, that we cannot even suppose the will and power of the Deity to be able to work the *contradiction*. (ERCE 72; 50)

What have appeared to some people to be violations of the laws of nature must actually have involved causes that, unknown to them because of their limited powers of observation, were *not* exactly similar to causes they had previously experienced. Instead of asserting that a violation of the laws of nature has occurred, they should only have asserted that an 'exception to the *apparent* course of nature' has occurred (EPEU 332; 221). And *those* kinds of exceptions are clearly possible. Thus there *may* be cases where we should believe a witness who says that a 'marvellous' event happened that was contrary to previous experience of the course of nature. What we should conclude from such trustworthy accounts is that God acted as 'an additional *cause*, equal to the alleged variety of effects' (EPEU 329; 220). That is, rather than God making exactly identical causes bring about different effects (which is impossible), God adds his own power to the action of some cause, so that a *new* cause brings about a never-before-observed effect.

Like her critique of Hume's views on miracles, Shepherd's arguments for belief in God are also based in her theory of causation. She offers two different arguments. The first is suggested in the first section of Chapter 7 of the 1827 *Essays* (**Selection H**), where she writes that just as our belief in an external world is based on 'what we conceive to be the consistent relations of ideas present in the mind... It is upon similar premises that we build the foundation of our belief in Deity' (EPEU 151; 227). She writes,

> ...after some contemplation upon the phenomena of nature, we conclude, that in order to account for the facts we perceive, 'there must needs be' one continuous existence, one uninterrupted essentially existing cause, one intelligent being, 'ever ready to appear' as the renovating power for all the dependent

effects, all the secondary causes beneath our view. (EPEU 151–2; 227)

A comment she makes later, in Essay 11, clarifies what she means. She writes there that to deny that there is a God

> is to imagine the existence of a series of dependent effects without a continuous being of which they are the qualities, and is equal to the supposition of the possibility of every thing springing up as we see it, from an absolute blank and nonentity of existence. (EPEU 391; 250)

So Shepherd suggests that this proof of God's existence takes the form of a *reductio ad absurdum*: if we assume that God does *not* exist, a contradiction follows, and so we are forced to conclude that God necessarily exists. This argument is therefore a 'demonstration', one that confers complete certainty on the conclusion.

Shepherd's second argument for God's existence is a teleological argument, which by nature is analogical rather than demonstrative. Teleological arguments have a long history, stretching back to the Stoics, and, in Shepherd's day, had been recently defended by William Paley in his 1802 *Natural Theology: Or, Evidences of the Existence and Attributes of the Deity, Collected from the Appearances of Nature*. Shepherd was familiar with Paley's argument,[24] which appeals to the 'complexity, subtlety, and curiosity' to be found in nature (such as an animal's eye), analogous to that which we see in mechanisms we know to be designed (such as a telescope), in order to argue that the universe must have been created by an '*intelligent* author'.[25] Her own version of the argument occurs in Essay 9 (**Selection I**). Her primary aim in that essay is to rebut unnamed materialists who argue that natural phenomena can be fully explained by purely material causes, with no need to invoke a deity. Shepherd argues that it is reasonable to believe that natural phenomena were created by an intelligent being.

She notes that we know from our own experience that to be a 'final cause' — that is, to produce something that has an

---

[24] She cites his book in a footnote (EPEU 391; 250 n9).
[25] William Paley, *Natural Theology*, ed. Matthew D. Eddy and David Knight (Oxford: Oxford University Press, 2006), pp. 16 and 215.

intended purpose—requires thought. Specifically, it requires thinking about what motions we need to perform on matter in order to create something that can fulfil the desired purpose (EPEU 347; 228). But no empirical test of an object can ever reveal to us whether such a thought was involved in its production: 'it is not to be descried by any sense or instrument, chemical, or mechanical, in our power' (EPEU 348; 228). In the case of a human activity such as building a ship, for example, all we can discern are 'the mere action of the brain, the nerves, and the muscles', which is not enough to know whether there was 'PERCEPTION *of happiness, or utility*, and the chosen direction of the eye, the ear, or the arm, in consequence' (EPEU 348; 229).

Shepherd's point is that while we know from our own experience that desires and intentions (which are mental states, or sensations) play a role in what *we* cause to exist, a purely materialist explanation of natural phenomena by its very nature denies a role to any such sensations. Thus if natural phenomena *do* have a purpose conferred on them by a creator with an intention in mind, the materialist's approach will not be able to identify that intention; the materialist simply cannot know that mind was in fact the 'final cause'.

Since no amount of empirical examination of natural phenomena will detect whether a final cause was at work in their production, we can only settle the question by reasoning analogically, comparing natural phenomena to those of our own creations. To decide whether some object shows evidence of design, it must 'always be examined *a posteriori* and be judged of by a sound mind, observing its analogies, its tendencies, its bearings upon others, &c' (EPEU 356; 232); once we have decided that it does show signs of design, we have reason to think that it had a final cause. And, she says, natural phenomena *do* appear to have purposes; there is an '*appearance* of contrivance in the universe' (EPEU 346; 228). Therefore, we should conclude that 'the beautiful arrangements of the heavens and the earth' received 'the beginning and direction of their motion' from 'a cause in action like in kind to that which I know of, but different in degree'—that is, from a deity (EPEU 370–1; 238; see also Essay 11).

Shepherd's applications of her theory of causation to theological issues are in her 1827 book, but her *Essay Upon the*

Relation of Cause and Effect does take up one theologically-motivated objection to her account of causation: namely, that if, as she claims, causes 'act as the junctions of different qualities' (ERCE 96; 61), and God is the ultimate cause of all other causes in the universe, it seems to follow that God and the universe are one. Interestingly, Shepherd does not dispute the opponent's inference. Instead, she suggests that her account of causation applies as much to God's actions as to natural phenomena, suggesting that the deity 'must nevertheless have attributes; or in other words, its own peculiar qualities, which required no former beings, *to give birth to them*', but which produce other beings by mixing and coalescing in the same way that natural causes do:

> *The unions of such qualities among themselves*, might well be equal to the going forth of the great Creation! The union of *wisdom*, with benevolence; and of these with the *'power'* arising out of the inexhaustible resources of his essence, might well occasion the 'starting forth' of innumerable beings. (ERCE 96–7; 61)

6. Mind and Body

In Chapter 7 of the first essay in *Essays on the Perception of an External Universe* (**Selection J**) and in Essays 10 and 11 from the second part of that book (**Selection K**), Shepherd addresses the distinction between mind and body, personal identity, and the immortality and immateriality of the mind.

Shepherd's characterization of mind and body are striking. Mind and body are not, as Descartes claimed, substances; they are 'capacities' or 'causes'. She writes,

> BODY is the *continually exciting cause*, for the exhibition of the perception of *extension* and *solidity* on the mind in particular; and MIND is the CAPACITY or CAUSE, for *sensation in general*. (EPEU 155; 240)

A capacity, for Shepherd, is a causal notion; it is a *power* to produce something. To be an external object is to have certain capacities to cause sensations of various kinds in sentient beings, and to be a mind is to have a capacity to have various sensations. Presumably, saying that something is a capacity implies that the capacity inheres in something else; capacities, after all, are not free-floating. Shepherd calls the underlying stuff in which the capacities inhere 'nature', 'existence', or 'beings'. We can distinguish between 'insentient nature' and 'sentient nature' (LMSM 701; 203–4), and she allows that we may legitimately call insentient nature 'material' and sentient nature 'immaterial', but the terms 'material' and 'immaterial' do not indicate anything further about the natures we so designate; they are just labels for the two kinds of capacities:

> Now those beings which do not yield any signs of mind or capacities of sensation, but exhibit upon our minds solid extension and other qualities in particular, are termed *material* things; — whilst such beings as yield the notion of their possessing life and understanding, are termed *im*material things. (EPEU 113–4; 141)

In sum, we can know that matter and mind are capacities that inhere in *something*, but 'the real essences of matter and mind we know not' (EPEU 244; 189).

In characterizing mind as a capacity for sensation 'in general' (or as a 'simple capacity for general sensation' [EPEU 15; 101]), Shepherd is contrasting mind with *particular* sensory perceptions (EPEU 15; 101). Mind is a capacity; sensations are actualizations of that capacity. Since sensations are, by definition, conscious acts of the mind (EPEU 6–7; 97), mind can be described as a capacity to produce conscious states. This is another important difference between Shepherd's account of the mind and a Cartesian account of mind as a substance that thinks: consciousness does not characterize mind itself; it characterizes the *sensations* that mind causes (either as a partial cause, working together with external objects, the sense organs, and other causes to bring about sensory perceptions, or on its own, when sensations result from memory, imagination, or reasoning).

Interestingly, Shepherd suggests that mind, like the external world, exists continually. She writes that

> ...the mind must be a *continued* and *exterior* capacity fitted to each change, upon any present state being interfered with by another object; and thus the pronoun *I* is ever *abstract*, and stands for a BEING *exterior* to, and independent of all the changes of which it is conscious. (EPEU 56–7; 119)

In saying that the mind is 'exterior', Shepherd means that the mind (the *capacity* to sense and think) is distinct from the actual sensations that result from the exercise of that capacity. In saying that the pronoun 'I' is 'abstract', she means that it is something separate from its sensations:[26] the mind is an ongoing, uninterrupted capacity for sensation, not the series of sensations that this capacity helps to produce.

Shepherd even suggests in Essay 10 that mind is eternal: it is an 'eternal power in nature, and as immortal for the future, as it must have been without beginning in the past' (EPEU 377; 244). Each individual thinking human shares in this eternal power; she refers elsewhere to 'minor portions of mind', saying that God unites a 'finite portion of mental power' and matter in the creation of humans (EPEU 400), and she writes of the 'mysterious eternal power of feeling, which has been conveyed to each animal as its inheritance from the commencement of its species' (EPEU 376-7; 244). This means, she says, that the human soul is immortal—but it does not settle the question of whether, after the death of the body, the finite portion of the 'eternal ocean of mind' (EPEU 378; 244) that was associated with that body retains its individuality and its memories of previous sensations and thoughts:

> The proper question, therefore, concerning the immortality of the soul, is not whether it can survive the body as a continuous existence—for it must be eternally independent of any particular set of organs in past, as in future time.—But the inquiry should be, whether when the organs which are in relation to any individual capacity, undergo the change called DEATH, if the *continuing mental* capacity become simple in its aptitudes again, or, whether it remain so far in an altered state by what it has gone through in the present life, that it continues as the result of that modification? (EPEU 378-9; 245)

Shepherd argues that analogical reasoning based on our experiences with other cases where memory is preserved or lost

---

[26] Shepherd elsewhere indicates that she uses the verb 'to abstract' to mean 'to separate' (EPEU 85; 130), so to say that the mind is abstract is to say that it is separate from something else—and, as Shepherd makes clear, it is separate from its sensations.

cannot settle the question, but that Scripture reveals that memories, and thus personal identity, are preserved after death: 'under the balance of these analogies the testimony of scripture in favour of the renewal of conscious memory is as a casting die' (EPEU 384; 247).

Towards the end of the *Essay Upon the Relation of Cause and Effect* (**Selection L**), in her discussion of the views of William Lawrence, Shepherd takes up the question of what conditions are necessary for an organism to be sentient. There must be a nervous system, sense organs, and life, and a materialist may claim that this is enough. But Shepherd insists that 'nature affords not experiment, or data enough to show, what are the *whole* causes necessary; i.e. *all* the objects required, whose *junction* is necessary to *sentiency as the result*' (ERCE 168; 253). There is thus reason to think that *mind* is also necessary:

> If indeed the powers of matter in general, (whatever matter may be), were sufficient to elicit sentiency when placed under *arrangement* and mixed with life, then the true causes for it are assigned, and found. But we cannot *prove* this. If on the contrary, the essential qualities of matter arranged and in motion be not thought sufficient to account for so extraordinary a difference as that between conscious and unconscious being, then there must be a *particular* cause for it: which cause must be considered an immaterial cause, that is, a *principle, power, being,* an unknown quality *denied* to exist in matter. — This must have a name, and may be called *soul,* or *spirit*. (ERCE 169; 253)

Since mind and body are two kinds of causal capacity rather than distinct substances, Shepherd maintains that mind–body interaction in a human (or other thinking being) is a 'combination of powers' (EPEU 158; 241). The body (brain and sense organs) and the mind work together, 'mixing' (ERCE 42n; 36) and 'coalescing' (ERCE 179), to cause sensations. And since causation is synchronous, every action of the brain occurs simultaneously with the mental sensation it helps to cause:

> as I have said, that in order to form the *proximate cause* of any event, *a junction or mutual mixture of all* the objects *necessary to it must take place*; so I conceive it to be impossible, but that a *distinct* and *different* action of the brain (without which organ there is no sensation in man, and all thought is but a mode of it)

must be *synchronous* with whatever other powers are also necessary for that result; viz. sensation and thought with their varieties. I say, the junction must be *synchronous* — for sensation is an *effect*, and must require the union of those objects whose mixed qualities elicit it. (ERCE 170-1; 254)

Mind and body thus act in concert, simultaneously.

It is this simultaneity of action that Shepherd seems to mean when she characterizes the brain-mind relationship as the brain being the 'exponent' of the soul (EPEU 36 and ERCE 171; 110 and 254). The *Oxford English Dictionary*'s entry for 'exponent' lists usage in an 1846 book by William Grove that illuminates Shepherd's meaning. Grove writes that 'The motion of the mass becomes the exponent of the amount of heat of the molecules'.[27] What Grove means is that A is an exponent of B when A and B vary in proportion to each other, and when, while we cannot directly observe or measure B, we *can* observe or measure A, thereby allowing us to infer something about B. While Grove's book was published after Shepherd's work, similar usage also appears in David Hartley's 1749 *Observations on Man*. There, Hartley presents a theory in which vibrations in the brain correlate with sensations, and he says that we can say either that vibrations are the exponent of sensations or that sensations are the exponent of vibrations, 'as best suits the enquiry'.[28] Given that Shepherd writes that 'the brain becomes the *exponent of the soul*; or is *in the same proportion in its actions*, as the actions of mind' (ERCE 171; 254), there is good reason to think that she means that actions in the brain (nerves firing, for example) are *correlated with* sensations in the mind. As we saw earlier (see §5, 'Religion'), Shepherd holds that sensations can never be detected by empirical means. However, if sensations are correlated with brain states, then observations of the brain can allow us to make certain inferences about sensations: a change in

---

[27] *The Oxford English Dictionary* cites William Grove, *On the Correlation of Physical Forces*, 2nd ed. (London: Samuel Highley, 1850), p. 25. See 'exponent, adj. and n.', *OED Online* (March 2018), http://www.oed.com.

[28] David Hartley, *Observations on Man, His Frame, His Duty, and His Expectations* (London: Printed by S. Richardson for James Leake and Wm. Frederick, 1749), p. 33.

brain-state (assuming all else remains the same) is an 'exponent', or indicator, of a change in the conscious sensation; as the brain-state varies, so the *sensation* varies.

7. Vision

In the final essay of *Essays on the Perception of an External Universe* (**Selection M**), Shepherd turns to two issues that Thomas Reid had discussed in his *Inquiry Into the Human Mind*. First, Shepherd asks, why does our having two eyes not result in double vision? Second, why do we see objects as erect when they are depicted – or, as it was then common to say, 'painted'[29] – as inverted on the retina? Reid's explanations for these phenomena drew on his views about principles of common sense; seeing objects single with two eyes is either 'a primary law of our constitution, or the consequence of some more general law which is not yet discovered',[30] and it is a 'law of nature, or a law of our constitution, of which law our seeing objects erect by inverted images, is a necessary consequence'.[31]

Unsurprisingly, Shepherd rejects Reid's explanations. The correct explanation of single vision is obvious, she suggests. She notes that in our visual field we distinguish two objects when there is a change in colour that forms '*a line of demarcation around its edges*' (EPEU pp. 408-9; 257). There only seems to be a puzzle about why we don't see single items as double because we tend to think that the space between our eyes *also* causes there to be a space between the two images on the retinas (EPEU 410); if there were a space between the two images, there would be what she calls a 'line of demarcation', and we would perceive the single object as two. However, there is in fact no image on the retina of the space between our eyes; we do not see the space between our eyes. Thus the images from the two retinas are superimposed, one on the other, with no line of demarcation between them, and so we perceive only one object (EPEU 410; 258). As for why we do not perceive objects as

---

[29] See Robert Smith, *A Compleat System of Opticks In Four Books, viz. a Popular, a Mathematical, a Mechanical, and a Philosophical Treatise* (Cambridge: 1738). Smith refers to images being 'painted upon the retina' (p. 29).

[30] Reid, *Inquiry* 6.19 (p. 166).

[31] Reid, *Inquiry* 6.12 (p. 123).

inverted, as are their images on the retina, Shepherd again suggests that there is no real puzzle: 'The real fact is, the painting of objects, though they be inverted, does not alter the painting of their *relative* positions; the *whole* colouring of *all* within the sphere of vision, maintains precisely the same position of things towards each other' (EPEU 413; 259).

Shepherd further explains her thoughts on vision in an essay (**Selection N**) that she published in *The Philosophical Magazine and Annals of Philosophy* the following year (and which was evidently deemed of sufficient interest that it was reprinted in *The Kaleidoscope; or, Literary and Scientific Mirror*). The 1828 essay is nearly four times as long as the 1827 one. Additions include five 'metaphysical positions in relation to vision' that Shepherd thinks will help prevent 'confused ideas, hypothetical assumptions, and inconclusive reasonings on optical experiments and facts'.[32] Her explanations of the visual puzzles are essentially the same as in the earlier essay, but now Shepherd situates that explanation in her broader theory of perception, according to which '*the proportions and relations of unperceived things are known from the relations of the corresponding sensations they create*' (EPEU 20; 103).

8. Textual Notes

Shepherd's two books have been digitized by Google and are freely available as PDF files on the internet. I used those PDF scans to prepare this volume, as well as consulting an original copy of *An Essay Upon the Relation of Cause and Effect* from Yale University and an original copy of *Essays on the Perception of an External Universe* from Harvard University (call number Phil 270.13). 'Lady Mary Shepherd's Metaphysics', published in the 1832 edition of *Fraser's Magazine for Town and Country*, has also been digitized by and is available through Google Books. The 1828 volume of *The Philosophical Magazine and Annals of Philosophy* containing Shepherd's essay on vision has been digitized by the Natural History Museum Library and is freely available at the Biodiversity Heritage Library web site (https://www.bio diversitylibrary.org). The July 1828 issues of *The Kaleidoscope; or,*

---

32 Mary Shepherd, 'On the Causes of Single and Erect Vision', *The Philosophical Magazine and Annals of Philosophy* (June 1828), p. 406.

Literary and Scientific Mirror containing the reprint of that essay have been digitized by Google Books.

To keep this volume within a manageable length, I have omitted some sections of Shepherd's writings, primarily those in which she repeats points made elsewhere, quotes at length from other authors, or is primarily arguing against an opponent rather than explicating her own positive accounts. Omitted passages of text are indicated by '[...]'. All italicized and capitalized words are Shepherd's own. I have included all of Shepherd's footnotes; my explanatory notes are indicated by square brackets. Since Shepherd's spelling, punctuation, and capitalization generally conform to our contemporary standards, editorial changes have been minimal, but I have silently modernized some spellings and have inserted some missing punctuation marks. Shepherd included errata sheets with both books; I have silently incorporated the changes she wanted.

References to the original sources are indicated at the beginning of each selection.

I would like to thank Gordon Graham for his invitation to include Lady Mary Shepherd's work in the Library of Scottish Philosophy series; to Maura Boyle for her help in preparing the text; to Alison Peterman for her feedback on the introduction; to Gail Terry for preparing the index; and to Terry and Sheila Meyers for their support of the project.

Further Reading

Primary Sources

Shepherd, Mary, *An Essay upon the Relation of Cause and Effect, controverting the Doctrine of Mr. Hume, concerning the Nature of that Relation; with Observations upon the Opinions of Dr. Brown and Mr. Lawrence, connected with the same subject*, London: Printed for T. Hookham, 1824.

Shepherd, Mary, *Essays on the Perception of an External Universe and Other Subjects Connected with the Doctrine of Causation*, London: John Hatchard and Son, 1827.

Shepherd, Mary, 'Lady Mary Shepherd's Metaphysics', *Fraser's Magazine for Town and Country* 5, no. 30 (1832), pp. 697–708.

Shepherd, Mary, 'Observations by Lady Mary Shepherd on the "First Lines of the Human Mind"', in *Parriana: or Notices of the Rev. Samuel Parr*, Vol. 1, pp. 624–627, London: Henry Colburn, 1828.

Shepherd, Mary, 'On the Causes of Single and Erect Vision', *The Kaleidoscope; or, Literary and Scientific Mirror*, Vol. 9, no. 420 (15 July 1828), p. 13, and Vol. 9, no. 421 (22 July 1828), pp. 22–23.

Shepherd, Mary, 'On the Causes of Single and Erect Vision', *The Philosophical Magazine and Annals of Philosophy* (June 1828), pp. 406–416.

Secondary Sources

Atherton, Margaret, 'Lady Mary Shepherd's Case Against George Berkeley', *British Journal for the History of Philosophy* 4, no. 2 (1996), pp. 347–366.

Atherton, Margaret, 'Reading Lady Mary Shepherd', *The Harvard Review of Philosophy* 8, no. 2 (2005), pp. 73–85.

Atherton, Margaret, 'Shepherd, Mary (née Primrose: 1777–1847)', in *The Continuum Encyclopedia of British Philosophy*, Vol. 4, pp. 2901–2903, edited by A.C. Grayling, Naomi Goulder, and Andrew Pyle, Bristol: Thoemmes Continuum, 2006.

Bolton, Martha Brandt, 'Causality and Causal Induction: The Necessitarian Theory of Lady Mary Shepherd', in *Causation and*

Modern Philosophy, pp. 242–261, edited by Keith Allen and Tom Stoneham, New York: Routledge, 2011.

Bolton, Martha, 'Mary Shepherd', *Stanford Encyclopedia of Philosophy*, 2017, https://plato.stanford.edu/entries/mary-shepherd/.

Boyle, Deborah, 'Expanding the Canon: The Case for Adding Lady Mary Shepherd', *The Journal of Scottish Philosophy* 15, no. 3 (2017), pp. 275–293.

Fantl, Jeremy, 'Mary Shepherd on Causal Necessity', *Metaphysica* 17, no. 1 (2016), pp. 87–108.

McRobert, Jennifer, 'Introduction', in *Philosophical Works of Lady Mary Shepherd*, Vol. 1, pp. v–xxvi, Bristol: Thoemmes Press, 2000.

McRobert, Jennifer, 'Mary Shepherd and the Causal Relation', 2002; revised 2014, http://philpapers.org/rec/MCRMSA.

Paoletti, Cristina, 'Restoring Necessary Connections: Lady Mary Shepherd on Hume and the Early Nineteenth-Century Debate on Causality', in *Hume, Nuovi Saggi [Hume, New Essays]*, pp. 47–59, Padova: Il Poligrafo, 2011.

Perkins, Mary Anne, 'Shepherd (née Primrose), Lady Mary (1777– 1847), philosopher', *Oxford Dictionary of National Biography*, 2004, www.oxforddnb.com.

Rickless, Samuel C., 'Is Shepherd's Pen Mightier than Berkeley's Word?', *British Journal for the History of Philosophy* 26, no. 2 (2018), pp. 317–330.

One

Causation

Selection A

(Excerpted from *An Essay Upon the Relation of Cause and Effect* [1824], pp. 27–135, pp. 141–4, and pp. 186–94.)

Chapter the Second

Having now made an abstract of Mr. Hume's Treatise and Essays on the subject of the relation of Cause and Effect,[1] I shall proceed to examine each part in as regular an order as I conveniently can; and endeavour to answer the two questions first proposed, in a more popular, and, I hope, not more illogical method than Mr. Hume has followed, by attempting to prove,

FIRST, That *reason*, not *fancy* and 'custom', leads us to the knowledge, That every thing which begins to exist must have a Cause. — SECONDLY, That *reason* forces the mind to perceive, that *similar causes* must necessarily produce *similar effects*. — THIRDLY, I shall thence establish a more philosophical definition of the relation of Cause and Effect. — FOURTHLY, show, in what respects Mr. Hume's definition is faulty. — FIFTHLY, proceed to prove that Nature cannot be supposed to alter her Course without a contradiction in terms; and, finally, show, that

---

[1]   [The first chapter consists of quotations from Hume's *Treatise of Human Nature* (primarily from Book 1, Part 3) and *Enquiry Concerning Human Understanding* (primarily from Part 4, with some reference to Parts 5 and 7). See David Hume, *A Treatise of Human Nature*, ed. David Fate Norton and Mary J. Norton (Oxford: Oxford University Press, 2000), hereafter cited as *Treatise*, followed by book, part, section, and paragraph number, with page number; and David Hume, *An Enquiry Concerning Human Understanding*, ed. Tom L. Beauchamp (Oxford: Oxford University Press, 2000), hereafter cited as *Enquiry*, followed by section and paragraph number, with page numbers.]

Custom and Habit alone are not our guides; but chiefly reason, for the regulation of our expectations in ordinary life.

[...]

Section the First

First, then, let me show, why Mr. Hume's argument, in favour of the possibility of beings commencing their own existence is sophistical; as well as his attempted confutation of those philosophers who have argued to the contrary. Mr. Hume says, the proposition, 'that whatever has a beginning, has also a Cause of existence, cannot be demonstrated', because the ideas of Cause and Effect are 'distinct' and 'separable'; and it will be easy to conceive 'any object to be non-existent this minute', and 'existent the next'; without 'conjoining to it the idea of a Cause, or a productive principle'.[2]—This imagination is plausible, and may perhaps appear well founded until thoroughly sifted. On a first impression, Causes and their Effects may seem separable, because two things are mentioned; one is distinct from the other, and may be *imagined* separated from it.

They may also *seem* to follow one another, and *time* to elapse between the *operation of the Cause*, and the *appearance of the Effect*; so that during the interval of the supposed period, the effect might be *imagined in suspense,* and so indifferent to existence or non-existence; but upon a strict and rigid attention to the real nature of a thing in opposition to its accidental appearances, one cannot, for a moment, suppose that the circumstances here mentioned, namely, of antecedency of Cause and subsequency of Effect; or of that *distinctness of language* which occasions two words to be used for two ideas; should in any degree render it possible for causes and their effects to exist apart in nature. That it is impossible for them to do so, without involving a direct contradiction in terms, is a proposition I hope to prove in the course of this Essay.

But before examining into this notion, concerning the possibility of effects being held in suspense, and then of being liable to begin their own existence, or, in Mr. Hume's words, 'of the separation of the idea of a cause from that of a beginning of existence', it will be necessary to render the expressions in

---

2 [See Hume, *Treatise* 1.3.3.1–3 (p. 56).]

which it is conveyed more intelligible. This can in no way be done so long as the *definition of the word effect* presupposes a cause; for the supposition of the objection lies, in its being possible for *effects* to be held in suspense: but in order that this should be possible, the meaning of the word *effect* must be altered. Then, if the ideas are altered that lie under the term, according as the varied occasion seems to require, there can be no philosophy; and it never can be insisted on, that the *effects*, which are *supposed to be conjoined* with their causes at one period of time; and to require, in order to their exhibition, those causes or others; and to receive the name of *effects*, on account of requiring causes; can again, upon another occasion, not be *effects*, nor require *causes*, be held in suspense, and be *imagined* capable of *beginning their existence by themselves*, without conjoining to them the distinct idea of any 'productive principle'. — It might as well be reckoned sound reasoning, after defining the figure 2 to be a sign signifying that two units are necessary to its composition, to maintain, that because it stands *singly*, it can be *imagined an unit itself*, without a contradiction; so that it *does not* stand in need of 2 units to its composition: — that is, a word may be taken in two contradictory senses, and then it may be reasonable to predicate of each, affections that belong only to the other; and so to form any contradictory scheme in the world. To make, therefore anything like a rational meaning in this sentence of Mr. Hume's, nothing more can be intended by it, than that we should imagine, those existences which we always observe conjoined with others in such a manner, that they *appear* to be their effects, properties, or qualities, to owe them *no real existence or dependence*; and therefore capable of being independent objects, and of beginning their own existence. In like manner, it may be said of *causes*, that although the word signifies something calculated to introduce a certain quality, yet that in fact it does not introduce a new quality; thus naming the object in one sense, and imagining its essence in another sense.

This also is as though we should agree to designate each unit by the figure 1; and to assert, that the union of two units introduces a compound notion, which shall be made known by the sign 2; and on account of this relation, the union of the units shall be called the cause of the compound quality two, under a single term; and the sign 2 shall be named its *effect;* and afterwards assert, that we can *imagine* the cause, that is the *union of the two units*, to exist without, and separate from, the effect, the result 2. All this cannot take place whilst we assign the same meaning to our words; and if we use the terms in different senses, there can be no philosophy. — Therefore, to make any meaning whatever of the proposition, 'We may imagine causes to exist separate from their effects'; the objects we call *causes* are not to be imagined as *causes,* but may be supposed *not to cause any thing,* but to exist without *determining their own effects,* or *any others*; that is, causes and their effects are so evidently distinct, that they may be imagined to be unconnected objects, that are *not causes and effects,* and to exist separately without a contradiction, though they are named expressly as signs of the ideas we have, that they are necessary to one another.

Thus, the original question, namely, 'Whether every thing which begins to exist requires a cause for its existence?' resolves itself into two others; viz.

First, Whether objects called EFFECTS, necessarily require causes for their existence? or, whether they may begin to exist with, or without them indifferently? — As also,

Secondly, Whether any objects whatever, without being considered as having the *nature of effects,* can begin their existences?

It may be plainly seen, that the first of these questions is sunk in the latter, because, if objects *usually considered as effects* need not be considered as effects, then they are forced to begin their existences *of themselves*: for, conjoined or not to their causes, we know by our senses that they do begin to exist: we will, therefore, immediately hasten to the consideration of the second question, which may be stated in the following terms: Whether every object which begins to exist must owe its existence to a cause?

Let the object which we suppose to begin its existence of itself be imagined, abstracted from the nature of all objects we are acquainted with, saving in its capacity for existence; let us suppose it to be *no effect*; there shall be no prevening[3] circumstances whatever that affect it, nor any existence in the universe: let it be so; let there be nought but a blank; and a mass of

3   prevening] preceding.

whatsoever can be supposed not to require a cause START FORTH into existence, and make the first breach on the wide nonentity around; — now, what is this starting forth, beginning, coming into existence, but an action, which is a quality of an object not yet in being, and so not possible to have its qualities determined, nevertheless exhibiting its qualities?

If, indeed, it should be shown, that there is no proposition whatever taken as a ground on which to build an argument in this question, neither one conclusion nor the other can be supported; and there need be no attempt at reasoning. — But, if my adversary allows that, no existence being supposed previously in the universe, existence, in order to be, must *begin to be*, and that the notion of *beginning an action* (the being that *begins* it not supposed yet in existence), involves a *contradiction in terms*; then this *beginning* to exist cannot appear but as a *capacity some nature hath* to alter the presupposed nonentity, and to act for itself, whilst itself is not in being. — The original assumption may deny, as much as it pleases, all cause of existence; but, whilst in its very idea, the commencement of existence is an effect predicated of some supposed *cause,* (*because the quality of an object* which must be *in existence to possess it*), we must conclude that *there is no object which begins to exist, but must owe its existence to some cause.*

For this reason it is, that the answers to Dr. Clarke and Mr. Locke are unsound, in as far as they are an endeavour to show, that their arguments are altogether sophistical.[4] — Mr. Hume objects to them, that the existence supposed to begin by itself, 'is not to be considered as an *effect*; and that these authors assume what is not granted, viz. that the existence in question requires *a cause*'; as where Dr. Clarke shows it is an absurdity to imagine an object its *own cause*, and Mr. Locke asserts that it is equally so, to conceive of *nothing* as a cause. It is undoubtedly true, that these authors assumed that which was in question; namely, that every existence must have a cause: but, as every thing not yet in existence, *to exist at all*, must *begin*, and as the

---

4 [Shepherd alludes to Hume's objections in *Treatise* 1.3.3.5–7 (p. 57) to arguments of Samuel Clarke and John Locke. The quotation Shepherd ascribe to Hume in the next sentence is her paraphrase of his objections.]

beginning of any thing must always be supposed, by the *nature of the action*, to be a quality of something in existence, which existence is yet DENIED by the statement of the question, these philosophers felt the involved absurdity so great, that they passed over the first question as too ridiculous, probably, to consider formally; then showed, that the mind of man was forced to look upon all things which begin to exist as *dependent* QUALITIES; and thus, that an object could neither depend upon *itself for existence*, nor yet upon *nothing*.

Let it be remembered, too, that although Mr. Hume inveighs against this method as sophistical, by conceiving it begs the question, yet his own argument, the whole way, consists in the possibility of imagining an *effect 'non-existent* this minute', and 'existing the next'; and does not himself consider any other 'sort of being' possible; and has no other way of supporting his own notion of the beginning of existence by itself, except under the *idea of an effect in suspense*; which is still a *relative term*, and begs the question for the necessity of its correlative, i.e. its *cause*, just as much as he asserts his adversaries do, whom he declares to be illogical reasoners.

If then (as I hope I have shown) all objects whatever, which *begin to exist*, must owe their *existence to some cause*, those we usually consider as *effects* CANNOT be held in suspense; suddenly alter their nature; be '*non-existent* this minute, and existent the next'; and, though always introduced as *qualities of other objects*, be easily separated from the ideas of their causes, and require no 'productive principle'.

'That Cause and Effect are distinct and separable'; so 'that any object may be conceived, as therefore *capable of beginning its own existence*', must be considered as among the notions adopted in *the Essays*: what else is the meaning of such propositions as these: 'There appears not throughout all nature, any one instance of connection, as conceivable by us'; 'one event follows another', 'but we never can observe *any tye between them*, &c.'[5] Indeed, the not admitting '*any relations of ideas*', or '*any reasonings a priori*', (so as to be capable of supporting the idea of CAUSATION as a *creating principle* absolutely necessary

---

[5]   Essays, Sec. 7. p. 77. [See Hume, *Enquiry* 7.26 (pp. 143–4).]

in the universe) is but repeating 'the *juvenile ideas*' of the Treatise, and '*casting them anew in these later pieces*'.[6]

Before I proceed further, I wish my reader to grant the proposition, 'That a Being cannot begin its existence of itself'; because I mean to make use of it in my further reply to Mr. Hume's doctrines; and, unless this step is allowed, I can make no further progress in this argument.

Section the Second

We will now proceed to the second part of the original enquiry; that is, Why we conclude that such particular Causes must necessarily have such particular Effects; and what is the nature of that inference we draw from one to the other, and of the belief we repose in it? The question, however, ought to stand thus, 'why LIKE CAUSES must necessarily have LIKE EFFECTS?' because what is really enquired into, is the *general notion of necessary connexion*, between *all like* Cause and Effect; and by thus putting the question respecting *particulars only*, although they might be included in an universal answer, yet no answer applicable to them MERELY, could authorize an *universal axiom*. The manner of stating the enquiry in *the Essays*, is also too vaguely expressed, (although it be evident that it is the *general relation* which is enquired, into). Mr. Hume says, 'we will now enquire, how we arrive at the *knowledge of Cause and Effect*.'[7] It ought to be stated, how we arrive at the knowledge of the *necessary connexion*, between *like* Cause and Effect?

Let it be remembered, that Mr. Hume says, 'this principle is nothing but custom and habit'; that 'belief in necessary connexion is nothing but an intense and steady conception, arising from the customary conjunction of the object with something present to the memory or senses; that when flame and heat, cold and snow, have always been conjoined together, there is such a customary conjunction between them, that when flame and snow are anew presented to the senses, the mind is carried by custom to expect heat and cold.'[8]

---

6   See advertisement to the Essays. [See Hume, *Enquiry* (p. 83).]

7   Essays, Sec. 4. p. 27. [See Hume, *Enquiry* 4.5 (p. 109).]

8   [Shepherd paraphrases and combines Hume, *Enquiry* 5.13 (p. 126) and 5.8 (p. 123).]

'That *reason* can never show us the connexion of one object with other, though aided by experience; for we can at least *conceive a change in the course of nature*. That necessary connexion is nothing but an internal act of the mind, determined to carry its thoughts from one object to another.'[9] Thus *necessary connexion* of cause and effect is only a custom of the mind! *Power* is only a custom of the mind! Expectations, and experience, are only customs of the mind! The consequence of which doctrine is, that as a *custom of the mind*, is entirely a different circumstance from the *operation of nature*, we may '*conceive*' at least the contrary of what we have been accustomed to may take place, — we may conceive the 'course of nature to change'.

Now it is my intention to shew, in contradiction to these ideas of Mr. Hume, that it is *Reason*, and not *Custom*, which guides our minds in forming the notions of necessary connexion of belief and of expectation.[10]

In order to this let us bear in mind the reasoning already adduced in the foregoing Chapter, and it thence immediately follows, that objects which we know by our senses do begin their existences, and by our reason know they cannot begin it of themselves, must begin it by the operation of some *other beings* in existence, producing these new qualities in nature, and introducing them to our observation. The very meaning of the word Cause, is *Producer* or *Creator*; of Effect, the *Produced* or *Created* —

---

9   [Shepherd paraphrases Hume, *Treatise* 1.3.6.5 (p. 62) and 1.3.6.12 (p. 64).]

10   I conceive it impossible to have a complete conviction that every Effect is inherent, or contained in its Cause, until the mind be imbued with the knowledge, that objects are but unknown circumstances in Nature, when unperceived by the senses; which when perceived, exhibit their appropriate qualities accordingly; and which then appear in certain defined masses, as to the different senses they affect, as to their figure, &c.; and receive an arbitrary name for their assemblage. They must have also among each other certain proportions. When these unknown circumstances, (or affections, or substances,) in nature, *mix*, and are thereby *altered, the qualities which affect the senses* are in the *same proportions* altered, and are necessarily included in those objects as their Effects. But this part of the subject, is of such moment that a separate consideration of it is intended.

and the idea is gained by such an observance of nature, as we think is efficient in any given case, to an *experimentum crucis*.[11]

Long observation of the invariableness of antecedency, and subsequency, is not wanted; many trials are not wanted, to generate the notion of *producing power*.

One trial is enough, in such circumstances, as will bring the mind to the following reasoning.

Here is a new quality, which appears to my senses:

But it could not arise of itself; nor could any surrounding objects, but one (or more) affect it; therefore that one, (or more) have occasioned it, for there is nothing else to make a difference; and a *difference* could not *'begin of itself'*.

This is an argument, which all persons, however illiterate, feel the force of. It is the only foundation for the demonstrations of the laboratory of the chymist; which all life resembles, and so closely, in many instances, that the philosopher, and the vulgar, are equally sure of what cause is absolutely necessary to the production of certain effects; for instance, each knows that in certain given circumstances, *the closing of the Eye* will eclipse the prospect of nature; and the slight motion of reopening it, will restore all the objects to view. Therefore, the Eye (in these circumstances), is the *Cause* or *Producer of vision*. ONE trial would be enough, under certain *known* circumstances.[12] Why? not from *'custom'*, because there has been *one trial only*; but from *Reason*, because vision not being able *to produce itself, nor any of the surrounding objects by the supposition*; it is the *Eye* which must necessarily perform the operation; for there is nothing else to make a difference; and a different quality could not *'begin its own existence'*. It is this sort of REASONING UPON EXPERIMENT, which takes place in every man's mind, concerning every affair in life, which generates the notion of Power, and necessary Connexion; and gives birth to that maxim, *'a like*

---

11 *experimentum crucis*] crucial experiment. [The phrase famously appeared in a letter from Newton to the Royal Society of London about his optical experiments and the nature of light; see 'A Letter of Mr. Isaac Newton …containing his New Theory about Light and Colours', *Philosophical Transactions of the Royal Society* 6, no. 80 (1671/72): 3075-87.]

12 When more trials are needed than ONE, it is in order to *detect* the circumstances, not to lay a *foundation for the general principle*, that a LIKE Cause repeated, a LIKE Effect will take place.

Cause must produce a like Effect'. The circumstances being supposed the same on a second occasion as on a former one, and carefully observed to be so; the Eye when opened would be expected to let in light, and all her objects. 'I observe (says the mind) in this or any other case, all the prevening circumstances the same as before; for there is nothing to make a difference; and a difference cannot arise without something to occasion it; else there would be a *beginning of existence* by itself, which is impossible.'

It is this compound idea, therefore, *the result of the experience of what does take place upon any given trial*, MIXED *with the reasoning that nothing else could ensue*, unless on the one hand, *efficient causes were allowed for the alteration*; or, on the other, that things could *'alter their existences* FOR THEMSELVES'; which generates the notion of *power or 'producing principle'*, *and for which we have formed the word.*

It is in vain to say that a habit of association of ideas from observing *'contiguity in time, and place'*, between objects is all we know of *power*; a habit of the mind will not *begin existence*, will not *introduce a quality*. The really philosophical method of viewing the subject is this: that objects in relation to us, are nothing but masses of certain qualities, affecting certain of our senses; and which, when independent of our senses, are *unknown* powers or qualities in nature. These masses change their qualities by their mixture with any other mass, and then the corresponding qualities determined to the senses must of course also change. These changed qualities, are termed *effects*; or *consequents*; but are really no more than NEW QUALITIES arising from *new objects*, which have been formed by the *junctions of other objects* (previously formed) or might be considered as the *unobserved* qualities of *existing objects*; which *shall be observed when properly exhibited.*

If then an existence now in being, *conjoined with any other*, forms thereby *a new nature*, capable of exhibiting *new qualities*, these new qualities must enter into the definition of the objects; they become a part of their natures; and when by careful experiment, or judicious observation, no new prevening circumstances are supposed to make an alteration in the conjunction of the same bodies, the *new qualities*, that are named *effects*, are expected without a doubt to arise upon every such conjunction; because, they as much belong to this *newly combined nature*, as the original qualities did to each separate nature, before their conjunction. So little is custom the principle of cause and effect, that if upon the *first* and original trial of the element of fire, all surrounding circumstances were put away from having any influence over it, saving the body it destroyed; that power of *discerptibility*[13] would be ever after considered as one of its qualities; as much as its colour or its light, or its warmth, without the presence of which, it would not be fire.

This conjunction with a grosser material than itself, is the new circumstance, on which it exhibits its essential and permanent quality of discerptibility to the senses; now if the trial be complete, when upon a second occasion an object having the same sensible qualities as fire hath, known also to have been elicited from the same prevening circumstances, meets with the same gross body as heretofore, it must of *necessity* consume it. There is nothing to make a *difference*. A *difference* is an *Effect*, a *change of being*, an *altered existence*, an existence which *cannot 'begin of itself'* any more than any other in Nature; could the fire be supposed not to consume the gross body, there would be a *difference* of qualities, that is, new qualities, which by the data there is no cause for. The original circumstances, of which fire is the compound Effect, from which it results as a *formed object*, are supposed to be ordered the same as on a former occasion; these are necessarily compelled to be attended with the same effects or combined qualities; otherwise there would be the *'beginnings of existence'* by themselves, which has before been shown to be impossible. But the *combined qualities*, are the whole qualities that fire in every circumstance, is capable of producing. Meeting, therefore, with a gross body, which on any one occasion, in certain circumstances, it once consumed; under the same circumstances, it must necessarily again consume it. That DIFFERENCES OF EXISTENCE cannot begin of themselves; is therefore the second conclusion supposed to be established.

'Antecedency and subsequency', are therefore immaterial to the proper definition of Cause and Effect; on the contrary, although an object, in order to act as a Cause, must be in Being antecedently to such action; yet when it *acts as a Cause*, its *Effects* are *synchronous with that action*, and are *included in it*; which a close

---

[13] discerptibility] divisibility.

inspection into the nature of cause will prove. For effects are no more than the new qualities, of newly formed objects. Each conjunction of bodies, (now separately in existence, and of certain defined qualities), produces upon their union those new natures, whose qualities must necessarily *be in*, and *with them, in the very moment of their formation.*

Thus *the union of two distinct natures,* is the *cause, producer* or *creator* of another; which must instantly, and immediately, have all its peculiar qualities; but the cause has not acted, is not completed, till the *union* has taken place, and the new nature is formed with all its qualities, *in,* and *about it. Cause producing Effect,* therefore, under the strict eye of philosophical scrutiny, is a *new object* exhibiting *new qualities;* or shortly, the formation of a new *mass of qualities.* A *chain of conjunctions of bodies,* of course, *occupies time;* and is the reason why the careless observation of philosophers, enabling them to take notice only of some one distinct effect, (after perhaps innumerable successive conjunctions of bodies), occasions the mistake, by which they consider *subsequency of effect,* as a part of the *essential definition* of that term; and *priority,* as *essential* to the nature of Cause.

As a short illustration of the doctrine unfolded, let us take the idea of nourishment, considered as the effect, subsequent to the taking of food, its cause. Here the *nature* of nourishment, is *a process* which begins to act immediately that food is in conjunction with the stomach. 'That we are nourished'; is only the last result of a continuous chain of causes and effects, in formation from the first moment the food enters the stomach, to that, in which every particle is absorbed and deposited in the proper place in the body. Here, the capacity of food to exhibit certain qualities, when in conjunction with the body, is shown; the nature of the human body, to exhibit certain other qualities, in consequence of that conjunction, is also shown; but the *effect of nourishment,* being *subsequent* to, and at such a distance of time from, the original Cause, is only so, on account of its being the effect of a vast number of causes, or unions of objects in succession, of which the union of the stomach and the food was first in order.

Our deficient observation, is apt to prevent our taking notice of the 2d, 3d, or indefinite number of effects; which arise in consequence of as many conjunctions of objects.

But the first, and other *effects* successively, are as much and entirely synchronous with their *causes*, as any other quality of any single object, which is always exhibited along with it.

2dly. It is also quite immaterial to the definition of this relation, whether an untried, or unobserved quality, be called *quality*, or *effect*. The unknown or at present undetermined quality, which is termed an effect, might always change its place with some *known quality*, and not bear the name of effect; and *vice versa*: Thus, a blind man may call the object which warmed, or burned him, fire; but his eyes being supposed suddenly to open, he would consider the flame and its brilliant colour as the *effects* of fire; whilst he who sees fire constantly, being able always to take notice of its flame and colour, con- siders them as the constant and unvarying *qualities* of fire, and which render the substance before him worthy of bearing that name; but the quality of burning, which he does not *constantly* experience, he names an *effect* or *consequence* of fire previously being in existence. But the true method of looking upon the subject is this — that fire, in order to deserve the name it bears, must comprehend all its qualities *tried* and *untried*; *observed* and *unobserved*; *determined* and *undetermined*; it deserves the name only on account of its being a certain defined object; *elicited from certain causes observed to be efficient to its production*; and by the very conditions of the question, is allowed to be *the same*. But an object is nothing else (in relation to *us*) than a mass of peculiar qualities; and when observations inform us, that any known mass is produced by similar circumstances, on various occasions; such mass or object must necessarily contain all its qualities, and be equal to exhibit all its effects in hitherto untried events. Upon any occasion where we are either certain, or have a high probability, that an object presented to us is truly similar to a former one, and was created by the same causes; we expect all tried qualities to be the same as before, and any *untried* quality, (that is, any quality not in present operation, though previously ascertained), must belong ever after to its definition. All that is necessary is to be correct, as to the pre- vening or influencing circumstances which gave *birth to the object*. They being the same on any two or more occasions, the object elicited must necessarily be the same — but it is not the same, unless it hath all its *qualities*, and no other than its qualities. Therefore fire, in order to have a right to the sign of the word fire, for an expression of its attributes, in order to be a *'like cause'*, must of necessity burn as much as it must be red, otherwise the red object were not fire; and *could not have been produced by those causes that elicit that element*. I mean therefore to conclude, that Effects are but the qualities of an object not experienced by some of the senses of the human frame, whilst certain others at present touch it; *the knowledge of which last*, being joined to the observation of the WHENCE the object was produced, beget the knowledge of what new untried qualities may be expected in future under given circumstances. It becomes therefore part of the definition of fire to burn certain bodies, to melt others; of bread to nourish the human body; of snow to be cold, and white; and these qualities they must have, in order to compose that entire *enumeration of qualities*, for which appropriate names have been formed, and to the exhibition of which similar and efficient causes have been in action.

If it should be said, that in considering objects as masses of combined qualities, the *result* of like Causes previously in action, we beg the question not yet supposed to be granted, — I answer; that *like* Causes, that is, *like* objects, are by the supposition admitted, and then the question arises, whether it is demonstrable they must have like effects or qualities, *under like circumstances in future?* I answer, they must have like effects, or qualities, because there is nothing else *given* that can be supposed to make a difference; and a difference of qualities could not arise of *itself,* could not begin its own existence; and I add, not only, there is nothing else *supposed* that can make a difference; but that when we also know that in the FORMATION of any object no difference took place; then, *there is no ground whatever,* for imagining the *possibility* of an *alteration* in *the effects of that object*. But although it be very difficult in the analysis of this question, not to use the word *cause* in its intended sense, before the definition of the word is given, and although it be true that in this last observation I may have done so in saying, *that objects must be the same which are elicited from like causes; i.e. from the junction of like prevening circumstances;* (and which position will be fully borne out in the process of the argument); yet a fastidious reader may omit every such reference to the notion of Cause; for the argument is perfect without it, and stands thus:

Effects are nothing but those *same conjunctions of qualities,* which in other words are admitted as *similar causes,* in the supposition of the question. The objects (whose *union is necessary* to a given result) must certainly exist, *antecedent* to such an union. But it is *in their* UNION, there exist those *newly formed objects,* or masses of qualities called *Effects,* which are therefore *identical* with the *similar cause;* for in *this union,* Cause and Effect are *synchronous,* and they are but different words for the same *Essence.* Fire and wood must be antecedent to combustion, no doubt; but in the *union of Fire and Wood,* there exists immediately *combustion* as a new event in nature; — also in this union exists the similar *cause* allowed by the *data,* whilst combustion is also termed the *Effect* of the union of Fire and Wood; but, however termed, an *effect,* is in fact a new but similar object as heretofore. A *similar* mass of qualities, in kind, which cannot therefore be a *different* mass of qualities in kind. — Equals added to equals upon any two occasions, the whole must be equal; add equal qualities to equal qualities, the sum of the qualities must be equal upon every repetition of the junction; — and the *sum* must be the *same result* taken *twice over,* not two *different,* or possibly *altered sums.* Therefore I repeat, that in the consideration of the nature of Cause and Effect, it is immaterial whether the yet unframed qualities of objects, previous to their junction, be named *effects;* they are to be considered as qualities; and qualities may be considered as *effects,* under any circumstances that prevent their usual exhibition. Effects when developed are no more than qualities; and qualities previous to their development are in our imagination considered as Effects.

3dly. Again, it is immaterial to the definition of the relation of Cause and Effect, that we are not acquainted with the 'secret powers' of natural objects,[14] either before or after experience; for when we find, that in any distinct and given circumstances they put on certain qualities to the senses, their secret powers and properties must be qualified in all *like circumstances* to be the

---

14 [Shepherd alludes to Hume's claim at *Enquiry* 4.16 (p. 113) that 'nature has kept us at a great distance from all her secrets, and has afforded us only the knowledge of a few superficial qualities of objects; while she conceals from us those powers and principles, on which the influence of these objects entirely depends.']

same, and are obliged to be so; because no contrary qualities could 'begin their existences of themselves'; and by the *supposition* there is no *cause in the circumstances*, to give rise to any *differences in the qualities*. Indeed, Mr. Hume makes a great mistake in supposing it necessary to demonstrate, in every particular instance, what *particular* Effect must necessarily flow from its object, in order to gain the idea of *necessary Connexion*. The *how* and the *why* have nothing to do with the general reasoning affecting the general proposition; for 'whether like Causes shall produce like Effects' is *not* a question exactly the same as whether 'such particular causes shall have such *particular* effects?' which Mr. Hume seems to consider as precisely of the same import;[15] whereas *one is a general* question, which however answered, in the *affirmative* or *negative*, would apply to *particulars*. But supposing in each *particular* instance under our notice, we could descry the '*secret powers of nature*', the general question concerning *all* like causes would still remain unanswered; and an universal conclusion could not logically be deduced from the particular premises concerning it: as will be more fully argued in the discussion upon Dr. Brown's reasoning.

If it should be asked, (as Mr. Hume presently does), how is it known when objects are similar upon any two occasions; the 'sensible qualities may be the same, and not the *secret powers, upon which the Effects depend?*'[16] I answer, this is to *shift* the question from the examination of *like Causes supposed*, to the consideration of the *method whereby their presence* may be *detected*.[17] But this difficulty is met, and considered in, its proper place; I shall only here say, that as the *secret powers* are the real external unknown Causes in Nature, which determine the sensible qualities, as well as *every other Effect*; so when we find

---

[15]   Compare Sec. 4. p. 30, with Sec. 4. p. 34. [Shepherd refers to Hume, *Enquiry* 4.12 (pp. 111–12) and 4.16 (pp. 113–14).]

[16]   [Shepherd paraphrases Hume, *Enquiry* 4.21 (p. 117).]

[17]   I should not here have taken notice of this objection, but that as Mr. Hume does suddenly shift the question, so I would not appear to avoid an answer to it: otherwise it is something too early to enter upon the subject; obliging me to make use of my argument previously to its complete development. But the reader may pass over to the next Section if he please.

the sensible qualities the same on any two occasions, we are sure the secret powers are similar *thus far,* and therefore fitted to exhibit their further similar effects; — (or *combined secret powers and sensible qualities*); and although some *unobserved* cause might creep in to alter the object, whilst appearing the same, yet this we do not *imagine* when we are not aware of it, especially in cases where the same sensible qualities have been regularly exhibited along with like secret powers; for this regularity is perceived as an *Effect,* for which there must be a proportional *Cause,* and begets a proportional belief accordingly. — We argue from the *regular Effects,* (the sensible qualities); to the *regular Causes* (the secret powers); which having been equal to certain other *Effects or properties,* we expect again the same, under similar circumstances. — We argue from the regular *ends* nature keeps in view, up to nature's God, who ordained them, and who must be supposed still to continue true to those ends; and along with the grander operations of nature, we may often in many cases observe our own actions and those of others, conspiring *only* to fashion similar objects. But when the *secret powers,* and sensible qualities, are known, or *supposed the same*, the conclusion is demonstrative; *so must be the Effects.* Whilst, were it possible to know the secret powers in each *particular* past instance, *universal* truth would not thence result. Neither has Mr. Hume any right to make this argument; because to conceive 'there may be secret powers which may change the Effects, dependent on them', is to make use of the relation between Cause and Effect, as of a really necessary connexion, in order to oppose his adversary: a principle which he previously refuses to admit. Also the objection forms an illogical argument in another way. For it virtually draws a general conclusion from *two negative premises.* To assert, that like sensible qualities merely, will NOT produce like Effects; and, that *like sensible qualities* are NOT *like Causes,* is to separate the middle term both from the subject and from the predicate of the general question. By *such an argument* Mr. Hume is certainly right in supposing, that REASON cannot support '*our conclusions concerning the operations of Cause and Effect'*.

Having thus cleared a way, towards the comprehension of this relation of Cause and Effect, we will proceed to a definition of those terms in the next Section.

Section the Third

A Cause, therefore, is such action of an object, as shall enable it, in conjunction with another, to form a new nature, capable of exhibiting qualities varying from those of either of the objects unconjoined. This is really to be a producer of new being. — This is a generation, or *creation*, of qualities not conceived of, antecedently to their existence; — and not merely an '*idea always followed by another*', on account of a 'customary association between them'.

An Effect is the produced quality exhibited to the senses, as the essential property of natures so conjoined. Necessary connexion of cause and effect is the obligation qualities have to inhere in their objects, and to exhibit their varieties according to the different human senses with which they come in contact. Power is but another word for efficient cause, or 'productive principle'; and signifies the *property* which lies in the *secret nature of objects*, when unobserved by the senses, and which determines the qualities that can be exhibited to them upon every new conjunction. — An *object* may be defined, a *combined mass of qualities*; the result of proportional unknown circumstances in nature, meeting with the human senses.

But Mr. Hume's three definitions of the relation of Cause and Effect are, in many respects, faulty, and not borne out by his own arguments; for he defines a Cause 'an object followed by another, and where all the objects similar to the first are followed by objects similar to the second'.[18] — Now, if he means an object that will in *future*, as in *past* times, be always followed by another; an *invariable* necessity in the antecedent to be followed by its subsequent, his whole argument tends to prove the *contrary*, and to show that experience has power to answer for the *past* only, and cannot for the future; for, that we may conceive a 'change in the course of nature', and that imagination supplies only the notion of *invariable* expectation from 'custom'; that this is the sense of the passage containing the original definition, we may be sure of, from what follows; for he goes on to say, 'or in other words, where if the first object had not been, the second never had existed'; but this idea expresses a much stricter necessity of connexion than does the relation of

---

18 [Hume's definitions of 'cause' are at *Enquiry* 7.29 (p. 146).]

any number of objects, which had only followed each other in *past time*, however often their antecedency and subsequency had been repeated. Such a necessity is contradicted the whole way by the argument. It is quite another sentiment, from that which arises from the ideas of always *before and after*. That which requires another object to its existence, must be *necessarily connected* with it; and I contend that it is so connected, as a *new quality* of an altered mode of existence. But Mr. Hume says, it is only connected, as an invariable subsequent, must always be understood to require its invariable antecedent. — But I retort, Why does the definition assume more than the argument can possibly bear out?

How can the *invariableness* of the future be answered for by the experience of any invariableness in the past? It is truly impossible that it should be so. Custom can only, at the most, lead us to *expect* that the future would be similar to the past; but it never could so sufficiently answer for it, as to enable us to form a definition concerning its *absolute* INVARIABLENESS *of phenomenon.*

Indeed, in many cases there are *single* exceptions to *universal* experience, and to any habit of expectation founded on it; which at once proves Mr. Hume's definition to be erroneous; for hence the *invariableness* of the sequence becomes altered, and custom shown to be utterly incapable of affording an *universal definition,* of the relation in question. — Now, *experiment* is what decides as to a real and necessary cause, under given circumstances. — When an event happens under one set of circumstances, not under another in all respects the same, save ONE; *that one* is a *true cause,* and a *necessary one*; and under the same circumstances, it must be invariably wanted to that end; and every mind feels it so, because it perceives that an *alteration,* could not begin of itself. This, and nothing but this, is a *strict necessity,* and can enable the mind to predicate for the future as for the past.

But the first definition is also faulty in another instance; because in every just definition, the ideas that are included in the terms, must not suit any other object. Now many objects are invariably antecedents and subsequents, that are not Causes and Effects; and it can be no good definition, to warrant the arguing in a circle, which *this definition* evidently does.

The second definition is also erroneous, because although similar causes must have similar effects, yet *diverse* causes may produce the same effects also — therefore the *second object might exist* without the first, by the operation of any other cause efficient to it.[19] The third definition, viz. 'an object followed by another, and whose appearance always conveys the *thought to that other'*, does not differ materially from the first — yet it is worthy of observation, that the thought always being carried by the appearance of one object to the idea of another, proves nothing but *an accidental, though strong association of ideas;* and is in like manner objectionable, on account of *suiting other objects than the things defined.* Every *Andrew* is not necessarily 'Simon Peter's Brother', although my thought always recurs to that idea, upon every mention of the name of *Andrew*.

Section the Fourth

It follows then from the definitions given in the preceding section, and the reasonings on which they are formed, that were a body, in all other respects resembling snow, to have the taste of salt and feeling of fire, it would be an extraordinary phenomenon, no doubt; and one which might for aught we know take place, but it would not be snow; and such a body could not fall from the clouds but by new causes efficient to its formation; — it would, therefore, be entirely a different object, and would require a new name; and the phenomenon could offer no ground for the conclusion, that *reason* does not afford an argument, for the expectation of similar effects from similar causes.

Nature, it is true, varies all her operations; but not in a manner that can ever make it appear otherwise than a contradiction to reason, that it should be through interferences with her regular course. For instance, something similar to the case imagined does take place; we all know that various substances fall from the clouds; but they are all named by various names accordingly; they are known *by reason* to be different *masses of*

---

19   I make this remark however, rather with respect to Mr. Hume's notion
      of Cause than my own; in order to shew there is an inconsistency
      between his argument and his definition; for *diverse antecedents* might
      invariably be *followed* by *similar subsequents;* then, in each separate case
      the second object might exist without the first.

qualities, different objects, which must have been produced by different circumstances. Such variety, therefore, offers no contradiction to our REASON, our EXPECTATIONS, or our TERMS. Yet Mr. Hume seems to think that nature, without a contradiction to our ideas, may be supposed to alter her course in the *determination of her qualities*; and occasion contrary and different qualities, from otherwise similar objects. Nature, no doubt, preserving in many objects certain appearances to some of the senses, may vary the remaining qualities.

But this cannot be, without her using prevening causes of an altered kind, efficient to the new production; and then it is a new object and must be *newly named*. Such events as these, which are nothing else than all the various events, in the universe, (for all things are *alike* to some of the senses, and *diverse* in others); nature is full of; but this does not prove, there is not a *necessary connexion* between CAUSE AND EFFECT; and that *custom* only guides our expectations. On the contrary, it is because there can be no '*beginnings* of *existences*' by themselves, that we know, when new phenomena arise, from *apparently* similar circumstances, that we must lie under a mistake; and that the new objects cannot be *the same objects altered*, and elicited from similar circumstances. We might as well deem meteoric stones to be snow, as a body, which had the taste of salt and the feeling of fire. Nature, therefore, cannot, when employing *like* causes in action, alter her course in determining different and contrary '*Effects*' from otherwise similar objects; because in such a case, these *new qualities* would absolutely be *uncaused*; *different* qualities would be exhibited from *precisely similar conjunctions of bodies*, i.e. *different* and *contrary* qualities, (or Effects) from otherwise similar objects, (or Causes) which is impossible.

Should it be said that nature is supposed to be employing *different* causes in action; by altering the '*secret powers*' (whilst the '*sensible qualities*' remain the same) that it is in this way she changes her course—then the prevening *conjunctions of bodies* which produced these secret powers, being supposed different; the *natures* of the objects are different; they are truly *other* objects, and there is no astonishment at the production of their altered Effects; *there is no alteration in the course of nature*; and the Phenomena will not support Mr. Hume's argument *against* REASON, and in favour of CUSTOM only; it follows, therefore, that if 'we imagine the course of nature *may change*', it must be under the notion of a *cause equivalent to it:—in which case there is no contradiction offered to the notion of causation as founded on* REASON. But for nature otherwise to change, and to vary either her '*Effects*', or '*Secret powers*', without varying the causes or prevening circumstances whose junction formed the objects, whence these result;—is so obviously impossible, that we cannot even suppose the will and power of the Deity to be able to work the *contradiction*. He could not make a finite quality, *dependent* upon himself or some other cause for its exhibition, to become *independent* and able to *exist of itself*; he could not otherwise than by himself altering the determination of the causes that form the objects; then there is a cause for the alleged change—the objects are not *similar* objects; the *whole* prevening circumstances are not the same; and it is only *unlike* causes again that beget *unlike* effects; unlike objects that vary in their qualities.

But the following sentence,[20] which contains the passage alluded to, involves an ambiguity of expression, which ought to be noticed, lest it should appear as though I had mistaken it, and consequently my answer not appear sufficiently applicable, viz. 'Nature may be supposed to change her course since it implies no contradiction, that an object SEEMINGLY like those which we have experienced, may be attended with different or contrary Effects.' There is here an ambiguity of sense on account of the expression 'SEEMINGLY'; for it may either intend, *an alteration in the determination of Effects from objects*, in ALL OTHER *respects similar, save in these* CONTRARY effects; or *an* 'ARBITRARY' *change in the* 'secret powers' 'which mix with the sensible qualities; and on which the effects entirely depend*' in either sense, such an arbitrary change in the course of nature, is a 'CONTRADICTION TO REASON', and an IMPOSSIBILITY.

Mr. Hume however seems to use it in either of these senses, as the occasion serves, and without conceiving there is much difference between them.

The former sense however appears to be that in which it is used, as applicable in the instance concerning the changes upon

---

[20]   Sec. 4, p. 36. [Shepherd quotes, with slight alterations, Hume, *Enquiry* 4.18 (p. 115).]

snow. Compare these *passages*,[21] 'may I not distinctly conceive, a body *in all other respects* resembling snow having the taste of salt, and feeling of fire',[22] 'Every Effect is a distinct event from its Cause; and ever after it is suggested, its conjunction must appear *arbitrary* with its Cause, since there are always many other effects, which to *reason* might seem fully as consistent and natural.' But it is in the latter sense, viz.: in the *'arbitrary'* alteration of the *secret powers, (in order to form* DIFFERENT *Causes for the determination of* DIFFERENT *Effects)*, which must explain the following passage:[23] 'Let the course of nature be allowed hitherto ever so regular proves not that for the future it will continue so.' 'The secret nature of objects, and consequently all their effects and influences, may change without any change in the sensible qualities'; In either of the senses in which Mr. Hume uses the notion in question, it is equally absurd; for as *Cause* is not by him granted, nature must be supposed to change her regular march *uncaused*; whether in striking off *different* and *contrary* qualities, from objects in *every other* respect similar, *save in these arbitrary and contrary determinations*; or in the mixing *different secret powers* amidst the *sensible qualities*. Nor will it answer for Mr. Hume to shift his position, and say; that the 'secret powers' may be considered, as *changed* by the *regular operations of nature*; and that, on account of our inability to detect them, we are necessarily obliged to consider, the *sensible qualities* ONLY, as *like Causes*; thereby concluding the *Effects* will be *similar* upon *insufficient grounds*; and thus REASON, not able to support the idea of a *really* necessary connexion between them.

For upon this supposition, the *real relation* of Cause and Effect, is *assumed as granted* —

1st. In order to account for the change in the secret powers.

2dly. To account for the change in the effects dependent upon them.

---

[21] Essays, Vol. 2. Sec. 4. p. 36. [The quotation after Shepherd's footnote is a slight alteration of Hume, *Enquiry* 4.18 (p. 115).]

[22] Ibid. p. 30. [The quotation after Shepherd's footnote is a slight alteration of Hume, *Enquiry* 4.11 (p. 111).]

[23] Ibid. p. 39. The method in which this idea begs the question, has been taken notice of before. [Both quotations are from Hume, *Enquiry* 4.21 (p. 117).]

And this is at once yielding the whole argument to the adversary![24] enabling him justly to retort, that he makes use of the general principle concerning Cause and Effect (which is now granted), and which he supports upon *'general reasoning'*, whereby in many instances to *suspect,* and in many others to *detect,* UNlike secret powers amidst the sensible qualities, by which means it becomes applicable, as an AXIOM founded on REASON, wherewith to try every kind of experience both in philosophy and common life—whilst also he can maintain;—that unless it were for the knowledge of such a general principle, *no knowledge* of the 'secret powers' of nature in ever so many *past* instances, could be of any material service to us *for the future.*

All mathematical demonstration is built upon the notion; that where quantities, or diagrams, resemble each other, the relations which are true, with respect to ONE of each kind will be true with respect to *all* others of a *like* kind; ONLY *because there is nothing to make a difference among them.* So, if in all *past time,* such *secret powers* could be shown necessarily connected with such *sensible qualities;* yet *in future* it could not thence be proved to continue so, *unless supported by the axioms;*—*that* LIKE Causes *must* EXHIBIT *like* Effects, and that DIFFERENCES CANNOT ARISE *of themselves.*

Upon the whole, therefore, Mr. Hume must be understood to mean, that as we know nothing of *'Cause and Effect'*, or of the *'secret processes of nature'*, so she might be supposed indifferently to strike off contrary Effects from similar prevening Causes, or else to alter their 'secret powers', whilst their FORMATION was produced by the same means as usual. Thus

---

24   This sort of argument forms a sophism which logicians term *'ignoratio elenchi'*; 'something being proved which is not necessarily inconsistent with the proposition maintained': See W. Logick, p. 240. And this is the real gist, of the whole of Mr. Hume's argument (*a posteriori*) and which is generally considered, I believe, as both acute and *logical*. [Shepherd alludes to Isaac Watts, *Logic, or, the Right Use of Reason in the Inquiry After Truth*, first published in 1725 and subsequently reprinted many times and widely used in both Great Britain and the United States. For discussion of Watts' *Logic*, see Wilbur Samuel Howell, *Eighteenth-Century British Logic and Rhetoric* (Princeton: Princeton University Press, 1971), pp. 331–45.]

that exactly the same circumstances might prevene the falling of snow, (precisely the same objects might unite to produce that object), upon any two occasions, yet, it might have the taste of salt or feeling of fire! That the 'secret powers' of vegetation might in future be altered; although the seasons should roll the same as before; and every power in nature be only equal to the contrary supposition!

To all which I answer, nature cannot alter her course when she is employing *similar means* in the formation of objects, by changing any of the 'Secret powers', or altering any Effects; because the prevening circumstances being supposed in any two cases similar, there would be no assignable reason for the difference. A difference, or change, *either* in the '*secret powers*' of objects, or the *Effects* of Causes, (other things remaining the same) is exactly equal to the CREATION of so *many new qualities*, which could not, without a CONTRADICTION, *arise of themselves.*

I can conceive it said by some, although Mr. Hume would have no right to do so, that a miraculous interference might alter the course of nature; not so, not in determining the production of similar objects from similar causes. No miracle could form an *uncaused* change in nature (which is the notion in question).

A miraculous interference, that is, an interference of God as a cause, might alter the production of objects, yet still there is a *cause* equivalent to the *change*, and again *unlike* objects beget *unlike* qualities: I therefore draw a conclusion from the whole of this reasoning, exactly contrary to Mr. Hume's inference from his; admitting indeed with him, that before experience we cannot know what *particular* effects will flow from given causes; yet *after experience* I judge that it is '*reason* which guides us in our expectations; because it convinces us, that instances' (of *Effects*), 'of which we have had no experience must resemble' (when Causes are similar) 'those of which we have had experience, for that the course of nature must continue uniformly the same', *by the regular determination of like Cause and Effect.*

The same kind of answer will serve for other paradoxical questions which Mr. Hume puts in these Essays.

Is there, says he, any more intelligible proposition than to affirm, that all the trees will flourish in December and January, and decay in May and June?[25] Certainly not, to those who conceive that the 'course of nature may without an implied contradiction alter the determination of Effects that proceed from like Causes', or, which is the same thing, exhibit different or contrary qualities, from similar objects. But according to the method I have laid down of viewing the operations of nature, there cannot be a more *unintelligible proposition* than to assert of those trees, which have usually flourished in May and June, that they may cease to do so, and only thrive in December and January.

So far from the mind being able distinctly '*to conceive*' such a change in their qualities, when the proof has been once afforded, that it is their nature to require warmth for their growth; and that cold kills their blossoms; it must be ever after considered impossible for these objects to affect qualities not originally included in their *natures*;—or, for their *natures* to alter, without a cause equivalent to the alteration—or a cause equivalent to it to be *supposed*, without REASON being the foundation of the whole principle of CAUSATION.

To suppose that the circumstances which at first stamped them the objects they are, could enable them to preserve themselves similar objects, and yet arbitrarily put on wholly contrary qualities, seems to be about as reasonable as to assert that black may become white, and white become black, and yet each colour merit its original name, of *black* or *white*; whilst, at the same time, these changes take place on account of such a 'change in the course of nature', as determine that although all the causes in action are sufficient only to produce black, yet white shall appear; and *vice versa*. Indeed, before '*nature could be conceived to alter her course*'; the question about which Mr. Hume is *examining experience* (namely, whether she will support the knowledge of the necessary connexion of like objects and their qualities), must be supposed to be *already* answered in the *negative*; and that it is KNOWN *that nature may be supposed* to exhibit *similar* antecedents *followed* by *different* subsequents, or in other words that there is *no necessary connexion* between like objects

---

[25]   [Shepherd alludes to Hume, *Enquiry* 4.18 (p. 115).]

and like qualities; which is begging the question; and in a different way from that in which he means to answer it, for he means to support the doctrine of necessary connexion, though upon principles peculiarly his own. Should it be said that I assume the contrary position, I answer, I do not *assume* it; but have previously proved the general conclusion, that 'all like causes must have like effects'; (because otherwise, *objects would begin of themselves*): in order purposely to show that 'nature cannot alter her course'. Mr. Hume makes also a great mistake in supposing because we can conceive in the fancy the existence of objects contrary to our experience, that therefore they may really exist in nature; for it by no means follows that things which are incongruous in nature, may not be contemplated by the imagination, and received as possible until reason shows the contrary. Indeed, the fallacy, on which his whole sceptical doctrines are *built*, may be seen at the very outset of his first Essay. He imagines it impossible to conceive the *contrary* to any *known relation* in quantities; but that we may *conceive* the *contrary of every matter of fact as possible*[26] — impossible, under *the same circumstances*, and if the *circumstances alter*, the fact is a *different fact*; but not a *contrary one* — any more than the *different* relations of various quantities are not *contrary* to each other. Mr. Hume did not perceive that all objects whatever in relation to us, are but masses of certain qualities elicited from certain prevening circumstances, and therefore incapable of having different qualities, (or of showing diverse effects) whilst yet they remain similar objects *born under like circumstances*. He did not perceive that the '*productive principle*', or *the Cause of an Effect*, is to be found *in the junction of objects already existing*, by which new objects are formed; but conceiving the nature of the operation of this principle to be wholly unknown, he imagined and alleged all things to be only '*conjoined* and *not connected*'; and that they might change their places fortuitously; custom only connecting them in the fancy; and a contrary fancy as capable of unconnecting them again.

Strange philosophy! 'Effects may be supposed non-existent this minute, and existent the next';[27] (and so in suspense), and

---

26 [Shepherd alludes to Hume, *Enquiry* 4.1–2 (p. 108).]
27 [Shepherd paraphrases Hume, *Treatise* 1.3.3.3 (p. 56).]

may therefore 'begin their existence by themselves'.—If this be so, undoubtedly we want no Causes for our Effects; our Rose-trees may suspend their blossoms in June; the flower require no warmth for its expansion, and remain non-existent till December!

That different objects have different qualities, all are well acquainted with;—The Chinese rose, and the holly, can thrive in Winter; but the same kind of rose, that hitherto has grown only in spring, and flourished in summer, can no more put forth its leaves and expand its blossoms in winter, than the mercury in a *tried* thermometer can suddenly contract to the freezing point, in a burning summer's day.

Let us however, before quitting this important and interesting argument, chuse an example to prove, that 'nature cannot without a contradiction be imagined to alter her course'. Let a receiver be imagined void of every substance whatever; and nothing but an *uncoloured space* within it. Now it is surely the 'course of nature', for this uncoloured space *to remain as it is,* without some *cause steps in to alter it;* and if *some cause steps in to alter it,* 'nature does *not* alter her course'. Then let nature be supposed to alter her course, and a *scarlet colour uncaused* to enter. Does not every reader perceive the impossibility that scarlet uncaused could enter? that it could 'start of itself into existence'? yet such is the idea that is veiled under Mr. Hume's argument;—that different and contrary qualities can take place in similar circumstances; that a rose may blow[28] in winter, when the causes were efficient to its blowing only in June! No circumstances are supposed changed; and yet '*of itself',* the nature of the rose may change!—and so may a new phenomenon take place in an *empty receiver,* as the entrance of a scarlet colour, or of a dove, or any other imaginable being, without an equivalent change of circumstances for its introduction.

The sum of Mr. Hume's argument is, that we knowing nothing of the 'secrets of nature', we cannot know there is really a necessary connexion between objects; but *imagining* there is, this *imagination* arises, from a CUSTOMARY OBSERVATION, of *the invariableness of their antecedence and subsequence;*—which invariableness, however, does not prove, that each connexion

---

28   blow] bloom.

may be more than an *insulated casual event*; not obligatory in nature; therefore *other subsequent* events might, without a contradiction, be imagined to happen after *similar antecedents*, and a *different order of events* might be supposed in the 'course of nature'.

Now shortly the whole of this reasoning concerning the *possibility of nature altering her course*, is but a circle! for the argument is invented to show that CUSTOM *not* REASON, must be the only ground of our belief in the relation of Cause and Effect. — But it is *impossible to imagine such a change in nature*, unless *reason* were previously excluded as the principle of that relation; — *and it is impossible to exclude reason as the principle of that relation*, except by supposing *that nature may alter her course.* —Thus the idea of *causation*, is founded only on *experience*,[29] experience is supplied with arguments by *custom* not by *reason*[30] and custom is supported in her authority by a supposed change in nature,[31] *impossible* to any idea of causation,[32] unless ALREADY SUPPOSED TO BE MERELY THE EFFECT OF CUSTOM.[33]

Nor must we conclude this branch of the subject, without observing the contradiction that lies in the very endeavour to persuade the world that *custom is the true* 'CAUSE *of* BELIEF' *in necessary connexion*, when before assenting to such a doctrine it must give up all usual habits of thinking upon the subject and believe upon Mr. Hume's reasoning, what it never before believed! —

---

[29] 'The opinion that a cause is necessary to every new production arises from experience.' — TREATISE. [See Hume, *Treatise* 1.3.3.9 (p. 58).]

[30] 'All inferences from experience are Effects of *custom*, not of *reasoning*.' — ESSAYS. [See Hume, *Enquiry* 5.5 (p. 121).]

[31] 'Since it implies no contradiction that the course of nature may change, there can be no demonstrative arguments in the case.' — ESSAYS. [See Hume, *Enquiry* 4.18 (p. 115).]

'Wherever there is a propensity without being impelled by any reasoning we say this propensity is the *Effect* of custom.' — ESSAYS. [See Hume, *Enquiry* 5.5 (p. 121).]

[32] 'If *there* were nothing to bind objects together the inferences from present facts would be entirely precarious.' — ESSAYS. [See Hume, *Enquiry* 4.4 (p. 109).]

[33] 'Our belief in *causation* is the Effect of custom.' — ESSAYS. [Shepherd paraphrases Hume, *Enquiry* 5.5 (p. 121).]

Mr. Hume himself recapitulates his argument thus:

'Every idea is copied from some preceding impression (idea being an Effect *derived* from impression as its Cause). In all single instances of the operation of bodies there is nothing that produces, nor consequently can suggest the idea of necessary connexion. But when *many* instances appear, we *feel* a new impression, a customary connexion in the thought, between one object and its usual attendant.'[34]

Now this method of placing the argument is but the statement of *another circle*; for *causation* is used as the very principle which lies at the foundation of the whole system; and afterwards we are desired to search for the *impression*, which is the CAUSE of that EFFECT, viz. the *idea causation*.

And it is no answer to say that the notion of causation is spoken of in his own sense, not in his adversary's; for in either sense it is equally illogical, to prove the conclusion by the premises, and the premises by the conclusion.

What should we think of an author, who, in attempting to account for the original discovery of metals, proved that it was effected by the use of instruments framed from a material termed *iron*, drawn from the bowels of the earth?

In like manner there is *a want of logical precision* in referring all the principles which connect our ideas to three kinds of associations amongst them; of which *causation* is ranked as one; — and then (in order to account for causation), shewing the power that lies in the associations of ideas. Such a notion ends in the formation of a mere identical proposition; *viz.* a certain association of ideas is causation; and causation consists in an association of ideas.

But there is still another passage in Mr. Hume's Essays, of greater consequence than any I have quoted, or argued on; and which I shall yet detain the reader for a few moments in order to consider; it is this following:

'As reason is incapable of any variation, the conclusions which it draws from one circle, are the same which it would

---

[34]   Compare the Treatise and Essays, — in both works *impressions* are considered as absolutely necessary to *cause* ideas — to create them; — to *produce* them; — they are considered as the truly 'productive principle' of ideas — *Objects* without which they could not exist.

form from surveying all the circles in the universe. But no man having seen one body move after being impelled by another would infer, that *every body* will move after a like impulse.'[35]

This passage I consider as containing the whole gist of Mr. Hume's error, and therefore it points out where my answer should meet it. The error consists, in making an *incomplete comparison* between the two subjects compared. *Every body* is taken in an indefinite sense for every *kind of body;* but *circle* is not taken for every *kind of figure.* The reason whence the CONCLUSIONS concerning all circles are *general,* is upon the very principle of Cause and Effect; for I know by experience; that upon the first study of Mathematical science, I found much difficulty in a philosophical objection I could not easily answer; namely that the relations of the quantities in one figure did not seem *necessarily* applicable to *all* of a like kind; until I perceived that the affections of *all,* were INVOLVED in *one* of *each kind;* as there was nothing to occasion a *difference* amidst their relations. Now then let the data be the same, and the IMPULSE *given* not only be *like,* but the BODY *given be like;* and I conceive that every man, and every child, would expect, upon a second trial, that the same body would move in the same manner as before. The inference would be drawn from the mind perceiving, (in the first instance), that no motion would have taken place except from the conjunction of the body with the impulsive force; and in the second case would add to the memory of this Effect, the reasoning, that there being nothing else to make a difference, a like Effect would again take place. Nay, I am persuaded, that reason might go so far as, from calculating the proportions of the impulse used, and the body moved, to conclude the varieties, which would take place under proportionably different circumstances.

Mr. Hume draws two inferences of much consequence from his doctrine; 1st, that as our *custom of thinking* is not the *operation of nature,* so we have no positive proof, that a cause is wanted for the existence of the universe as of a *truly 'productive principle'.* 2dly, That it is *unreasonable to believe in miracles,* because it is foolish to allow of our *customary habits of thinking,*

---

35   Essays, Vol. 2. Sec. 5, p. 47. [Shepherd quotes, with slight variations, Hume, *Enquiry* 5.5 (p. 121).]

which arise from 'experience in the course of nature', to be interfered with by an *'experience of a less frequent occurrence'*; which dependence upon testimony can only afford. This latter inference he professes in his Essay against Miracles. The former opinion is less openly acknowledged; not being stated in explicit terms, but of immediate inference from the doctrine; and which he was well aware of, was the case.

The sum of my answer and argument is, that although we know not the 'secrets of nature', yet we know that nothing can 'begin its own existence'; therefore there must truly be a 'productive principle', a cause necessary for every new existence in nature; — that we gain the knowledge of a 'necessary connexion between Cause and Effect', by an *experimentum crucis*, and therefore no greater number of invariable antecedents and consequents are wanted, than what is necessary, in order *to observe* what circumstances *affect* each other, or the contrary. That neither *fancy* nor *custom* creates the notion by an association of ideas; but the UNDERSTANDING gains it, by an observation of what is *that circumstance, without which a new object does not exist.* Things therefore could not change their places, nor nature alter her course, without a contradiction.

Hence it is that a cause is wanted in the universe equivalent to the change from non-existence to existence! And also that it is not more unreasonable to believe in miracles than in any other extraordinary phenomena in nature, when we may suppose, that *efficient Causes have been in action*, towards their production; and that *final causes are of sufficient weight to justify the altered work of Providence.*

But a minute investigation of Mr. Hume's Essay on Miracles is much wanted. The purport of it, and the method by which it is drawn out as a consequence from the three preceding Essays, has not (that I know of) been observed by the learned. One would think at first sight that Mr. Hume, in admitting that the 'course of nature might change', conceded much to the Christians. Instead of which he adroitly turns round upon them, and says, 'so it may in fact'; but in 'custom' you *think it cannot*, therefore it is absurd to allow this custom of thought to be overthrown by testimony. In this struggle of fancy, against fancy, the more powerful must and ought to prevail! If these pages should find favour before the public, an examination of the Essay on Miracles is intended to follow them; without which the answer to these on Cause and Effect is hardly complete.[36]

Should an objection arise to my doctrine, that on account of supposing causes to act as the junctions of different qualities, and yet by pushing back all causes to the ONE UNCAUSED ESSENCE; I thereby prevent the idea of him being reposed in as a Cause; as he forms ONE object only: I answer, that the uncaused essence, however mysterious in his nature, and however awful and distant to our speculations, must nevertheless have attributes; or in other words, its own peculiar qualities, which required no former beings, to *give birth to them.*

The unions of such qualities among themselves, might well be equal to the going forth of the great Creation! The union of *wisdom,* with benevolence; and of these with the *'power'* arising out of the inexhaustible resources of his essence, might well occasion the 'starting forth' of innumerable beings; the highest orders of which, without the slightest philosophical contradiction, might be considered as coeval and coequal with the Father 'as touching the Godhead'.[37] But after this, the wide universe, with all its gradations of wonderful beings, with all its powers of life and heat, and motion, must have come out from him according to the laws with which they were endowed. And although the original undivided essence, whose qualities were equal to such creation, must be considered as antecedent to his own work; yet the *operation* of that essence must ever have been the same from all eternity; and in that point of view, the *junction* of wisdom and benevolence, with whatever *'capacities'* of that essence were efficient to their ends, must have been accompanied with their instant synchronous Effects; — the *formation of inferior beings.* 'Let there be light,' said God, 'and there was light.'[38]

Thus God, the universal Father, and with him any noble *manifestations* of his essence; then archangel, and angel; man (or beings analogous to him) and animals; mind, and matter; may be considered as having existed eternally, coming forth from him, living in him, and supported by him; whilst an analogous

---

[36] [For Shepherd's essay on miracles, see pp. 219–26 in this volume.]

[37] [Shepherd quotes the Athanasian Creed.]

[38] [Gen. 1:3.]

state of being must be expected to continue eternally, in like manner—and it may also be expected as a circumstance consistent and probable with the whole of so grand an arrangement, that some inferior orders of beings may be raised in the scale of nature, to be inhabitants of a kindlier world than this; with enlarged capacities for happiness and virtue.

The consideration of the method the understanding has recourse to, in order to judge of the probable presence of similar causes on the contrary, will come under our view in the next Chapter.

Chapter the Third

I shall now proceed to apply the principles already laid down, to the examination of the question concerning the guidance of our expectations in ordinary life, which question forms the subject of the Essay entitled Sceptical Doubts concerning the operations of the Understanding. The question itself might be shortly stated thus:—why does the operation of the apparent qualities of an object upon the senses, lead the mind to expect the action of its untried qualities, when placed in fit circumstances for their operation?

Why should bread, on account of its formerly nourishing the body, be expected to nourish it again? why may it not, whilst it preserves 'its colour, consistence, &c.' nevertheless destroy the human frame?

In my answer to these questions, I shall allow to Mr. Hume, that the memory of the sensible and *apparent* qualities of any object, is necessary to the acknowledgment of it as the same body, upon every acquaintance with it; also that the *memory of what its qualities will be*, when conjoined with any other, is also requisite to the *expectation* of any farther qualities arising from it.

The idea of these must be associated with the sensible qualities; but the knowledge that they will assuredly take place, when existing in like circumstances, is founded upon much stronger principles than those of custom and habit.

It is founded—

First,—Upon a quick, steady, accurate observation, *whether the prevening causes are the* SAME, *from which an object is elicited in any* PRESENT *instance, as upon a* FORMER *one;—and,*

2dly,—Upon a demonstration, that if the observation hath been correct, the result—(i.e. the *whole* effects or qualities) must necessarily be the same as heretofore; otherwise contrary qualities, as already discussed, would arise without a cause, i.e. a *difference begin of itself*, which has been shown to be impossible.[39] Thus the first step the mind takes, in order to be satisfied that the same *apparent qualities* in any object will be attended with like 'secret powers', is the consideration, from the surrounding circumstances, of what the prevening causes were, which gave *birth to the object*; and therefore whether the *apparent qualities* are *truly* the accompaniments of the *same nature* or not. —As for instance, we can form a notion almost with certainty, whether the substance placed upon the table has been truly elicited from such causes, as could alone produce the compound object bread. Whether the pure liquid offered, be the result of such circumstances as render it water, or of such others, as may prove it, (notwithstanding its apparent quality to the eye), to be spirits of ammonia? &c. It is not the *mere* appearance of the external qualities, which can determine the mind to expect certain effects; it is only that *appearance in conjunction with the recollection of the probable causes, that have produced the objects in question*, and which lead the mind to suppose the said objects to be truly bread, water, or hartshorn; and therefore impossible not to be capable of exhibiting all their qualities, and none other than their qualities.

The first step belongs to those combined qualities of mind called good sense; and will always be made with an assurance and propriety in proportion to it. The nature of its operation is this;—the mind knows that different objects have the same apparent qualities to some of the senses, which cannot afford a sufficient test concerning the farther exhibition of others;—but observation enables it to judge, when an object is presented, what *causes have been used in its formation*; and if it perceives that the causes have been similar, it *knows* that the whole effects or

---

39 It has already been shown upon mathematical principles, that a *difference* in the *result* of equal unions, can no more arise out of the *mixtures of any other qualities of objects*, than from the *junctions of those of number*. If ONE added to ONE, bear out the result TWO, *once*; it must ever do so; and if a certain proportion of *blue and yellow particles* form a mixture termed GREEN, *once*; GREEN in like manner shall ever *thence* result.

qualities must necessarily be similar; otherwise there might be an uncaused 'change in the course of nature'; which, although sometimes *philosophers* imagine possible, *no ordinary minds* ever do, because they never think a *change* can take place of itself; or in other words, qualities begin their own existences.

It is nothing but this reasoning concerning the *causes*, used in the *formation of an object*, which makes us argue to the 'secret powers', and the similar appearances only guide us, in as far as they form a proof that they are truly the same objects, with respect to those appearances; for SIMILAR *objects* could not have *different appearances*.

The way to try the case is to observe the action of the mind, when two objects are presented of precisely similar appearance, but which may be thought, on account of the uncertainty as to the circumstances which elicited them, possibly, to possess different properties.

We always enquire, in such cases, as to some *leading circumstance*, which may enable us to judge what causes were used in their formation.

If an ignorant person, for instance, whom we perceived could not read, were about to serve us in a chymist's shop with *Epsom salts*; we, being aware that *oxalic acid* had the same *apparent* qualities, should not feel an assurance in the *'secret powers'*; but would cautiously enquire for some mark, by which to be guided in our notion as to their *original* FORMATION; — i.e. as to what mass of qualities *apparent*, and *secret*, had been combined by the hand of nature, or art, in the object before us. It is here that Mr. Hume's mistake is evident in the statement of what he deems an irresolvable difficulty, concerning the method of the mind in the *guidance* of its expectation with respect to the *untried qualities*, or 'Effects', of the objects presented to it.

These are his words, —

'The two following propositions are far from being the same; I have found that such an object has always been attended with such an Effect; and I foresee that all other objects, in *appearance similar*, will be attended with similar effects.'[40] The connexion between the two propositions is not intuitive; of

---

[40] [Shepherd quotes Hume, *Enquiry* 4.16 (p. 114).]

what nature is it then? I answer, WE NEVER DO MAKE THE CONNEXION—*we never do foresee that objects similar in appearance* ONLY, will be attended with *similar Effects.*—But as *truly similar* objects, must necessarily *appear* the same, we combine these acknowledged similarities, with the circumstances which we are aware of, as *most probable to have been used in their formation*, and thence judge whether the object be *truly* a mass of similar Effects or qualities, elicited from like causes in action, or the contrary.

If the causes in action have been the same; (and we are pretty good judges if they have, or have not, in the vast variety of ordinary cases with which we have to do), then the objects in question must necessarily possess the whole qualities which belong to their natures, whether taken *singly*, and acting *alone* on the senses; or acting in *conjunction with another object*, and exhibiting those *further qualities*, which are usually termed '*Effects*'.

Thus Mr. Hume's statement—'I have found such an object has always been attended with such an effect; and I foresee other objects, in *appearance* similar, will be attended with similar effects'; is not the state of the human mind in any given circumstance. It should rather run thus, (although the familiarity we have from infancy with the objects of life prevent the notion from being so distinctly formed, much less expressed, as to be easily detected when called upon).

Here is an object which has been the result of LIKE CAUSES IN ACTION, *now* as *formerly*. The *whole* mass of Effects, which *those causes once* produced, must necessarily *be again* capable of being exhibited in like appropriate circumstances.

It may also be added, that when an object in nature is, on account of some governing circumstance relating to it, considered as a similar object with another; because that governing circumstance points out the creating causes of it; then the 'Effects', as well as the *apparent* qualities, enter into its definition, and *bread* stands as a sign of *all the ideas under the term*, and of *nothing but the ideas*.

It receives that name on account of its *tried qualities*, and it retains it, when *known to have been formed by those creating causes*, that necessarily can only determine *similar effects*.

If the human body is in the same state on any occasion, as on that when bread nourished it; there is as great a necessity it should again *nourish,* as that it should be *white.*

Thus all experimental reasoning consists in an *observation,* and a *demonstration,* as has before been shown; — an *observation,* whether the circumstances from which an object is produced, and in which it is placed, are the same upon one occasion as upon another; — and a *demonstration,* that if it is so, *all its exhibitions will be the same.* But Mr. Hume asks in another question of the same nature, why we judge *otherwise* concerning the 'Effects', (or untried qualities), following the apparent qualities, in some other objects.

'Nothing, says he, so like as eggs; yet no one, on account of this apparent similarity, expects the same taste and relish in all of them'; 'Now where is that process of reasoning, which from one instance, draws a conclusion so different from that which it infers from a hundred others?'[41]

The reason is, because it is one of the *tried, known, qualities* of eggs, to become soon changed in their flavour; without any great indication of such change becoming apparent to the eye — therefore again, there is *not* a connexion between the apparent qualities, and 'secret powers', and we should enquire if *we doubted;* concerning *some circumstance before tasting* that might afford *a discreet judgment,* some ground for conceiving that *only* those causes, had hitherto been in action, which had been likely to produce *fresh eggs.*

This instance forms an argument on my side of the question, rather than on Mr. Hume's; as it shows there is not an absolute connexion, (and that the mind never thinks there is), between *the mere* APPEARANCES, and the '*Effects' of an object;* — but that we judge concerning the probability of the method in which an object has been *formed,* and of *the circumstances it may have been placed in afterwards, as likely or not to alter it;* before we announce, whether the *apparent* qualities are indications of those '*secret powers, on which the Effects entirely depend'.*

Thus I not only assert, that *these are* 'the steps' the mind takes, from *experiment* to *expectation;* namely, ONE OF A HIGH PROBABILITY, that the prevening circumstances which

---

[41] [Shepherd quotes, with slight alterations, Hume, *Enquiry* 4.20 (p. 116).]

determine those *masses of Effects*, (or qualities) called *objects*, have rendered them *the same* upon a present occasion, as upon a past; AND ONE OF DEMONSTRATION, that IF they are the same objects, *all* the *unexhibited* qualities, or *effects*, must also be THE SAME; but I also affirm, that *'custom'* is not, cannot, be the principle on which the notion of necessary connexion between Cause and Effect, is really founded; and that with respect to the most familiar objects of our life it has only a partial operation, in governing our expectations of the future. I grant that custom or an association of ideas, arising from those habits which infix ideas in the mind, is the foundation of all *memory*; and therefore similar appearances, suggest the *remembered unexhibited accompanying qualities* of objects; but it will not suit *all* the phenomena; it will not give the *assurance* that the accompanying untried qualities, must of necessity take place; and that the object in question merits the name assigned to it. In order to prove this proposition, let us try any of the various strongly associated circumstances, which govern the mind, where clearly the suggestion to the imagination, can arise from nothing else but association of ideas. The ideas of these may always be disjoined from each other, without any apparent inconceivableness to the fancy; which is always the case, in endeavouring to imagine a *similar cause* to take place with *one we have before known*, and a *different Effect* follow, from *that* which had *previously followed it*.

Let any school-boy, who always joins the first two lines in Virgil together, endeavour to imagine one line only written, without the other; he can do it; or that Virgil might have made another line, the first remaining the same; he can; one is not the *cause* of the other; nor, are they necessarily connected. But when he says, twice 2 are 4, he finds that the consequence of two units being taken two times over, necessarily exhibit four units to the mind; and cannot be disjoined from that result, while the terms are spoken of in the same sense.

Like Causes necessarily *include,* and therefore *produce* and *exhibit* their *Effects*. The mind indeed may be forced from every recollection of habit, and consider the qualities of an object apart from each other, as in any other association: but the mind never can consider them as *possible* to exist *apart in nature*; it never for a moment supposes it but *inconceivable*, and impossible, that they should be 'non-existent this moment', and 'existent the next' without conjoining to them the idea of a cause or 'productive principle'.

The only difficulty the mind has to do with, in forming a right judgment concerning its expectations of the qualities of objects, is the probability, or the contrary, whether the circumstances which formed them, are the same as heretofore or not. — But this part of the question, we always consider with more or less nicety of induction; and do not believe them to be so, from external appearances only, but from those circumstances which enable us to know, what *course nature was taking, when she stamped them such as we see them.*

We judge in short that nature, in the continuance of her plan, is constant still to her own great ends; where the first beginnings of the work are wholly out of our cognizance.

We judge from the memory, of the parts we have ourselves taken in the disposition of Causes.

We judge from the knowledge we have had of the actions of others, and of the parts they have also been performing in their disposition; and when these are all in the affirmative, towards the probability of like Causes having been in action, in the formation of any object immediately concerning us; then we judge that the similar appearances, are qualities, of a like object, which only remains to be tried, to justify the assumption that *it is the same*; and that it deserves *the name* which has been bestowed on it accordingly. I think this answers the whole argument, and is sufficient to prove, that '*reason*' not '*custom*' is the great guide of human life; convincing us, that the 'instances of which we have had no experience, must resemble those of which we have had experience; for that the course of nature must continue uniformly the same'.

Section the Second

In the course of writing these pages, I have met with some passages in the works of Mr. Locke, which when compared with the whole of Mr. Hume's argument, (*a posteriori*), must be considered as forming the basis of that elaborate and inconclusive reasoning. Mr. Locke says, 'there is a supposition, that *nature works regularly* in the production of things, and sets the boundaries to each species; — whereas any one who observes their different qualities, can hardly doubt that many of the individuals called by the same name, are in their *internal constitution* different from one another.'[42]

Again; 'Let the complex idea of gold, be made up of whatever other qualities you please, malleableness will not appear to depend on that complex idea. The connexion that malleableness has with those other qualities, being only by the intervention of the real collection of its insensible parts; which since we know not, it is impossible we should perceive that connection, &c.'[43]

In another place he has; 'But we are so far from being admitted into the *secrets of nature*, that we scarce so much as ever approach the first step towards them.'[44]

The parallel passages in Mr. Hume's writings I need not again quote, especially as, if the reader has been interested in the course of this discussion, they will immediately recur to his memory.

Now Mr. Locke never meant to say that the differences of species could take place, excepting by the *regular operations of* CAUSES, *necessarily connected with their* EFFECTS; for he considered the sensible qualities of bodies, as dependent upon their internal constitution; which is both to acknowledge the relation of Cause and Effect, as also to conceive the *sensible qualities*, to be the EFFECTS of the *secret powers*.[45]

Both of these principles Mr. Hume denies; saying expressly of the latter—'It is acknowledged on all hands, there is no connection between the sensible qualities, and those secret powers of objects, on which the effects entirely depend.'[46]— Which latter remark I consider not only as erroneous, but astonishing! in as much as the ideas in this part of his Essay, are an obvious expansion of those of Mr. Locke, who is an *exception*

---

42 [Shepherd quotes John Locke, *An Essay Concerning Human Understanding*, ed. Peter H. Nidditch (Oxford: Clarendon Press, 1975), 3.10.20 (pp. 501-2), hereafter cited as *Essay*, followed by book, chapter, and section number, with page numbers.]

43 [Shepherd quotes, with slight alterations, Locke, *Essay* 4.6.9 (p. 583).]

44 [Shepherd quotes, with slight alterations, Locke, *Essay* 4.6.11 (p. 585).]

45 'That every thing has a real constitution, whereby it is, what it is, and on which its sensible qualities depend, is past doubt.'—Locke's Essay on the Human Understanding. [Shepherd quotes Locke, *Essay* 3.10.20 (p. 502).]

46 [Shepherd quotes, with slight alterations, Hume, *Enquiry* 4.16 (p. 114).]

to the notion of an universal agreement to this opinion; (being *one*, at least, and in authority equal to many, who does not acknowledge it). The doubt however which Mr. Locke throws out, although it does in no respect affect the general principles concerning causation; yet it regards the difficulty there is in the *detection* of like objects, on account of our inability to form a judgment concerning their *internal constitutions*, from the *mere appearance* of their sensible qualities.

I consider Mr. Locke renders the difficulty something greater than it need be; although he acknowledges that a similarity in the sensible qualities forms an argument of high probability, (though short of demonstration), in favour of the presence of truly similar objects.

For as the secret, external, unknown powers or qualities, in nature; determine the sensible qualities as their *effects,* as well as every other effect, or property; so when we perceive the sensible qualities in any instances to be *like,* we know that *as far as they go,* they are LIKE *Effects,* from like SECRET *constitutions;* which *secret constitutions* having been once able to determine certain effects, may do the same again; and not only *may,* but *must* do so again, *unless something has* occurred unobserved to make a difference among them.

In order to form a judgment if any thing is likely to have occurred towards making such an *alteration;* the mind has recourse to several observations and reasonings. — For considering that a certain figured, limited, portion of extended matter in nature, does by the action of the *self same particles,* exhibit different qualities, according to the different senses they meet, or variety of objects with which they mix; so it applies these masses to the examination of more senses than one, for an higher certainly in this matter; knowing it to be very rare, but that a diversity is detected among the particles, by some *one* sense, at least. The senses, therefore, are considered capable of *nearly* detecting the similarity of internal constitutions; — and this upon such a *regularity in fact* of the course of nature, which must itself be looked upon as a general Effect, from a general Cause.

Nevertheless the proposition founded on these trials, is but a probability, although a high one.

But, 2dly. The mind has always a regard to the *method* taken by *nature* and *art* in the FORMATION of an object. When these are similar; the MASSES of *Effects*, or *objects*, are necessarily similar; and SUCH therefore will be *their* Effects in *their turn*. Then these *forming objects* are still silently traced backwards; in order to perceive if their production hath been similar — till we rest at last in those grand objects and operations in nature, which we have found so universally regular to certain ends, that upon the *general relation* of Cause and Effect, (as applicable to this particular case), we *conclude*, that such a *regular like Effect*, can only be the result of a *like* continual cause; which shall not alter as long as the GREAT FIRST CAUSE doth not alter his pleasure therein. Thus we trace the *sensible qualities* of bread to the SECRET CONSTITUTIONS which have partly been put in action, by the sower and reaper of corn, the operations of the miller and the baker; and beyond these to the influence of the air, the sun, and the juices of the earth; which objects as they originally seem to have 'come forth from the Father of man'[47] for his use, so have they ever continued too true to their destination, not to be considered as dependent on that 'God of seasons',[48] who has ordained the nourishment of his children to arise from '*bread, earned by the sweat of their brow*'.[49]

It is, on account of these reasons, (that in answer to Mr. Hume) I say, that 'other bread will also nourish, when a body of a like colour and consistency has frequently done so; and which remains free from the suspicion of any other beings having been concerned in its FORMATION than those alluded to'. *Frequency of repetition*, abstracted from the *principle of* CAUSATION *as a* CONCLUSION *already drawn* from '*general reasoning*', is not a circumstance sufficient to generate such a principle, either from *custom*, or aught else; but being previously known and believed in; *frequency of repetition* becomes legitimately to be considered as an *Effect*, from a *Cause*, equally constant and general in its exhibition; and thereby begets a *reasonable*, as well as a customary dependence, upon the *necessary connexion*, that is between such regular Cause and Effect.

---

[47]   [John 16:28.]
[48]   [Shepherd may be quoting from Scottish poet James Thomson's 'A Hymn' in his oft-reprinted volume *The Seasons*.]
[49]   [Gen. 3:19.]

Thus the most ignorant conceive; *first* that qualities cannot begin of themselves; for there is as quick and accurate a perception, of natural contradictions in terms, amidst the least as the most learned of men: they therefore believe in *Cause*, as a 'productive principle' in general. Secondly, they believe that regularity in nature is an Effect whose *Cause* they may regularly depend on, as a corollary with the preceding principle. Thirdly, they believe there is the intimate connexion of Cause and Effect between the secret powers, and sensible qualities of objects; conceiving that an OUTWARD *indefinite object*, which when it meets with the eye presents to it a certain colour, and with the touch a certain consistency, and which they believe to be FORMED from certain materials, will *also*, upon trial, be palatable to the taste, agreeable to the stomach, and nourishing to the body.

Thus when Mr. Hume says, 'I require *for my information* what reasoning it is that leads men, from the mere sensible qualities of things to expect their future Effects?'[50] he requires the statement of an argument, which in fact is never made; for men conceive that it is *something indefinite*; i.e. a certain mass of particles determined into that mass by forming powers equivalent to it, which meeting with the eyes, is seen of a defined colour, with the touch yields the sense of a certain consistency, and when entering the stomach shall be enjoyed as a satisfaction to hunger.[51] *None ever suppose,* that it is what is *first* seen and felt — that it is *colour and consistency*, which *afterwards* NOURISHES. — *They suppose it is that which is sown and reaped, and kneaded and baked*; which seen, or *unseen*; touched or *untouched*; is FITTED TO NOURISH; but being seen, shall be white or brown; and being felt, shall be of a less or greater compressibility. The sensible qualities are only considered as SIGNS of the secret powers, — which *secret powers* are understood to be determined by certain similar processes of *art*, mixed with the grand and regular operations of nature. When

---

50   [Shepherd paraphrases Hume, *Enquiry* 4.20 (p. 116).]
51   This part of the subject again touches upon the Berkleyan theory, concerning external nature; and the opinions ordinary minds have of the *external existence*, or the contrary, of the sensible qualities: upon *which point* Hume and Berkeley are at variance.

the *formation* of objects can be less accurately detected; their similarity of internal constitution becomes more doubtful, from the mere appearance of *some* of the sensible qualities only; — for, the greater number of qualities which are exhibited as similar to the senses, the higher does the proof become, of the secret powers being also similar.

Fourthly. — The mind, (of ordinary persons especially), though appearing to reason upon this subject in a *circle*, yet in reality escapes the sophism and proceeds by a method involving much practical result and rational evidence. For instance; if there were an *appearance* of fire, doubted, as to its being more than a *mere* appearance of it; — the moment it were known to have been elicited from the concussion of flint and steel, there would no longer be a doubt on that matter. Then if in any case did the question arise, whether those objects usually considered as *flint and steel*, were truly such, it would be thought a proof in the affirmative, if upon their concussion they could elicit a *sensible* spark. Philosophers might imagine the *secret powers* of the *whole* to be altered; but plain understandings would consider the *entire coincidence* to be too great and remarkable to arise from *chance*. Such *sensible causes*, giving birth to such *sensible effects*, they would suppose formed a connection of the highest probability, whence to form a judgment, that the whole secret powers of each were similar. And in cases of high probability the mind is as much *determined* to action, as by demonstration. It cannot stand hesitating, and therefore 'takes a step', (in arguing from the sensible qualities to the future effects of things), governed by a *high probability* founded on REASONING 'that *they* ARE' connected with like secret *powers, on which the Effects entirely depend.*

Nor is this argument in a circle, for the mind does not reason from the Effects to the Causes; and from the Causes back again to the Effects, but considers in each of these cases, that the *invariable regularity* of nature is a POWER that may be depended upon; and from which fact of *invariableness* the reasonable argument is framed, that the same secret powers will accompany the sensible qualities which have ever done so, when elicited from like *apparent Causes*. It is an additional proof added to the APPEARANCE *of fire*, that it is REALLY such, if found to be the result not only of *apparently* like Causes in action, but of such that have *never been known to* MISS FIRE, when they have *seemed* to kindle it. Whilst should the temper of steel lie under any suspicion, of incapacity as to the determination of its Effects; if upon trial, the spark be immediately emitted, the conclusion is as immediate that this Effect is similar in the secret powers, which nature in no instance ever failed, to determine along with such sensible qualities.

In moral feelings also, I might argue that had I a friend whose absence might suggest a dread, lest the *powers* of his friendship had become weakened; if upon his return I observed the same *sensible manifestations* of regard as heretofore I should have very reasonable ground to judge, that they were the symptoms of a *heart*, as true to me as ever, whose faith was always found to shew itself *in similar demonstrations of kindness.*

It is one of the most ordinary modes of reasoning that the generality of mankind possess; to consider invariability of recurrence as incapable of arising from *chance.* — The meaning of which is, that having the principle of general causation already in their minds, they judge that invariable regularity cannot be *undesigned* and without an end in view, (as well as that it is itself an *Effect*, and must therefore have its own Cause, i.e. a *regular* invariable Cause of whose very *essence* it is, only to determine similar Effects). And it is remarkable that this idea and in the *very same language* expressing it, is used as the beginning of Mr. Hume's '*Treatise*', as the sole foundation of a system expressly undertaken to prove that the mind never *reasons*, from experience to expectation. His words are to this purpose; '*this coincidence*', (viz. of an IDEA always requiring an IMPRESSION to prevene it), 'IS TOO GREAT TO ARISE FROM CHANCE'![52]

To return to Mr. Locke, he merely meant to say, that nature in her regular and usual modes of operation, from Cause and Effect might form *irregular collections of qualities*, not to be detected by mere appearances; and therefore unworthy *on that account only*, of retaining the *names* of regular species, which are *also named* on account of their *tried* Effects and properties. But every man acquainted with Mr. Locke's writings must consider him, as far from wishing to authorize in future times such a scheme as that of Mr. Hume's. Nor do I think he would dissent

---

[52]   [Shepherd paraphrases Hume, *Treatise* 1.1.1.8 (p. 9).]

from my notions, that the method the mind takes to judge of the kind of objects which are present is:

1stly: — By tracing the *manner* of their formation.

2dly. — By considering an invariable regularity in nature as reasonable to be depended upon, being itself an invariable effect from an equal Cause.

3dly. — By the application of various senses to the affections of the particles.

4thly. — By the consideration that the sensible qualities being similar is a presumption in favour of similar secret powers, as *truly* similar objects would necessarily *appear* the same.

5thly. — That in like manner when *Effects* are *apparently* similar a presumption is formed in favour of apparently similar causes, having given birth to *like secret powers* in the EFFECTS, as well as *their sensible qualities.*

6thly. — That the mind quickly and habitually surveys these things; so that the understanding being *accomplished* in such latent, and constant reasoning; may uniformly blend and use it, although it may find a difficulty of analysing it when called for.

7thly. — That after the application of an exact experiment, it is impossible to imagine a difference of qualities to arise under the same circumstances.

It is strange that a system at once so unstable and confused, as Mr. Hume's, should ever have been built upon any notions of Mr. Locke, whose moral conclusions are so much at variance with his. Divest Mr. Hume's ideas of the air, of science and grace, which he throws around them, and present them in a plain and popular manner, they will appear thus. — 'The mind cannot become acquainted with the knowledge of a necessary connexion between Cause and Effect; for there exists no relations amidst things, of which an *idea* can be conveyed to it, except by the means of an original *impression.*'

'But in nature events are entirely *unconnected*, therefore not capable of conveying an *impression* of *necessary connexion*, or of POWER; yet men conceive that events, are *not thus unconnected* — in which idea they are mistaken; as *experience*, which is the ONLY field for their observation in this matter, merely offers to view certain similar sensible qualities, which are *frequently*, although not *invariably* followed by other similar sensible qualities. In certain cases, however, there have been such *invariable* sequences (though "of *loose, casual, unconnected events*") that a definition of Cause and Effect, as of an *invariable* sequence, may be *framed thereon.*'

'In as much as it is only like sensible qualities with which we are acquainted, so they alone are considered as like *Causes* or *antecedents*; and they have *no connexion* with the *secret powers of objects,*—which secret powers, are *nevertheless the only true Causes on which the Effects entirely depend:*—therefore *like* sensible qualities NOT being like Causes might be followed by *different* Effects.'

'Hence the *Custom* of the observance of those sequences of sensible qualities, which are similar, can alone convey the *impression*, whence the *idea* of causation results; and thence *necessary connexion* is a "fancy of the mind", not a relation in nature.'

'To prove that *Custom* is the only "*Cause*" of our *belief in causation*; it is perfectly *reasonable* to suppose, that such an *invariable sequence might be interrupted*, for there is no contradiction in imagining an "ARBITRARY" *change in the course of nature.* Yet should a contrary *imagination* resist *reason*, and not conceive *in fact* this interruption as possible to take place; she may again *reconsider* the possibility of nature altering her course, forming no contradiction to *reason.*'

I appeal to those who are acquainted with Mr. Hume's Essays, if this statement be not the sum of the argument—and I also appeal to every man capable of logical accuracy, if it doth not involve every species of illogical sophistry; for,

lst.—There is drawn a general negative conclusion; from an examination of particular instances only. If the adversary may not draw from particular experience the general affirmative conclusion, that *there is a necessary connexion;* neither can Mr. Hume infer a general negative position, that there is *not a necessary connexion* between Cause and Effect. He also deduces a general affirmative conclusion, viz. '*that the future shall invariably resemble the past*'; from *particular* instances only.[53]

2dly.—The mind is directed to infer a conclusion against the general relation of Cause and Effect, by the demonstration of a proposition in nowise inconsistent with it; namely, that *like*

---

[53]   See p. 66, of this Essay. [See p. 47 in this volume.]

sensible qualities, NOT being *like* Causes, might be followed by DIFFERENT Effects.[54]

3dly. – A general negative conclusion is in fact drawn from negative premises, merely; – (however the illogical method may be disguised both as to manner and diction), for it is concluded there is no proof for the existence of the general relation of Cause and Effect between objects; – because experience shows that like sensible qualities are *not* like Causes; and are therefore *not* necessarily connected with like Effects![55]

4thly. – The question is *shifted* from the examination of the general relation of Cause and Effect, to that of the criterion for ascertaining the presence of like Causes.[56]

5thly. – The very proposition is admitted, which is in dispute; in order to serve the purpose of his argument; – first, in the statement that *impressions are the productive Causes of ideas;* – secondly, in supposing the secret powers of an object to be alone *the real productive Causes of its future properties,* – thirdly, in conceiving Nature may alter her course for the express purpose of changing the secret powers; *and that they are changed by such alteration;* – and lastly, in alleging *custom to be the sole Cause* (i.e. producing generating principle) *of the IDEA of causation.*[57,58]

6thly. – The proposition that 'the course of nature may be supposed to change', is used *ambiguously*, signifying

---

54 See p. 76, ibid. [See pp. 51–2 in this volume.]

55 It may be seen, that on account of these *particular* and *negative* propositions, (which after all include *that proposition which is in question*) he *really* deduces *there is no such existence*, in this relation AMIDST THINGS – for in the place of the *reality of its existence in nature*, (supposed by their statement to be disproved to reason, and therefore disproved altogether) a *'fancy of it in the mind alone'* is obliged to be substituted in its stead. This 'FANCY' is *no connexion* between objects.

56 See further, p. 60, and 62, of this Essay. [See pp. 44 and 45 in this volume.]

57 In these several instances it cannot be contended that Mr. Hume's idea of Cause, is only that of an antecedent; IMPRESSION is supposed not merely *to go before*, but to *create* IDEA; i.e. to be an object absolutely necessary and completely efficient to its production, &c.

58 See pages 76, 90, and 146, &c. of this Essay. [See pp. 51–2 and 58 in this volume.]

indifferently either an uncaused alteration of the SUBSEQUENT *sensible qualities* or of the ANTECEDENT *secret powers*.[59]

7thly, and lastly.—The two chief propositions of the argument are in opposition to each other; for Mr. Hume attempts to establish, *that CUSTOM not reason is the principle of causation*, whilst he allows REASON to be the sole ground and necessary Cause of this belief.

In presenting the foregoing observations to the reader's attention, I have endeavoured, I hope, without presumption, to show that Mr. Hume's reputation for logical correctness has been overrated. The effect of his work is to astonish by its boldness and novelty;—to allure us by its grace and lightness; his propositions are arranged so artfully, that their illogical connexion is not perceived, and the understanding, without being satisfied, is gradually drawn into inferences from which it would *gladly* but cannot *readily* escape.

If any reader should agree with me in conceiving this scheme to be fallacious, when minutely analysed, and is thereby enabled to overcome its influence on his mind, I shall consider myself more than repaid for the labour of thought spent in an endeavour towards so desirable an end.

Chapter the Fourth: Observations on Dr. Brown's Essay on the Doctrine of Mr. Hume[60]

[...]

To represent the relation of Cause and Effect, as A *followed* by B, is a *false view* of the matter. Cause and Effect, might be represented rather by $A \times B = C$, therefore C *is* INCLUDED *in the* MIXTURE OF THE OBJECTS called CAUSE. If C arises once from the *junction of any two bodies*; C must upon every other *like conjunction*, be the *result*; because there is *no alteration in the proportions of the quantities to make a difference*;—C is really

---

[59]   See p. 73, ibid. [See p. 50 in this volume.]

[60]   [Thomas Brown wrote the pamphlet *Observations on the Nature and Tendency of the Doctrine of Mr. Hume, Concerning the Relation of Cause and Effect* (Edinburgh: Mundell and Son, 1805), expanded and revised in a second edition of 1806, and further expanded and revised as the *Inquiry into the Relation of Cause and Effect* (Edinburgh: Archibald Constable, 1818).]

included in the MIXTURE *of* A *and* B, although, to our senses, we are forced to *note down* (as it were) the SUM arising from their union, *after the observance of their coalescence.* In like manner the results of all arithmetical combinations are *included* in their statements; yet we are obliged to take notice of them separately and subsequently, owing to the imperfection of our senses, in not observing them with sufficient quickness, and *time* being requisite to bring them out to full view and *apparent* in some DISTINCT *shape.* Indeed my whole notion, of the relation of Cause and Effect, is aptly imagined, by the nature of the necessary results, included in the juxtaposition of quantities.

But as long as Cause shall be considered ONLY *as an antecedent*; the FUTURE can never be proved to be *included in the* PAST, which yet is truly the case. — For, when it comes to be observed, that *Cause means, and really is the creation of* NEW QUALITIES, (from new conjunctions in matter or mind), then it is perceived that the future is 'involved in the past'; for when existing objects *are the same,* they must put on SIMILAR QUALITIES; otherwise *contrary qualities or differences,* would arise of themselves; and 'begin their own existences', which *is impossible,* and *conveys a contradiction in terms.*[61] All that *experience* has to do, is to show us, by what passes within ourselves, that there is a *contradiction* in the supposition of *qualities beginning their own existence*; and A CONTRADICTION is never admitted in the *relation of any ideas* that present themselves. The very act of reasoning consists, in such a comparison of our ideas, as will, not permit of *inconsistent propositions*;[62] which would be the case, if 'like Causes could produce *other* than like Effects'.

---

61 No mathematical reasoning can ever be driven further back, than by showing that the *contrary* of an asserted proposition, is a *contradiction in terms.*

62 The beginning of every quality is perceived to be only a *change,* upon some objects already in existence, and therefore cannot convey the same notion to the mind, as the *beginning of a quality,* supposed to be *independent of other objects* and NOT to be a change. THE BEGINNING OF EXISTENCE, therefore, cannot appear otherwise than *contrary* to the idea of its *independency* of those objects of which it is a *change.*

So then REASON does establish this beautiful and certain proposition, which is the foundation of all our knowledge;— *That like Causes must ever produce like Effects.*

[...]

Chapter the Sixth

[...]

Section the Fourth

But as long as the notions of Mr. Hume shall prevail, enquiries of this nature will be instituted in vain; nor indeed is there any received doctrine upon the relation of Cause and Effect, which can be securely used, as an efficient instrument in the advancement of science.

Bishop Berkeley thought a Cause must necessarily be *active*, and so a *spirit*! And it is universally imagined that a Cause is, in its very essence, *before* its Effects.

There is also, a notion that one object is *sufficient* to an event; when many are perhaps wanted in order to produce it.

I pretend not to have found the whole nature of this relation;—But I shortly recapitulate what I have advanced.

1st.—The junction of two or more qualities or objects is wanted to every new creation of a new quality.

2dly.—That any *one* of the qualities or objects needful in order to the formation of another, may be termed a *Cause*, because *absolutely necessary*, and, when all the other needful circumstances are duly placed with which it is to unite, *efficient* to its production.

But, 3dly. The *whole* number of objects existing, which are necessary to it, may also, under one complex idea, be deemed *the one whole* cause necessary.

4thly.—The *union of these*, is the proximate Cause of, and is *one* with the Effect.

5thly.—The *objects* therefore are *before* the Effects, but the *union of them* is *in* and *with* the Effects.

This ambiguity, arising from the necessity of naming each object, wanted to an end, and all that are wanted to it, and the junction necessary to it, the *Cause* of it, is a fruitful source of error in every branch of analytical philosophy.

6thly. — When Effects or *new qualities* are once formed, they may re-act as Causes, in order to keep up the original objects, which contributed to their formation.

7thly. — Although the very word Effect implies a *change* in qualities, yet among a set of new qualities formed, *all* of them are not therefore entirely changed.

The spark first elicited from the tinder, is kept separate, as to its appearance, its warmth and light, amidst all the alteration, in which it involves the objects it approaches.

8thly. — *It is not necessary, however,* that *any* of the Effects, *should resemble any of the objects,* by whose union they are caused; — and in general, an entire mixture, junction and con-cussion of qualities, involves the whole original objects in ruins, whilst it strikes out a vast many new and altered ones, creating other masses, other complex objects, totally unlike those whose union was their Cause. On the other hand, it sometimes appears that nature intends to render one individual essence, the prime object intended to be preserved; and therefore in its mixture with others, ordains that they shall only administer to it, by contributing to the perpetual nourishment, support, and increase of its qualities; as in the growth of plants and animals; or the vigour, improvement, character, individuality, &c. of the sentient principle.

[...]

Section the Sixth

What probable arguments may be advanced upon the matter, is foreign to the object of this Essay, and I shall not now enter upon them; but conclude by expressing my astonishment, that Mr. Hume's and Dr. Brown's definition of the relation of *Cause* and Effect, should have continued so long, admired, adopted, and unanswered.

The necessary connexion of Cause and Effect, and our knowledge of it, in opposition to mere *fancy or custom,* is the governing proposition in every science. In vain should we look for improvement in any, *could we run the risk of so vital* a mistake, as to suppose that objects, however frequently con-joined, were *therefore necessarily connected,* or, on the contrary, that in the necessary production of qualities, there was no more than an experienced conjunction of them, and that they might change their places by a 'change in the course of nature'.

I have endeavoured to show, that any one junction of bodies in fit circumstances for what is termed the *experimentum crucis*, may be sufficient to establish where the power lies towards the production of certain qualities – that ordinary life affords such experiment to the mind; and that without it, constant conjunctions of antecedent and subsequent objects, will not prove where the Cause of an Effect is. Conjunctions, however frequent, may be separable both in fact and fancy; Cause and Effect, a changed object with its changed qualities, are inseparable in both.

Let then the following just propositions be again received –

That objects cannot begin their own existences.

That like objects, must ever have like qualities.

That like Causes, must generate like Effects.

And that objects, of which we have had no experience, must resemble those of which we have had experience, for that the course of Nature continues uniformly the same.

These are the only true foundations of scientific research, of practical knowledge, and of belief in a creating and presiding Deity.

Selection B

(Excerpted from *Essays on the Perception of an External Universe* [1827], pp. 304-24.)

Essay 6: That Sensible Qualities Cannot Be Causes

[...]

By denying *abstractions*, Berkeley denied analysis – by denying analysis, he truly kept up the *associations* of the vulgar, who *conjoin* the sensible qualities exterior causes create, with those causes themselves; – the very error he wrote to combat.

Now it is the *formation* of the particles, (whatever particles may be), which renders exterior objects such as they are, and of any certain definite constitution; and this formation we can trace in, and by the means of sensible qualities, as *signs* of the things that are hid. It is the exterior unknown particles of fire, it is a certain principle disengaged and elicited by certain defined means, which rendering by its *appearance* certain perceptions to the mind, will, when in connection with the live flesh, disperse its particles with violent pain; or meeting with the unknown powers, whose sensible qualities, when formed, are termed *wood*, disperse the particles of that substance without including in the action the idea of pain.

In like manner, '*It is not whiteness and consistency which nourish; it is that which is sown, reaped, kneaded, and baked*, which seen or unseen is fitted to nourish.'[63] The appearance of fire, it is true, will antecede the burning of the hand, if seen before it is touched; but its appearance, and its power of discerptibility, are but successive and conjoined effects; and in the latter instance, if bread be seen and touched before it is eaten, the colour and consistency will precede its nourishment; but they are but conjoined and successive effects. Such action of cause and effect must be the same throughout all nature.

Thus, I consider it to be the want of separating our *perceptions* from their causes, which has given occasion to the false notion, viz. that of the *successive effects perceived*, the *antecedent* are causes and the *subsequent* are effects.

A, *after* A is formed, and determined upon the senses, when it is *followed* by B,[64] cannot be B's *cause* in any sense whatever; but if A and B have been determined to the senses by any external object in nature, A will be the effect of that external object acting on one sense, and B of the same object acting on another sense; and so long as this object acts on these senses shall A be followed by B, and the appearance of one will ever guide rational minds to expect the appearance of the other,[65] without expectation being so great and mysterious an act of the mind upon such occasions, as Mr. Hume supposes.

I find several men of science agree with me in thinking that this view of the matter may be considered as of practical importance. It bears immediately upon every part of physiology, and very materially upon the treatment of mental and bodily disorders, upon the nature of chemical actions, &c. as it opens a different view of the nature of the action which goes on between matter, (as it is termed), and mind.

---

[63] See the 'Essay on Cause and Effect', p. 121. [See p. 72 in this volume.]
[64] See Dr. Brown's Essay on Hume's doctrine. [See p. 78 n60.]
[65] Mr. Hume says, 'I ask for information', &c. See sec. 4, 'Sceptical doubts', &c. [Shepherd alludes to Hume, *Enquiry* 4.20 (p. 116).]

The ancients, in order to explain the mystery of this phenomenon, *invented* the notion of sensible species; but the modern phrases, of perceiving things, or knowing them by the ideas of them, imply no more than that we know certain definite varieties of mind, must be occasioned by equal varieties in external nature. Most men, however, are not able to conceive otherwise than that those changes of mind, called primary qualities, exist by themselves *externally*. Now the moderns have found by observation and experiment, that by the means of every organ of sense, there is truly an interaction between the corporeal part of the senses, and the external objects of nature, whence it is matter of surprise to me, how it can be still maintained as a point of the highest perfection in philosophy, to be able to explain the nature of external perception.

Now, I dare venture to say, however bold it may appear, that if the doctrine I have proposed upon causation be ever received, it will help to throw light upon this subject, hitherto supposed to lie beyond the reach of human discovery.

From a practical knowledge of cause and effect, we measure the heavens, and foretell their revolutions;—if a scientific knowledge of its principle be obtained, we may perhaps be enabled to understand and imitate nature, better than we have hitherto done.

In the modern metaphysics 'things that go together are defined and *esteemed* to be causes and effects', and, at the same time, are considered as NOT *necessarily connected*,[66] which is a contradiction to the understanding. But when a rigorous analysis of those complex notions which are formed and associated by nature takes place, proximate cause and effect will be perceived to be synchronous, and to be nothing more than a change of qualities from the *interferences* which take

---

[66] See D. Stewart, E.P.H. Mind, vol. 2, p. 222, &c. Lawrence's Lectures, pp. 79, 81. [Shepherd refers to Dugald Stewart's discussion of the metaphorical use of the term 'law' in the physical sciences, *Elements of the Philosophy of the Human Mind*, Vol. 2, 2nd ed. (Edinburgh: Archibald Constable and Co., 1816), chapter 2, section 4, part 2 (pp. 221–5); and to William Lawrence, *Lectures on Physiology, Zoology, and the Natural History of Man, Delivered at the Royal College of Surgeons* (London: Printed for J. Callow, 1819), pp. 79 and 81. She paraphrases rather than quotes directly from either text.]

place amidst the qualities of different objects.[67] There seems to me little difficulty in apprehending different parts of the human frame, the external extremities of the organs of sense to interact with the particles of external nature and become changed thereby; which frame being sentient must consciously notice these changes, and which changes can neither be *like* external nature, nor the parts of the human frame — nor like the *principle* of sensation, soul, mind, spirit, or by whatever name may be designated the capacity for sensation in general, and consciousness.

Now, indeed, the nature of *body* and *soul* is supposed to be so well known, that the *body* is considered to act 'BEFORE *the soul and* UPON it', and vice versa, '*the soul* BEFORE *the body, and also* UPON it',[68] and contradictory inexplicable propositions are framed, concerning *essentially* different natures, mutually affecting each other in some manner beyond our scrutiny; for though some action must take place in some manner, yet philosophers are very apt to reject every proposed manner as equally nugatory and absurd; so that virtually no *manner* of action whatever is supposed possible. But let it be considered, that the qualities of body and mind are equally unknown, save that mind is a capacity or cause for sensation in general, when that capacity shall meet with some other object to draw it forth; (for in sound sleep there seems no inherent *sentiency*, though there be animation);[69] and body, a capacity fitted to determine the *particular* feelings, or perceptions, of extension, colour, smell, taste, &c. upon the capacity for sensation in general; — then there appears no more contradiction to me, that they should thus act in, and with each other, than that any one event or object in nature should take place according to the condition of its essence.

---

[67] This I have spoken of at large in the 'Essay on Cause and Effect'.

[68] [Shepherd could be referring here to Descartes, although various dualist philosophers have held such a view.]

[69] See Locke. [Shepherd may have in mind Locke's claim that 'you find the mind in Sleep, retired as it were from the Senses, and out of the reach of those Motions made on the Organs of Sense, which at other times produce very vivid and sensible Ideas' (Locke, *Essay* 2.19.4 (p. 228)).]

For there must always be a natural necessity in the inter-change of qualities according to their original formation; so that the contradiction would be to imagine them otherwise than they are, when *once* experience informs us of their appearances: therefore, muscular action, nervous influence, and in short, all actions of the human frame; all the actions of nature, are to be explained after one and the same method, namely, by con-ceiving cause and effect as synchronous in each step of the *series* of actions[70] which take place, from the first junction or mutual affection of the external senses, with the particles of external bodies, to the last sensation of animated consciousness.

Nor is this idea a mere arbitrary hypothesis; the knowledge of causation is got by a strict analysis, as well as the knowledge of the dissimilitude there must necessarily be, between any mental sensations, and any external qualities whatever; by which discoveries the synthesis is afterwards formed, which shows that a successive series of unions, and mutual affections of qualities,[71] *will be equal* to the *formation* of *sensation* and muscular action.

---

[70] To prevent the trouble of the reader in looking for the argument in the first essay for the proof of the simultaneous action of cause and effect, let him reflect, That every object would remain as it existed at any given moment unless it were interfered with; and an interference cannot be either *before* or *after* itself; but must be in and with the same moment of the change occasioned by it.

[71] It is not meant that qualities must always unite, but that they mutually affect each other; for whatever may be the nature of their interaction, the argument equally holds good. No arbitrary *law* can create a mutual interference of qualities. Indeed, I have in vain endeavoured to find what philosophers exactly mean by the word *law*; the only rational signification is that mode of being, or action, or relation of qualities, which as Mr. Locke says, 'renders an essence that which it is and not another'. But it appears to me, as though they mean it to signify an arbitrary rule which matter would observe without there being a necessity for it in any physical cause. This is impossible. [Shepherd probably alludes to Locke, *Essay* 3.10.21 (p. 502).]

Essay 7: That Children Can Perceive the Relation of Cause and Effect, on Account of Their Being Capable of a Latent Comparison of Ideas

First principles are the perceptions of the corollaries, inclusions, or necessary relations of our simple impressions; and infants who have not a capacity fitted to generate such perceptions, are born idiots.

Idiotcy appears to be little else, than an incapacity for further perception than what resides in the immediate impressions created by the use of the five organs of sense, and the power of motion.

Now the necessary connection of cause and effect, resolves itself into the identical proposition, that 'same things are same'; and children perceive the relation of ideas which determines that conception upon the mind, and depend upon it, in all their understandings; for children are too simple to perceive any difference between *effects* and *qualities*; and although I must allow that they do not, cannot argue formally on the subject; yet, I am fully persuaded, their understandings take notice of, (i.e. their latent powers of observation enable them to perceive), certain simple relations included in those ideas of sensation, which are determined to their minds by the organs of sense.[72] And this they very soon do, as readily as they distinguish by which organ it is that any new impression of sense is conveyed. It is not therefore necessary to have recourse to any *instinct* or principle of nature, which we know nothing of, in order to explain the source of those ideas which govern their expectations.

To the question which enquires, 'Whence it is, the child supposes a candle will burn his finger upon a second trial, as upon a previous occasion?'[73] I answer, that the child considers, upon the second *appearance of a candle*, that the *candle* is a *candle*.

---

72 M. Destutt de Tracy says, 'Un enfant apperçoit un rapport, comme il apperçoit une couleur.' ['A child perceives a relation [among his ideas] as soon as he perceives a colour.' Shepherd refers to Antoine Destutt de Tracy, *Eléments d'idéologie, Première partie: Idéologie proprement dite* (Paris: Lévi, 1824).]

73 See Hume's Essays, vol. 2, sect. 4, p. 40. [Shepherd paraphrases Hume, *Enquiry* 4.23 (p. 118)].

He knows nothing about 'secret powers', 'methods of formation', &c. but owing to the sensible qualities being precisely
alike, he considers the object presented to him to be a similar
one to that, which he formerly observed of the same appearance; he therefore *expects* it will prove itself the same in all its
qualities. The burning of his finger he considers to be as much a
part of the same *whole*, as the light which shines before him.
There is thus a secret reference made with more or less distinctness to those exterior causes of its figure, motion, and brilliancy,
which are associated with these qualities—their effects; thereby
forming one whole: and as these exterior causes, were[74] on a
former occasion capable of burning the flesh upon the application of touch, so they must again be considered as capable of
that further quality, or effect, which must necessarily belong to
them.

No child or ignorant person supposes that it is the motion,
figure, brilliancy, or colour of fire, (when separated from the
outward permanent causes of these qualities), which efficiently
governs the burning of the flesh; for that these antecedent
qualities *after* being determined upon the mind, *are the only
causes of any subsequent burning,* is a *discovery* which they leave
to philosophers to make; but they conceive that *some* object,
which *is not in themselves,* and which affects their eyes with
figure, light, &c. will also affect their touch with the painful
sense of burning. They conceive that an exterior brilliant object
is what they see; and that they see it because it is brilliant and
like what they see; they also think the *same* object is a *burning*
object, and will therefore burn them. There is thus a false
association made no doubt in conceiving the archetypes of
sensible qualities to be the permanent causes of the sensible
qualities, the effects;[75]—but still their expectations depend upon
the notion, that when a *part* of the *whole effects* belonging to one
similar exterior cause or object takes place, that the remainder
will do so, if nothing arise to prevent it.

---

[74] To dispel this association was the object of Berkeley. Its intimate
indissoluble nature formed the foundation on which Hume reared his
doctrine of causation.

[75] It is this association which Mr. Stewart, Dr. Reid, and indeed, almost all
men, still make concerning the primary qualities.

Thus it is really the case, that children possess a truer philosophy than that contained in the modern theories, concerning cause, viz. '*that invariable antecedency of sensible qualities is the definition of cause*'; for they consider the *successive* sensible qualities which arise from the application of our different senses to the same exterior object, to be merely *successive effects*, on account of that object meeting successively with different senses.

But to prove that the child, as well as the peasant, (and even the philosopher when withdrawn from his books), considers the successive effects imprinted on the senses, as truly but concomitant effects arising from one common object, meeting with various human senses; it may be observed, that if any one were to shut his eyes for a moment, being aware at the same time, that a candle which he had immediately seen placed before him, was neither removed nor extinguished; he would expect upon re-opening them to see its light, &c. again. Why? for when his eyes are shut the whole qualities of the candle become but as so many future effects; and thence such an expectation lies open to Mr. Hume's query; namely, 'Why he expects in any case similar sensible qualities to be *followed* by similar sensible qualities?' for in this case, the darkness upon the shutting of the eyes is the similar sensible quality which may be supposed to have taken place upon a former occasion? I answer to this query, that the expectation of seeing the candle upon opening the eyes, when it is known, not to have been either removed or extinguished, is because, *Like causes (or objects) being supposed and* GRANTED *as* PRESENT; *like effects (or qualities) are known to be only capable of existing*.

The child, &c. upon such an occasion would consider there was a similar object present, and which he would immediately perceive could not be a *similar* object, and yet a *different* one; and which nevertheless would be the case, could it do *other* than yield those *future* effects, of its light, brilliancy, motion, and colour.

Expectation of future sensible qualities, is thus founded upon the notion of a similar object being in existence, when it is perceived to be similar, as far as concerns each impression made upon each organ of sense; for although some unperceived cause might alter the exterior object as a whole, yet this is not much taken into the account, for it is perceived, that *if an object were really the same, it would necessarily appear the same;*[76] whilst also many circumstances secretly influence the judgment of even very young children on this head,—i.e. as to whether appearances are entirely to be depended upon; but however this may be, children's expectations are founded upon their conceiving a similar *exterior cause or object* to be placed before them as heretofore, and knowing and perceiving as well as adults do, '*that equals must be added to equals in order to render the whole equal*', they suppose when *parts* of certain *wholes* are present, that the *remainders* will also recur upon similar occasions; otherwise there would arise a *difference*, without any reason they could suppose for such an occurrence: and children never *imagine* that changes of qualities can arise without a reason for them; or that qualities can *begin* of themselves without a producing principle; or that there can be an *uncaused* change in the course of nature. These ideas appear to them to involve an impossibility; and indeed appear so to all, for I much doubt, although Mr. Hume said, 'We could at least *imagine* a change in the course of nature' (without a cause for it) whether he ever was able to stretch his *fancy* so far.

I grant that children, as well as others, too frequently consider objects as similar, upon insufficient data; for when things *appear* like, and the circumstances in which they are placed seem also to be similar, the imagination does not easily suggest a possible variety; for which, however, there may be some unperceived reason. Nevertheless, when any thing occurs different to that which was expected, such a change is supposed to be owing to some sufficient cause or reason, and the objects which yield such a difference in their effects, are considered as different objects. But the contradictory notion is never held by infants, who have not the misfortune to be born idiots, that objects can be *similar objects*, and nevertheless their *exhibitions be different*.

Thus no interval of *time*, can have any relation to any supposed difference, and the expectations of the *future* are thus *involved as identical* with the knowledge of the *present*. *Time*

---

[76] Similarity of appearance proves the presence of like proximate cause; *other things* therefore *being equal*, it proves the presence of a really similar object.

enters not into the ideas of the axiom – that equals added to equals, the whole must be equal. 'Add equal qualities to equal qualities (of whatever nature they may be) the sum of the qualities must be equal upon every repetition of the junction, and the sum must be equal to the *same* results taken twice over, and cannot possibly be two different or altered sums.'[77] Objects are but the same groups of qualities meeting together, and are therefore, to be considered as the same aggregates repeated over again. Thus children, peasants, and even brutes, perceive, that similar objects being supposed to meet, mix, or in any way affect each other, *no interval of time* which may elapse between the repetition of such mixtures, could prevent their being truly, the same identical objects in nature.

---

[77]   See 'Essay on the Relation of Cause and Effect', pp. 54, 55, &c. [See pp. 41-2 in this volume.]

Two

Knowledge of an External World

Selection C

(Excerpted from *Essays on the Perception of an External Universe* [1827], pp. xi–xvi, 1–149, and 160–91.)

Preface to the Essay on the Academical or Sceptical Philosophy

It was my intention in a former publication[1] to have introduced an appendix containing some enquiry into the nature and proof of the existence of matter, and of an external universe; deeming it necessary in order to the more enlarged comprehension of *that manner of action exerted in causation which renders it 'a producing principle'*, to have a right understanding of the idea of an *external* object; but finding the notions which suggested themselves would exceed the limits of that work, and of sufficient interest to be pursued beyond its immediate purpose, I have ventured to unfold them in the following essay.

Now the question concerning the *nature* and *reality* of external existence can only receive a satisfactory answer, derived from a knowledge of *the relation of Cause and Effect*. The conclusions therefore, deduced from *some* of the reasonings used in the former essay are the instruments employed in conducting the argument in this;—nevertheless it will not be reasoning in a circle, if by carefully defining the nature of *internal* and *external* existence of *objects perceived and unperceived*,

---

[1] An essay upon the relation of cause and effect.

we gain thereby clearer ideas of the *method and action of causation*. For in this discussion, taking the two essays together as one whole, the knowledge of Cause is supposed to be first, because previous to any belief in exteriority, one *internal* object would appear so necessary to another, that without its presence it would not arise; also every change of perception would be observed as a change of that being which was already in existence: — the action of *beginning* any existence would therefore appear as a quality of *self*, or the *accident* of a continuing existence; and it would be a manifest contradiction, to predicate of such a quality its self-existence. Thus, *to begin of itself*, would appear to every child under the faintest and most indistinct form of latent conception, to be a contradiction. But that *one object is necessary to the existence of another*, (by some kind or manner of action) and that *qualities cannot begin of themselves*, are those primaeval elements of the doctrine of cause, which regulate every opinion speculative and practical.

Then, secondly, those *causes* of our ideas, which are neither our senses nor our minds, are deduced *by inference* from a comparison of the ideas which experience yields, *by that method of argument which it is the intent of this Essay to show.*

Whilst thirdly, the *manner of the action of cause*, by which it is a PRODUCING PRINCIPLE, and has a necessary and invariable connection with its effects, becomes elicited by a separation of the ideas of the exterior causes of our sensations, and the ideas of the sensations themselves. Thus showing there are *two sets of* OBJECTS *in nature;* viz. the EXTERIOR OBJECTS, the acting causes of nature, independent of the senses; the INTERNAL OBJECTS, the sensible effects of these, when meeting with the human senses, and determining their specific qualities upon the mind.

The exhibition of the justness of this last conclusion, although hinted at in '*The essay on cause and effect*', p. 42,[2] could not be fully shown, until all sensations, all sensible qualities whatever, were exposed as themselves but a series of successive effects.

Thus the subjects of the two Essays are capable of being considered independently, yet of throwing a mutual light upon

---

[2]   [See p. 36 n10 in this volume.]

each other. To analyse the operations of our minds in such a manner as shall distinctly show the limit of 'what we know of body', will materially help the mind in forming an idea of how it operates when 'acting as a cause'; as also on the other hand, when the mind perceives by what passes within itself, that *no* quality, idea, or being whatever, can *begin* its own existence, it not only perceives the general necessity of a cause for every effect, but also thence deduces, that there must necessarily be a continually existing cause, for that *constantly recurring effect*, our *perception of extension;*[3] or in other words, the *existence of that*, which though *unperceived* and *independent*, merits the appellation of 'body'. The analysis, therefore, of the operations of mind from infancy, throws light upon the knowledge we have of cause and effect; and the relation of cause and effect when fully known and established, affords the only method of *proof* in our power, for the knowledge of external existence.

I propose in this essay as in the former one, to consider Mr. Hume's notions as expressed first of all in his '*Treatise upon Human Nature*', and afterwards as resumed in his essay entitled, 'On the Academical or Sceptical Philosophy'; yet to conduct the argument rather by stating what I conceive to be truth, than by a minute examination of his reasoning. In doing this if any thoughts should appear of such a nature as to afford a prospect that the doctrine first set up by Bishop Berkeley, is capable of being modified in such a manner as not to be at variance with the common experience of life, much less to afford a supply of arguments in favour of atheism, the author will be rewarded for the labour of thought which has been found necessary in the consideration of it.

---

[3] 'Essay on Cause and Effect', p. 34. [See p. 32 in this volume.]

Introductory Chapter

Section I

The question stated.

The question intended to be investigated in the following pages is thus stated in the 'Treatise on Human Nature',[4] 'Why we attribute a *continued* existence to objects even when they are not present to the senses?' And, 'why we suppose them to have an existence distinct from the mind; i.e. *external in their position,* and *independent* in their existence and operation?' Mr. Hume argues at great length, that it is *not* by means either of the *'senses,* or of *reason'*; that 'we are induced to believe in the existence of body'; but that we gain the notion entirely by an operation of the *'imagination'* which has 'a propensity to *feign* the continued existence of all sensible objects, and as this propensity arises from some lively impressions on the memory, it bestows a vivacity on that fiction, or in other words, makes us believe the continued existence of body'.[5] It is not my intention to analyse Mr. Hume's reasoning on this subject, which I conceive to be altogether erroneous, and which it would be very tedious to examine; I prefer, therefore, answering the question as it stands, according to my own views of it, setting down what experience and reflection suggest to my mind as the operations of nature in this matter; and I shall endeavour to point out what complication of objects, and what arrangement of them is necessary towards that result which appears to us from its familiarity and constancy of appearance, perfectly simple and easy to be understood. But first, I shall shortly observe, that Mr. Hume's error in general is similar to that in the essay on 'necessary connexion', viz. of substituting *'imagination'* and *'vivacity of thought'*, as a ground of belief, instead of *'reason'*. 'An idea', says Mr. Hume, 'acquires a vivacity by its

---

4   Part 4, sec. 2. [Shepherd quotes David Hume, *A Treatise of Human Nature*, ed. David Fate Norton and Mary J. Norton (Oxford: Oxford University Press, 2000), 1.4.2.2 (pp. 125–6). Hereafter cited as *Treatise*, followed by book, part, section, and paragraph number, with page numbers.]

5   [Shepherd quotes Hume, *Treatise* 1.4.2.42 (p. 138).]

relation to some present impression',[6] and this at once, according to him, forms the whole ground upon which our 'belief' rests, of the necessity there is, that *similar effects* should flow from *similar causes*, and *that objects should continue to exist unperceived*. It is my intention to shew here, as upon a former occasion, that as the very *act of reasoning consists in drawing out to observation the relations of things as they are included in their juxtaposition to each other;* so upon this question, concerning our 'knowledge of the existence of body', it is REASON, which taking notice of the *whole* of our perceptions, and of their *mutual relations*, affords those proofs 'of body' which first generate, and after examination will substantiate, the belief of its existence.

[...]

Section 2

1. Sensation a generic term, &c.
2. Question restated.
3. Generally answered and subdivided into three parts for further consideration.

I. In the discussion of this subject (*'as to our knowledge of the existence of body'*), I mean to follow the example of Dr. Berkeley in the use of the word *sensation* chiefly, instead of *perception;* because it is a *generic term*, comprehending every consciousness whatever. Dr. Reid[7] is most unphilosophical in supposing perception to be a power of the mind independent of sensation, and that it can be contradistinguished from it; whereas, although *every sensation* may not be *the perception of an exterior object*, acting on either of the five organs of sense, yet there can be *no perception* of such objects without that *inward act* of consciousness, which, as a consciousness, is in truth a sensation of the mind. When it is apprehended *that all we know* must be by means of *consciousnesses*, or *sensations*, then will be the time to

---

6   [Shepherd quotes Hume, *Treatise* 1.4.2.41 (p. 138).]

7   In the beginning of his argument against Mr. Hume in his Inquiry of the Human Mind. [See Thomas Reid, *An Inquiry Into the Human Mind on the Principles of Common Sense*, ed. Derek R. Brookes (University Park: Pennsylvania State University Press, 1997), 6.20 (pp. 167–74). Hereafter cited as *Inquiry*, followed by chapter and section number, with page numbers.]

analyse their various classes, to examine their relations, to notice their peculiarities, in order to discover by what means it is we come to the belief of *non-sentient* existences. I know, indeed, that it is usual to apply the term *sensation* to those perceptions only which are unaccompanied with the notion *of their inhering* in *an outward object*, as the pain arising from the incision of a sharp instrument is a sensation, which is *not in the instrument*. But in reality every thought, notion, idea, feeling, and perception, which distinguishes a sentient nature from unconscious existence, may be considered generally as sensation. Whereas perception, as used by some authors, (especially by Dr. Reid), begs the question under debate; i.e. of the existence of objects or masses of external qualities already *perceived*. For under any illusion of the senses, a person would say, (as of sight, for instance), 'I thought there had been a bird in this room; until I *perceived* it was only a painting': meaning that he made use of the *whole knowledge relating to the subject*, then in the mind, as an instrument, an inward eye, to correct the impressions at first received; and when the doctrine I propose becomes unfolded, the following is the conclusion to which I wish it may lead, viz., *That the relations of various sensations generate conclusions, which become new sensations or perceptions, and which, as so many inward objects of sense, afford an evidence of the existence of the exterior objects to which they refer, equal to the evidence there is for any existing sensation whatever, in the mere consciousness of its presence.* Mr. Hume uses the word *perception* in the sense I do that of *sensation*, i.e. for any consciousness whatever. But on account of the ambiguity to which that word is exposed, I prefer the latter term. However, when I occasionally use the word 'perception', I use it in the sense of a '*consciousness of sensation*', a SENSATION TAKEN NOTICE OF BY THE MIND, and this is the sense in which Mr. Locke defines the word.

2. Having said thus much for the sake of clearness, I proceed to state the question proposed, with some slight variation of expression, thus: *Whence is it, that many of the sensations with which we are acquainted are considered as objects continuous in their existence, outward from, and independent of our own,* when it is obvious, they are still upon the same footing as those are allowed to be, which are considered as interrupted, inward, and dependent beings; being all of them *equally perceptions,* or

feelings of a mind, which when *not perceiving,* or *feeling,* cannot take notice of any existence whatever?

3. I answer that we do not conceive our *sensations* so to exist, but by habit associate them with the notion of some sort of corresponding continuous existences, and that we gain the knowledge that there must needs be some *continuous (independent)* existences, beings that are *not* sensations, by the means of *reasoning,* which *reasoning itself* consists of other and *superinduced sensations,* arising from the comparison of the relations, of simple sensations among themselves, thus testifying the existence of the external objects it represents, as much as the experience of simple sensations (of colour, sound, &c.) testifies the existence of their respective internal objects; and that, although we be only conscious of our sensations, yet our whole combined sensations include in *their relations* the necessity, that there should be, and the proof that there are, other existences than the mere sensations themselves.

In order to discover *what these relations*[8] are, whence this result is deduced, let us enquire,

---

8   In dreams and madness the mind is not in a state to perceive and examine *these relations;* for, First, There is no remembrance of the *place* the percipient is in; therefore, *the relation of place* in regard to all those vivacious images which are moving in the fancy is wanting, which, did it exist, would show they were merely parcels of sensible qualities, independent of the action of the senses on external objects, and thus render the mind *conscious* it was in a delirium; a very peculiar state of mind no doubt, but one which experience proves may take place, and which at once renders futile that notion of Hume and Berkeley, that the *reality* of things consists only in the superior *vivacity* of their impressions.

Secondly, The mind is not in a fit state to perceive, that these masses of sensible qualities are not such as can return upon the sense when called for; and so are wanting in that proof of *continuous* existence.

Thirdly, The mind is not in a state to combine with these observations, the knowledge that these masses of sensible qualities cannot owe their existence to those methods of *formation* which in nature determine objects, independent of each man's sense in particular, and, therefore, wholly different beings from the creatures of one man's fancy in particular, the result of a lively, or disordered circulation of the blood.

This view of the subject will be further pursued in the discussion of this essay.

First, By what means it is we acquire the notion of CONTINUOUS *existences*, in opposition to the INTERRUPTED sensations, by which they appear to the mind?

Secondly, Examine the foundations, for considering such objects EXTERNAL to, instead of a part of, or included IN the perceiving mind.

Thirdly, Further consider, whence the notion originates, that such objects are entirely INDEPENDENT of our own existence; although we can only know them by our sensations, which themselves DEPEND upon our existence?

In the consideration of these three branches of the question, I shall take notice, how far the method nature takes to *generate* the notions of independent existence, *proves* it, and cursorily observe on the errors of Mr. Hume and Bishop Berkeley on these points, &c.

Chapter 1: On Continuous Existence

Section 1

Whence the knowledge of CONTINUOUS Existence unperceived?

First, I observe, that the *method* in which what are called external objects[9] introduce themselves to the mind, occasions it to judge, that the cause of *each sensation in particular*, is *different from the cause of sensation in general*, and so *may* CONTINUE *to exist* when *unperceived*. For by a *general* sensation present to the mind, it *always* possesses the notion of the *possibility* of the existence of unperceived objects; and from the facts which take place, it can only explain the appearance of objects, by the supposition that they actually do exist when unperceived or unfelt. For the mind perceives that unless they are *created purposely, ready to appear,* upon each irregular call of the senses, they must CONTINUE *to exist, ready to appear* to them upon such calls.

Also the mind knows there must necessarily be some sort of continually existing beings which are not perceptions, on account of their successively *vanishing*; for there needs must *continue sufficient objects to cause* a renewal of them; otherwise

---

9   i.e. The object which meeting with any sense excites its action.

they would each in their turn 'BEGIN *their own existences*', i.e. a relation of ideas would exist, which by the youngest minds is not embraced from its involving an intuitive contradiction.

Such is the latent reasoning silently generated in the minds of all men, from infancy;—by returning on their steps men can again recover the image of the house, the tree, they have just passed: Do these objects continue to exist in them; and is the eye put in action; and does motion take place in relation only to the mind; or more indefinitely to the object called self? (i.e. an individual capacity for sensation in general?)—No, in vain would sight, and motion, attempt to call up these images, unless as objects different from the mind, or object termed *self*, or simple capacity for general sensation, they were ready to appear in relation to those appropriate methods for their intro-duction, (viz. motion and the use of the eye); which cannot gain any appearance of them, by only applying such methods as call upon the inward sentient principle, termed mind. The *readiness, therefore, to appear when called for* by the use of the organs of sense, mixed with the reasoning, that the organs of sense and mind being the same, a *third* set of objects is needed in order to determine those perceptions *in particular* which are neither the organs of sense nor mind *in general,* forms together the familiar reason, (the superinduced sensation), which yields to all,—infants, and peasants, as much as to wise men, the notion of the *continual* existence of objects unperceived. Interrupted sensa-tions of mind, when the organs of sense are not used, are not ready to appear upon any *irregular call* of any power we are possessed of. But the mind is conscious of the *interruptions* of its sensations; therefore, the ultimate *causes* which exist ready and capable to renew them, must be UNINTERRUPTED *causes,* otherwise they would '*begin their own existences*'; a proposition which has at large been proved in the former essay to be impossible, for any being, or any affection of being to be capable of. The more refined kinds of reasoning, I grant, lie not in the compass of thinking, of which ordinary minds are capable; and as this essay is intended to explain the popular notion of all men, and to shew exactly what it is, and how far philosophy will support it, and how far dissent from it, so I shall chiefly dwell upon the method nature takes with all men. And, therefore, I repeat, that men take notice from their earliest infancy, that the *call of the organs of sense,* and the use of motion, are related to things *constantly ready* to *appear* in relation to them, and that the action of the organs of sense, and *motion,* have *nothing to do with,* and can *gain nothing* by applying themselves to that object they consider their minds. But this may easily be translated into philosophical language; and resolves itself into the consideration, that *that class of sensations,* called the *use of the senses,* and *motion,* will by *application however irregular* to some sort of existences, introduce the notice of them to the mind, and that these existences, being always *ready to appear* upon these irregular calls of the senses, and motion, must continue to exist when *not called upon,* in order to be *thus ready to appear.* But the sensations in which they appear to the mind, are by consciousness known to be *interrupted;* therefore, the existences which are *uninterrupted* and *continue to exist,* and which are in relation to the *senses* and *motion,* do *not* continue to exist *perceived* by the mind, but continue to exist *unperceived* by the mind. Moreover, the capacity for sensation in general being given with the use of any particular organ of sense, certain perceptions belonging to that sense do not arise; therefore, when these remain the same, and the perceptions in question do arise, they must be occasioned by *unperceived* causes affecting it, the existence of which causes is known, and is demonstrably *proved* by these their effects. These observations and reasonings when compounded together, give evidence for the *continued* and *unperceived* existences which are in relation to the senses, as much as the exhibition of any simple sensation whatever affords an evidence of the existence of that *new being in the universe, in which the sensation consists.* For colour, sound, &c. may be considered as so many beings; and every variety of them, as so many various beings, whose *existence* cannot be *disputed,* after a *consciousness of their appearance to the mind.* In like manner *the relations of the simple sensations* are equally true in their existence.

The existence of the *notion of four units* is not more certain under the immediate consciousness of it, than *all the relations* that are included in that number; and if in the examination of these relations, any *negative* ideas present themselves, these *negations* are upon the *same footing also;* and as *non-existences* are *proved not to exist,* as much as *positive* ones are proved to exist. Now the only objection that can be made to this reasoning, is the possibility of an *imperfect* or *false view* of the relations in question—and this I grant. But upon the supposition that the mind in this matter observes carefully enough the *relation of its simple sensations,* then the evidence for the existences which depend on them, is *upon the same footing as are the simple* sensations, and must render an equal confidence in it.

Now all that is wanted for the argument is to shew, that reason, (or the *observation of the relation of our simple sensations),* does as a new sensation of the mind, give evidence of unperceived existence, and therefore affords a solution to the difficulty which appears to be in the question—Whence we know of any *continued existence,* when we can *immediately* know nothing but our sensations, which are obviously only *interrupted existences?*

Section 2

1. *Several corollaries with the preceding statement – The association of the sensible qualities with the ideas of their unknown causes.*
2. *The error of Dr. Reid and others in separating primary and secondary qualities.*
3. *The error of Bishop Berkeley.*
4. *Time, &c. The near union of popular and philosophical notions on the subject.*
5. *The nature of dreams, and the difference between them and realities.*
6. *The reality of a future life.*
7. *The conclusion that the proportions and relations of unperceived things are known from the relations of the corresponding sensations they create, and find a fit illustration in the nature of algebraic signs.*

1. Hence it arises *first,* that it is owing to the intimate *union* and *association* of the sensible impressions, with the ideas of their *causes,* that these *causes,* (or objects), can never be contemplated, *excepting under the forms of those unions;* by which it comes to pass, that the *whole union* is considered in a popular way as *existing unperceived*: and it requires a philosophical examination to separate that natural junction of thought. This explains, I think, by an easier as well as truer method, than that of the *'feigned imagination'* to which Mr. Hume has recourse, whence it is, that colour, sound, &c. as well as extension and solidity; i.e.

all our perceptions of primary and secondary qualities, are thought to exist unperceived, when yet a *perception* certainly cannot exist *unperceived*, nor a sensation *unfelt*. It also explains why even philosophy does not readily give up the notion of the separate existence of primary sensible qualities unperceived; for, first, it is too great a stress for the imagination to separate all sensible images from the ideas of their causes; that which is left seems as nought, and the mind cannot bear that vacuity of thought: and, secondly, a number of arguments are lost, as men think, for *Creation*, for *Deity*, &c. which is really not the case; and if with minds equally removed from unfounded fears on the one hand, and insidious intentions on the other, men would pursue logical deductions, and rise above the weakness of keeping up a false philosophy in order to avoid the consequences of truth, they would come to clearer notions of all important truths, and establish them more firmly than they possibly can do, by the retention of any popular prejudice, however it appears to favour them.

Popular prejudice, it is true, leads frequently to a belief in those results, which reason, by different steps, may assure us to be correct. But the vicious mixture of philosophical analysis, with some erroneous notions, only gives birth to monstrous opinions; the old and common habits of thought are disturbed by it; the road, which before seemed so plain and direct, assumes a different appearance under the partial lights of a temporising philosophy, which are only sufficient to disclose the dangers through which we managed before to walk, blindly indeed, but with sufficient security for every ordinary purpose of life.

2. Dr. Reid's philosophy is not exempt from the fear alluded to, nor, in consequence, from error. It is the clearest and most logical reasoning possible, as long as he descants upon the nature of the secondary qualities, 'observing, that the causes for them being named by the sensations they create, occasions an ambiguity of thought as well as of expression, and that the nature of the causes is wholly unknown in their unperceived state'.[10] But he cannot regard the *primary* qualities as subject to

---

[10]   Inquiry into the human mind. [Shepherd paraphrases Reid, *Inquiry* 2.9 (pp. 40–3).]

the same reasoning; that there is an essential difference between them, for that the mind has clear conceptions of their *external nature*,[11] and therefore he yields in an instant all that would render his philosophy most valuable, by those contradictions which would endeavour to show, that extension, figure, hardness, softness, i.e. all primary qualities may be known distinctly as they exist when unperceived; that these perceptions are *suggested* by sensations; but that the perceptions themselves are not sensations, and though clearly '*conceived of*', '*do not resemble any sensation whatever*'; thus making the *perception* of primary qualities in their independent state, to be the result of the sensations which those primary qualities convey to the mind, whilst the perception *itself is not a sensation of mind*: – Considering *perception of visible figure*, to be capable of existing without such *conscious* vision being either an *idea, impression,* or *sensation;* conceiving it possible, '*immediately* and *objectively*', to *perceive* extension, hardness, figure, &c. when yet the organs of sense are to be used as a means of perception, and by whose use, and in whose conscious living feeling, there must be a modification of the objects, which must at least add something unto them, or in some way alter them from the state in which they were, when existing unperceived; overlooking entirely a certain fact in his appeal to the notions of the vulgar, concerning their *immediately* seeing 'the *real* sun and moon', (and not an image, impression, or idea of those objects), namely, *that the sun being blotted from the universe, would still be seen eight minutes after its destruction.*

3. Hence may be seen the error of Bishop Berkeley, who perceiving that the sensations of qualities, (commonly termed sensible qualities), could not exist unfelt, concluded that '*nothing material could exist unfelt*', so that 'all the furniture of heaven and earth were nothing without a mind';[12] and as his followers

---

11   Essay on the intellectual powers. [Shepherd paraphrases Thomas Reid, *Essays on the Intellectual Powers of Man: A Critical Edition*, ed. Derek R. Brookes (University Park: Pennsylvania State University Press, 2002), 2.17 (pp. 200–11). Hereafter cited as *Essays*, followed by essay and chapter number, with page numbers.]

12   [Shepherd slightly alters Berkeley's famous remark that 'all the choir of heaven and furniture of the earth, in a word all those bodies which compose the mighty frame of the world, have not any subsistence

conceive after him when they say, '*Time is nothing*', '*extension nothing, solidity and space equally nothing*'! That such propositions are professed is not a fancy, for I have heard the notions maintained in the conversations of the day, especially with regard to *time*, which as it was concluded to be *only* a quality in reference to a perception of mind, so it could not, (it was contended), be a *measure*, adequate to the allotment of any peculiar portion of existence, as necessary to the attainment of certain ends; such as the possibility of the events of a long life taking place in the short space of a moment, *of that twinkling of an eye, in which the eastern prince, with his head beneath the water*, COULD MARRY, AND BECOME THE FATHER OF A NUMEROUS FAMILY.[13]

I have heard it maintained by able men, that this Arabian fable is strictly philosophical; and in consequence of such contradictory ideas, it is supposed proved, that the author of it perfectly understood, in that early age, the nature of *time*, to be what these philosophers consider it, *a mere succession of ideas in a mind*.[14]

4. Hence may be seen, that the popular and philosophical notions nearly meet, for there must be a cause for every effect, and therefore continually existing causes for all the qualities ready to appear to the mind, upon the call of the organs of sense and motion; and these causes must have the *same proportions*, in relation to *each other among themselves*, as the *effects have to each other*; for the SENSES and MIND, (*or powers adequate to sensation in general*), being the same, the cause for the sense of *extension* cannot be the same as for the conception of *inextension*. The sense and mind being the same, the cause for a

---

without a mind.' See George Berkeley, *The Principles of Human Knowledge*, in Desmond Clarke, ed., *George Berkeley: Philosophical Writings* (Cambridge: Cambridge University Press, 2008), section 6 (p. 85). Hereafter cited as *Principles*, followed by section number and page number.]

[13] [Shepherd is probably alluding to the Japanese folktale of Urashima Taro, who was transported to an undersea kingdom, married a princess there, and returned home after what seemed a few days to discover that more than three hundred years had passed. A version of this story appeared in Engelbert Kaempfer's *History of Japan*, published in England in 1727 (Engelbert Kaempfer, trans. Johannes Casparus Scheuchzer [London, 1727], p. 176).]

[14] Bishop Berkeley's doctrine will be spoken of afterwards.

long *period of time*, cannot be the same with the cause for a *short period of time*; and time must be capable of being *measured* externally to the mind, by whatever could measure equality, such as the *beat of a pendulum*, &c.; and such a measure in *relation to other things*, than the *succession of ideas*, would measure off what portions of it were necessary to the existence of those things, in their formation and continuance, whether animate or inanimate; and even were there no creatures in existence, still this *capacity* of admeasurement must exist as a possible quality, capacity, or object in nature. Thus the existence of *time*, like every other existence in nature, is perceived by some quality it determines to the mind, but has not its whole existence merely in that individual perception. It is the existence of things, and therefore of *time*, which enables them to be perceived, not the perception of them which enables them to exist. Nevertheless, it is the latter most absurd and contrary proposition, (namely, that in the perception of objects their existence is contained), which is the basis of a modern philosophy; which, however contradictory even in its grammatical statement, does not seem likely to be overturned by observation and detection at the present day. The very words, *perception of a thing*, state a relation between two existences: whereas our modern philosophers consider *one* existence as created in that relation, which truly is a contradiction in terms; and one which Dr. Reid taking notice of, felt thereby an offence offered to his *common sense*; and one which he knew would have the same effect upon the minds of others, although he did not succeed in detecting the fallacy by which such offence was given.

5. It may here be seen, whence it is that in dreams, we mistake the qualities which present themselves for the qualities belonging to the continuously existing objects of sense—it is because they are combined in the same forms in which they appear in a waking hour; but on account of our ignorance of remaining in the same place during the time of the dream, the *relation of place* is wanting to enable us to correct the false inferences from these vivacious imaginations, and view them in their true character. They are considered therefore as owing their existences to *causes*, which will *respond to every future call of the senses*. A waking moment shews, that on account of our being *in the same place during the time of the dream*, these objects will not be able to *fulfil their whole definitions*; i.e. *be ready to*

appear upon the irregular call of the senses, or be taken notice of by more minds than one, &c.; and therefore are not the same objects which thus appear, are not the objects of *sense,* but of the *imagination.* The circumstance of objects *fulfilling their definitions, or not,* is what renders them REAL, or the contrary. It is not on account of the superior order, variety, and force in which they appear to the mind, as Berkeley and Hume contend to be the case; for a *real* object is that which comprehends all the qualities for which its name stands. And dreams do not present *real* things, because they cannot answer all the qualities expected of them after waking. Now because we perceive, when awake, that sensible qualities are no more than one set of the conjoined effects flowing from exterior objects, *which when meeting with various other circumstances,* are known to be capable of determining the remainder of their qualities; we therefore refer them to such compound objects as their causes, and as capable of their further effects; and this reasoning is the *step* the mind takes in arguing from the *present* sensible qualities of things to their *future* properties, and that which Hume eagerly enquires after,[15] denying the possibility of finding it.

It is not as Mr. Hume says, *in the case of bread,* that the sensible qualities of its colour and consistency lead us *immediately* to expect nourishment, or are its causes; *sensible qualities* are *effects,* and are always considered as such, and antecede, no doubt, *other effects,* which *invariably follow,* when the exterior causes and objects are put in action to that end.[16] In dreams and insanities, &c. this reference is made by the mind; for the sensible appearing qualities, the vivacious images of things, are considered to be what they usually are, in a waking state; i.e. *one set of the effects* which *are determined by compound* objects, equal to fulfilling the remainder of their definitions, and therefore real, or usual objects, for which certain names first stood. At the moment of waking, the understanding regains its

---

15   See Hume's Essays. [Shepherd refers to Hume's *Enquiry Concerning Human Understanding,* published in 1748, 1750, and 1751 under the title *Philosophical Essays Concerning Human Understanding,* and subsequently included in *Essays and Treatises,* which appeared in various editions between 1753 and 1777.]

16   See Essay on cause and effect, p. 121. Short Essay, 'Sensible Qualities', &c. of this publication [See p. 72 and pp. 82–6 in this volume.]

ascendency; and, perceiving that during the time of the dream, the mind had only been in one place, it justly concludes, that therefore the vivacious perceptions of sensible qualities could not be *similar effects* from similar objects or causes, but *partial effects from partial causes*, and therefore must necessarily be mere delusions. Wherefore new sets of sensible qualities, which rush in upon the mind, are also justly considered to be the true effects from *real, usual, continually existing things*, which now shall be capable of fulfilling their whole definition; for they do not appear to lie open to any objection to the contrary, whilst also the *superior accuracy* of the whole sensations, when compared with the former ones, gives the mind immediate security.

And if in any other state of being than this, all our knowledge of outward and independent things could be proved to have arisen only from an action of the brain, and so this life should be shewn to have been but a waking dream, (i.e. the perceptions to have been in relation to other causes than those imagined), still whatsoever should renew the memory of past life, with the then present sense, would continue the notion of our own continuous existence, although we might require further proof than what we had enjoyed for the assurance of the existence of other beings than ourselves. But I can conceive no method possible of conveying the assurances of other existences besides ourselves, than such as is analogous to what we enjoy; for such assurances must come through some means, some notions in the soul, some reasonings, some probabilities. *And if we will always say*, the notions are the things, and the things separate from the notions are not proved, it appears to me to exclude the possibility of proof upon the subject; for I hardly can conceive how the Deity himself, in granting proofs to us finite creatures, can go beyond affording us such sensations, and such relations of sensations, as are capable of the inference, *that 'in order to support the phenomena, there must needs be other continuous existences than ourselves'*; and that there must necessarily be continually existing *causes, for every variety of sensation*, which continues either to exist or to appear. Nevertheless, it is clear that objects are *real*, or the *contrary*, independently of any speculations concerning the *cause of our perceptions*; they are *real*, if they fulfil the *whole qualities* for which their names first stood — those are *delusions*, which *fall short of this*, but which, on account of their first appearances, are taken to be the *present qualities* of such objects, as will *realize all the others,* upon trial: whilst the mind is in that state which prevents it from detecting the fallacy, by perceiving the circumstances are such, that it is utterly impossible they can be the original objects for which certain names were originally formed. In dreams, we detect these circumstances on waking – in madness, after recovery.

Now the qualities wanting for the proper definitions of the objects, the absence of which prevents their being *continued,* and *external* existences, may be many; but the chief one is, that those objects called other men, do not testify to their existence; therefore they do not fulfil the quality of *outwardness,* or the capacity of being taken notice of by more than the perception of *one mind*; and therefore these cannot be the *same kind of objects* as those deemed *real,* because they do not possess *all* the qualities expected of them.

6. Sixthly, in religion, those notions which either alarm or console, are *real* or *the contrary,* according to their capacity of fulfilling their definitions, and can only be *proved* so, when a future life shall come; because it is not enough to prove them false, that their birth and decay, the vigour, or faintness, depends upon the organization and action of the brain. The action of the brain is the exponent of the powers of the soul; but every sensation of the soul is in itself simple; and whatever in futurity shall be sufficient to unite memory with the then present sense, will render reality of objects to its contemplation. It is of no consequence what are the signs of our ideas, or what *ideas* are the *signs of objects,* provided they fulfil the qualities for which their signs stand. The pointing of the compass is not itself the north in the heavens, yet we know which way to steer the ship; and there is a *real north* if upon the wide ocean, (notwithstanding the inadequacy of our ideas upon the subject), we have so guided our vessel as to find ourselves at last '*at the haven where we would be*'.[17]

Thus if our notions here shall lead us to a state of happiness hereafter, it is immaterial whether the action of the brain is partly the cause of our notions; or whether the future happiness shall be inspired without a brain.

---

[17]   [Ps. 107:30.]

The objects are *real*, if they either fulfil the positive hopes of virtuous minds; or inspire happiness by ways, 'such as the heart of man cannot conceive'.[18]

7. It may therefore be concluded, in contradiction to the idealists, who say, that we can have no notions but of our sensations or perceptions, and that exterior objects not being *sensations*, we can therefore have no notions *of them*; that *by our sensations*, (i.e. *by our reasonings*, which are a *certain set* of sensations), *we do have the notions of existences or objects*, which are *unperceived or unfelt* — nay, we can have the notions of things which have it not in their capacity to yield a sensation: such as of sound sleep and death, neither of which was ever *felt* by any one; yet the meaning of which we perfectly understand, by the *negative ideas* which stand as their signs, and by the words which stand as the signs of those ideas. And although it be true, that '*nothing can be like a sensation but a sensation*'; yet by perceiving that objects *unperceived* cannot be *like perceived objects, by that very notion we do predicate something concerning unperceived objects; and concerning our knowledge of them* in their *unperceived state*; viz. that they are *not* similar to our perceptions. And this knowledge arises from a reflection, which reflection is itself a sensation: and thus it may be hereby seen that the *whole* of our sensations does include our knowledge of CONTINUOUS existences, which are unperceived. *For all our ideas are as algebraic signs, which give evidence both of their own existence, and the quantities also signified; whose proportions among themselves are* known thereby, *as well as their positive value*.

Chapter 2: On External Existence

Section 1

1. *Knowledge of external existence, how gained, &c.*
2. *The nature and differences of external objects, how known?*
3. *Varieties in the sensations, which are effects, prove their causes proportionally various, &c.*

1. We now enter upon the second part of the question proposed, viz.

---

[18]   [1 Cor. 2:9.]

Whence is it that a judgment is formed by the mind, that some of its sensations or perceptions are *exterior* to, instead of *included in* the mind, when it is manifest that sensations *are* and *can* be only in the mind—as for instance, a coloured, figured, and extended object, is considered, by the generality of mankind, to continue to exist after being perceived, (although it should be obliterated from the memory, or left at a great distance), in its coloured, figured, and extended state— although its colour, figure, and extension be *perceptions*, and perception be the affection of a sentient being?

I answer as before, that by *reason* the mind judges that the *causes* of those sensations in particular, which come under the definition of external objects, must needs be *out* of, and distinct from the mind, or the *cause of sensation in general*; for the notion of *outward* existence does not suit the *definition* given to *inward existence*: *Inward existence* is the *capacity for sensation in general*; *outward* existence is the exciting cause for *some sensation in particular. The one* is the very mind itself, or the *power of thought and feeling; the other* is a *motive*, or *cause for a particular kind of it*, and therefore out of, and distinct from, the *continually existing essence of it. That is inward* existence, of which the individual only is conscious; *that is outward*, which is in relation to the *organs of sense*, and to *motion*, in order to be apprehended, and must be met by them before it becomes *inward*; and which is so situated as to meet the organs of sense, and reply to the motion *of others*, (others being supposed possible), as well as our own. But the *peculiar sensations* which outward existences can create as their *effects*, are the only forms under which the mind can contemplate them in *absence*, or expect their *reappearance* after separation; which circumstance forms so strong and indissoluble a connexion, or association, between the ideas of the causes and their effects, that they cannot be easily disjoined from the fancy; and never are disjoined until philosophy brings in some new light; shewing, that 'perceptions can only be in a perceiving mind', &c.; then an effort is made by the mind; and it readily allows, that colour, warmth, &c. i.e. the *secondary* qualities of bodies, cannot be *outward;* and for the most part, goes on to a false conclusion, that *all* for which those words stand must be *only* in the mind; whereas, there must be *causes for them*, and for *every variety of them, exterior to the mind's essence;* and though when unfelt, or unperceived, not *like* their sensations, or perceptions; yet incapable of being conceived of, except under the images of sensations, and as named by the names given to these appearances. For that which we call *ourselves*, and that which forms any individual mind, is a continued capacity in nature, which yields a *liability to sensation in general*. Then those we justly deem *inward objects of thought*, which are such, as give no symptoms of being the qualities of *continued* existences, capable of yielding the same images to *other minds* than *our own*, (such being supposed); and those are *outward objects*, which, having nothing in common with the capacity to sensation in general, must be out of, and not included in it.[19]

---

19 All these merely consist in being *successive effects*; successive consciousnesses, which are but *changes* resulting from prior and unconscious objects, uniting their qualities with those necessary for sensation, in order to their formation—for inasmuch as the *changes*, must be *changes* on that which *continues* to exist, (for any sensation passed into oblivion cannot be changed), so *continuous* existence is known by *inference*, not by *sensation*: for every sensation passes away, and another is created—but none of these, in its turn, could 'begin its own existence'; therefore they all are but changes upon the existences which are already in being —they are effects requiring causes. But as each mind could not change, unless *interfered* with, therefore the *interfering* object is *exterior* to the mind:—I have subjoined this remark, since writing the above, on account of having met with M. de Condillac's 'Traité des Sensations', which is at once, one of the most profound and poetic productions. Nevertheless, I consider his argument as not supporting his conclusions—for he supposes, that during the period in which *the statue* contemplates the first and most simple impressions arising from *successive* and various ideas, that the notion of SELF will be generated from the perception of the *memory of successive* scents merely. Now if *the statue* considered SELF to exist in *any memory*, or in any *sensation merely*, he would consider SELF to be capable of being annihilated, and again *beginning* of itself; which would appear to it a contradiction—for whenever it became capable of *reflecting* on its sensations, it would consider self as *continuing* to exist, and not to vanish for one single moment during whatever change might arise, and therefore as an existence independent of each scent in particular, and so not included in odour in general. [For Condillac's example of the statue that has a mind but cannot use its senses except in very limited ways, see Étienne Bonnot, Abbé de Condillac, *Traité des sensations*, Vol. 1 (London, 1754), hereafter cited as *Traité*. Shepherd might have read the French original, which was not translated into English until 1930; or she may have read an English translation of Condillac's 1746 *Essai sur l'origine des*

Inward thoughts are also beings, which when not thought of, and not contained in any given state of the mind, are nought; but *continually existing causes*, ready to appear, upon the application of the organs of sense, efficient to the production of certain sensations in *particular*, when operating upon the capacity for *sensation in general*, are *out of, and distinct from*, that is to say, *not included* in that capacity.

If a mirror were conscious, then it might know of its own constant existence, as separate from the objects brought for reflection on its surface; and by comparing the method and order, the appearance and re-appearance, &c. of the rays on its surface, might understand well enough, whether or not, they belonged to *continuous outward existences*; although it might *argue*, that it knew of *nothing but of incident and reflected rays;* and that incident and reflected rays, were not continued outward existences. The *primary* qualities, are subject to the same reasoning as those which are *secondary*; and cannot be *like the sensations* their causes create. Every sensation of mind whatever is an *effect*, and may be considered as a quality. *It begins to be*, and its cause which is *not* a sensation cannot be *like* it, and yet can only be *conceived of under the image it creates* as its effect, whilst the cause and effect being united by the mind, the compound is named as one object by one name.

Is it matter of surprise, therefore, that a coloured, figured, extended object, is considered as existing outwardly; when the continually existing *causes*, which are 'ready to appear' to the mind, under these forms, must in order to account for certain existing phenomena, be judged to exist outwardly? Is it matter of surprise when the mind discovers, that although the *effects* cannot exist outwardly, yet the *causes* must, that it should be so startled at the discovery as not to know how to settle and arrange its belief on the subject, and is filled with a thousand fears concerning the consequences of it? Hence various and inconsistent theories all supported by names of authority.

---

connaissances humaines, where the translator's preface describes the statue example (Thomas Nugent, trans., *An Essay on the Origin of Human Knowledge* [London: Printed for J. Nourse, 1756]).]

Thus *some* philosophers make *God create all the images at the moment they appear in every mind.*[20] Others conceive there is a pre-established harmony between the qualities of the external object, and our inward perception of it.[21] One considers the sensations arising from *some* of the senses, to exist *outwardly;* but *not those of others*, arising from the *rest* of the *senses.*[22]

Another gives up all outward existence whatever of objects and qualities.[23] And some suppose that if there be such things, that unless they be *like* our sensations, they are not worth talking about.[24]

Whereas it is evident, that in order to the formation of *all* the effects produced on the mind, through the senses, there must be *efficient causes, not included* in the *general essence* of the mind; and these are '*ever ready to appear*', and that in so *clear, vigorous,* and *uniform* a method, and fashion, as to the appearances of *figure, colour,* and *resistance;* or of *sound,* and *taste;* or of *beauty,* and *deformity;* or of *warmth,* and *cold;* or of *happiness,* and *misery,* or of *vice,* and *virtue;* that whatever they may be, however unknown, they may well be termed *objects, outward objects,* which the organs of sense, and their associations reveal, according to their peculiar bearings upon the mind. I repeat it, therefore, that the unknown causes of all our perceptions, are as the unknown quantities in. algebra, which yet may be measured, valued, reasoned on by their signs; and the signs of these outward objects are the sensations they can create; and they may always be spoken of, and compared together, as though they did *truly exist,* in *these forms* in which they appear to the mind.

For as the power of sensation is simple, and yet its *kinds* and *degrees various,* when the kinds and degrees relate to *outward continually existing objects,* fitted to create them, they may be compared in their bearings to each other, under the '*ideas and sensations*' they appear to the mind. Thus while the sentient principle observes scarlet, and blue; these two colours may be

---

[20] Malebranche.
[21] Leibnitz.
[22] Reid.
[23] Berkeley.
[24] Hume.

compared together as existences. Empty space, and solid extension, are two sensations, whose causes must have a pro-portional *variety*, and may, therefore, as outward beings, be examined as space, and solidity. The same with every other essence in nature; for the organs of sense and the mind being always the *same ingredients* thrown into the compound qualities presented to it, these varieties may be argued on as *they appear*, and are *known* to us when joined with them. The senses and mind, also, may be considered as *measures* of the proportions of exterior objects, and the measures being always the same, and the quantities and proportions being considered as *measured*, the faculties need not be strained to conceive of them still as unmeasured. Thus it may be seen the notions of the vulgar are not so far removed from truth as it is supposed. All men con-sider *objects*, as *continually existing outward beings*, appearing to the mind *through the senses*. Their only error is, their considering them to exist outwardly under the inward forms of the 'ideas and sensations' they create, through the strength of the associations.

Section 2

The notion of exteriority further considered. What the phenomena are which generate the idea of external existence.

But we must examine a little further in what consists the notion of outwardness, how it is generated, and what are those phenomena, which make us conclude, that the continually existing causes of our sensations are *outward*, and not included *in* that object whose definition we name mind? Now, I observe, that having the word 'outward' we must have the ideas the word stands for; and the ideas are negative ones. For *outward* existence means, existence *not* contained in the mind; and negations of being in any circumstance when the relations of existing things will not admit of the existence of the being in question, are proved as a consequence from these relations, as much as the affirmations of the existence of beings, are proved on account of *other* relations. The sum, or consequence of 5 *plus* 5, is 0 in the place of the units; to shew there are no units expected in their place; and the idea of '*no being*', conducts our expectations aright with respect to the total sum; and the *mark* the *zero*, conducts our ideas aright respecting the *particular difference,* between *this* and *any other number.* In like manner, from the phenomena it is judged, that the continually existing causes of those sensations called objects, are *not in the mind,* and so must be *out of it.* But this piece of reasoning to *justify the phenomena,* is an *inward* sensation, which testifies of the existence of those things which are not sensations, viz. 'outward beings'.

Section 3

The notion of exteriority further considered. The phenomena which generate the idea of outwardness.
1. The consciousness of sensation being uninterrupted.
2. The comparison of motion with a state of rest.
3. That tangible objects are beyond the limit of the skin of the body.
4. Exteriority as a sensation itself requires a cause of which it is the effect – observations on Berkeley, Reid – the application of the doctrine of cause and effect.

1. But what are the phenomena alluded to, which require outward existence in order to explain them?

First, the consciousness before spoken of, concerning the *interruption in fact of all* the sensations of the mind, and yet the necessity there should be *some continually existing causes, ready to renew them;* (else they would begin of themselves); and which must, therefore, be external to each sensation in particular, and its cause.[25]

For although the images produced in a certain associated train, which do *not* require in order to their exhibition *the use of the organs of sense,* we deem *in* the mind, and present to the mind during their exhibition; yet the *causes* of each of these previous to their exhibition, are as much exterior to the sensations themselves, and to the capacity of sensation in general, as are the *causes* of sensible qualities, previous to the sensation of sensible qualities. All things *not* in any given state of sensation

---

[25] It may be perceived that the notion of *externality* is not an hypothesis merely as Priestley supposes, but is a conclusion the result of reasoning. [Shepherd refers to Joseph Priestley, *An Examination of Dr. Reid's Inquiry into the Human Mind on the Principles of Common Sense,* 2nd ed. [London: J. Johnson, 1775], pp. lix–lx).]

of mind, but capable of having their appearances determined there, must truly have their causes exterior to each sensation in particular, and to every cause which may be necessary and efficient to each particular difference.

The question, therefore, concerning the reality of things, if put rigidly, should be: — *With respect to those things* which are OUT of the mind's consciousness, whence is the proof of the *continual* rather than of the *external* existence of the objects, which are in relation to the five organs of sense?

For the *causes* of the determination of the illusions of dreams, &c. are *out* of the mind, but they do not *continue* to exist; nor after an orderly and regular manner remain ready to reply upon the application of any regular instruments whatever.

Now the organs of sense, (although these powers should be considered as merely a class of particular sensations), yet are the causes of introducing these objects, which consciousness acquaints us were previously not present to, and in the mind. Also these *externally* existing objects are the same upon comparison, as those which must *continually* exist on account of their regular reply to the irregular calls of the organs of sense, and thus are justly regarded as *continually existing outward objects, ready to appear and to be introduced by the organs of sense to the perception of the mind.* Inasmuch also, as the organs of sense themselves are ready upon the call of the mind to act as such causes, so are they regarded as continuous existences, and justly and reasonably are so regarded; and although their immediate action be perceived, yet they are known necessarily to *continue* to exist *unperceived*, as instruments fitted to their office, and ready to answer the demands of the mind. So that the whole reasoning of the first chapter in behalf of continuous unperceived existences affords a like proof in behalf of the continuity of the existence of the organs of sense themselves; and so does the reasoning of this chapter in behalf of their exteriority.

The organs of sense are by all authors spoken of in a very vague manner, and their external, continued, and independent existence taken for granted.[26]

---

26   See Essay VI. [See pp. 82–6 in this volume.]

Berkeley speaks of the 'senses' in the popular use of that word, and employs it very conveniently, in a manner calculated to support a theory contrary to his own; for it is necessary, indeed, in order to support any theory whatever, to consider them as *something* more than either 'impressions or ideas'; or *'ideas and sensations in a mind perceiving them'*; for *although their action be perceived*, yet it is not in this consciousness that they exist as instruments of sense or by which they act as causes. It is not *the feeling as if we were using the eye* which gives *vision*. It is the eye as a *mechanical instrument* in relation to continually existing external objects. The same with respect to the rest of the organs of sense as well as motion. It is not the sensible qualities of any thing which can be causes.[27] The sensible qualities are always effects in the mind, and cannot, therefore, stand out again, and intermix with other objects as natural causes; and if it should be asked, whence the mind knows itself to be exterior to each sensation in particular, and continued in its existence, I answer from the same principle which enables it to judge other things as exterior to itself; namely, from that perception of the understanding which forces upon it the conclusion, that because each sensation in its turn vanishes, and new changes spring up, so there must necessarily be some *continued* existence the subject matter of these changes; otherwise, *'each change would* BEGIN *of itself'*.

Therefore the mind must be a *continued* and *exterior* capacity fitted to each change, upon any present state being interfered with by another object; and thus the pronoun *I* is ever *abstract*: and stands for a BEING *exterior* to, and independent of all the changes of which it is conscious.

Now the mind always referring the *sensible* action of any sense, to the *mechanical* action of its respective organ, (as an effect to its cause), and considering this mechanical action as existing in relation to those other objects, or causes, which are likewise needful to introduce the ideas of sensible qualities into the mind, does thereby truly perceive and detect the presence of such other objects as are external to, and independent of mind in general.

---

27   See Essay IV. [See pp. 189–200 in this volume.]

It is thus by a union of observation and reason, coalescing with the conscious use of the senses, that we are enabled justly to affirm, that 'outward objects are perceived immediately by sense'.

Secondly, I consider another (and that perhaps the chief) method which nature takes to impress the notion of outwardness, to be by means of motion. For the intimate sentiment of our own existence, separated from the ideas of our bodies, (which idea of body, again includes the idea of motion along its surface from point to point), has no relation to *space*, or place; *thought, sensation merely*, never suggests the occupation of space as essential to its existence; the *need of room*, or of the distinction of *here* and *there*. A dead body and a living one, take up the *same portion* of *space*. But the very impression of motion consists in the impression of passing through extended space, and as a corollary with it suggests to the mind, *here*, and *there*; and whilst the *mind* requires *no place*, nor *space*, to *comprehend it*, the sensation of passing through different points of space, suggests the notion, or rather inspires the immediate feeling of the *extension of space*, (or of an unresisting medium), but never that of the *extension of the sentient principle, the self*. This space or unresisting medium appears continually to exist, and to respond regularly to *motion*, as other objects do to other senses.[28] It is hence the immediate consequence of motion also to suggest the corollary that must be included in its essence, that is, the *reality* of distance or outwardness from the *sentient being*, the *self*; which has an equal relation to *rest*, and *motion*; and, therefore, knows of outward existence, as it does of *continued existence*, by a piece of reasoning; viz. that it needs must be in order to justify the possibility of motion when in a state of rest, as well as regularly to respond to its action upon demand.

Therefore, the soul has the *idea* (or conclusion from reasoning) of distance, mixed with the *sensible impression* of rest; which *mixture* gives occasion to that just result and consequence, the notion of *outward* and *inward* existence. Moreover, *motion* introduces sensations of touch concerning objects, only *seen* when at

---

[28] Kant imagines time and space to be only modes of the mind, which is mistaking the *causes* which determine a mode of the mind with the effect, viz. the mode of the mind.

rest, and which are the same as those which 'continually *exist ready to appear* upon *the irregular call of the senses*'.

But it must be observed further, that the *cause* of motion, or unperceived motion, is the *essence* of what motion is in nature; and in its unperceived state, we know that it *cannot be like its effect*, a perception; all we know is, that it is in its *unperceived state*, in which it must act as a *cause*, and that the perception of it must be an *effect*, and owe its existence to a prior cause; because it is a *dependent being*, and *begins to be*, even when *un*related to us; for we know our *sensation* of it does not cause it, therefore, something else does. I shall here observe, once for all, that *all sensations*, and all their varieties, must have causes or objects in nature as various as themselves which are the effects of those causes, or the qualities they occasion to the mind's perception. Contrary qualities also must have contrary causes. Thus the *cause* for motion cannot be the same as that for rest; nor for one place, (whatever place may be), as that for a different place.

Now the *names* for the qualities, may indifferently be applied to the *causes*, or *external objects*, or to the *effects* the *inward perceptions*; or to *both together*, as *compound beings*. It is in the latter sense they are *always popularly* applied, and on account of which circumstance there has been so much confusion in the minds of philosophers upon the subject. Especially as it seems to me in that of Dr. Reid.

It is, however, unavoidable that it should be so; for it is impossible to name unknown things so well by any other names, as by those given to their constant and invariable manifestation. The constant junction of the *ideas of the unknown causes*, and their *known effects*, forms the reason why the compound is supposed to be *placed externally*, and distant from the mind, as well as supposed continually to exist; and *in that compound state*, 'to be ready to be called upon';—which, although the whole world should think it, cannot in nature be the case. For objects are *minus* the senses and mind, and cannot be the same with that state, or sum, in which they exist when *plus* the senses and mind.

Thirdly, The notion of *outwardness* is gained by the observation, that the *causes* of such sensations, as require the use of the organs of sense in order to let their specific impressions enter the mind, are *out of*, (i.e. *not included in*), the definitions and limitations of our own bodies: and we consider *that as our own body*, which is within a bound, or certain limit, and is the source of *conscious* pleasure and pain, and this *limit* we call the skin, within which, is contained *all we call ourselves*, and being summed up, is the notion of the conscious sensation of the extension of the body, and of a sufficient cause for life and sensation in general. Because without any impression from what are called external things, or the use of the organs of sense, the general sensation of life can go on. But for *particular kinds* of sensation the organs of sense are to be used; which organs are in relation to things that appear *beyond the skin of the body*, and which also require motion, in order to apprehend their tangibility. Now if the mind does not here reason amiss, this method which nature takes to impress the notion of out-wardness, also contains a *proof* of its reality. For if a certain number of amassed causes are sufficient for a portion of sensation in general, (say a mere sense of life), and some other causes are wanted in order to excite particular definite kinds of it, then these become independent of each other; and the *use of the organs of sense* and the mechanical action of *motion*, being requisite to enable them to intermix with each other, are such circumstances as place them in that relation to each other, as may be deemed distance. For it must be ever remembered that *words are arbitrary*, and we may name distinct *classes of sensations* and their *causes*, and the *apparent limit* of their *causes*, by any name we please; and they can be *nothing else but what we do so name them*; and *such* we may say shall be called *inward*, and such other *outward* existence. Then the whole mass properly put together again, (after all this excruciating analysis), becomes our own, and other existences. It is owing to this circumstance of the *causes* of particular sensations being considered outward, that we look to them as capable of being useful or hurtful to us; that for instance, we consider there is a quality in water by which we may be drowned, instead of considering drowning, as *only* a sensation of mind, (a necessary consequence of an unmodified ideal system), whilst the perception of the mind by which it fails not to take notice that it can continue to exist, although this quality for drowning, which is a quality tending to death, still continues to exist in water, (*ready to appear, if called upon*), proves that the *causes* or objects of these two existences must be *external* to each other.

Fourthly. Also outwardness is represented in the mind as a sensation, (a perception of a quality), which as a capacity in nature, admits of motion, through an unresisting medium, towards objects at a distance; and a power of *seeing* this medium, by the difference of its colouring in comparison of those objects. In this sense, it is a quality common to all continually existing objects; and although the inward sense of it be a sensation, yet it must have its *cause*; and if it regularly return upon the senses as other qualities do, must be concluded also like them '*continually to exist*'. Moreover, things must appear to the judgment and the senses *as outward*, although inwardly conceived of, and that in respect both of primary and secondary qualities; because, when unperceived, the proportions and relations of things, must have their own position to each other; and these, when meeting with a sentient nature, must inspire the sensation of proportional positions. Now the limit of the conscious feelings of pleasure and pain, marked out by what is termed the skin of the body, will be taken as a centre, or at least as a certain defined point or standard to which other things will be referred; for the sentient nature itself must, in the perception or *imagination* of its own existence, become one of the objects it surveys; thus forming an inward perceived knowledge of the relative position of unperceived things. And when the unperceived cause of a certain quality called *extension*, is combined with another for *hardness*, a third for *colour*, a fourth for *sound*, a fifth for a certain relation deemed *distance*, in respect to the combined causes, for other masses of extension, figure, hardness, and colour; a sixth, for a *different degree of distance*, to what we deem or term our own body: it necessarily follows, that all qualities of continually existing objects, taken notice of by the senses, must be perceived outwardly, i.e. combined together in select masses, surrounded by that common quality called outwardness, which quality CONTINUES *to exist,* EXTERNALLY *to the capacity of sensation in general.* Now I repeat there is one sense in which it may be said that objects are perceived immediately, as existing *outwardly, by the senses.* It is this; *the conscious powers of the understanding* and the *senses,* are blended together in man; *we* are analysing them, *but in nature they are united as intimately as are the prismatic colours in one* uniform mass of light. This being the case, they are acting in concert when any object affects the senses. Therefore the understanding knowing the *simplicity* of mental sensation, it follows, that the *varieties* of the causes, (which create *varieties* in the effects), are instantly *perceived* and *detected,* and that *immediately* with the conscious use of the senses; whilst also the mind as *immediately* mixes that idea of which the understanding is aware; viz. that these varieties, as complex objects, continue to exist unperceived and independent, when unnoticed by the senses. The vulgar also, and all men in a popular way, unite with these notions, the constant and equally present sentiment, that the varieties are *like* what the senses render them, by a very natural and almost indissoluble association of ideas. Berkeley never affixed the names of objects to any thing, but the combined sensible qualities which the organs of sense helped to form; omitting the idea of their constant ability, to return upon the sense when called for, and of outwardness being equally a regular attendant upon their appearance, and a capacity in nature necessary to their existence in relation to us, and to our own in relation to them; which *circumstances are included* in their names. He wrote his theory of vision to obviate an objection that might be made on the score of *'visible distance'*, in order to prove it to be a sensation of *mind only,* suggested by tangibility, &c.; but this would not do to explain away that *condition* of *being,* which, when unperceived, must be a proportional relation and variety amongst unperceived objects, and capable of affecting the touch, sight, and other senses in its own way. This he omitted purposely, in order to have nothing to do with the *causes and objects which create sensations,* until he came to explain them after his own notions, as necessarily *active,* and therefore *spirit.* His method of incomplete definition, and naming only the combined sensible qualities the effects of things, when all men name them as united with the perceptions of the understanding, and the observations of experience, is the reason why his philosophy seems at once plausible, contradictory, and unanswerable. Hume denied that *'reason'* could prove, by the relation of our ideas, the knowledge of continued existences, and resolved all into 'custom and imagination'. Whilst Dr. Reid, when he asserted, that the primary qualities are *conceived* by clear ideas of them as *they exist when unperceived,* and unlike any sensation they yield, was not aware that he explained these conceptions of unperceived qualities, by other qualities which still require the senses, in order to their formation; and therefore such as could only exist in a sentient being. Thus he explained '*hardness*', as 'a firm cohesion of parts'; '*figure*', as 'the relation of parts to each other';—'*visible figure*', as 'the relation of parts in respect to the eye'; '*sound*', by 'the vibrations of the air', &c. &c.[29]—as though these things, after being perceived, could be planted as they appear to the inward sense and consciousness of the soul, *outwardly again*, as independent modes of existence, and objects of contemplation; as though the very system he is arguing against does not suppose cohesion, parts, vibrations, figure, &c. &c. &c. to be perceptions, which are inward; because all perception is conscious, and all consciousness is inward and sentient; thus assuming as his premises the very idea which is in question; and which premises involve the difficulty his argument is raised to answer.

It is matter of surprise to me that Mr. D. Stewart should call this 'luminous and logical reasoning'.[30] Dr. Reid all along considers 'extension, figure, and motion, as instinctive simple conceptions of understood qualities of external matter'.[31] Now the doctrine of the relation of cause and effect, as I have considered it in my former essay, throws light upon this part of the subject, and would, I think, if it once became familiar to the mind, explain the whole mystery of external and internal existence.

The union of the three following things are required to form the proximate cause for that great effect, the *formation* and *combination* of those aggregates of sensible qualities usually called objects; namely, first, the unknown, unnamed circumstances in nature, which are unperceived by the senses; secondly, the organs of sense, whose qualities mix with these; and thirdly, the living, conscious powers necessary to sensation in general.

In this union, and *with it,* is the *creation,* and *production of all sensible complex qualities called objects, such as we know them.* These objects are what Berkeley calls '*ideas*', and '*sensations in*

---

29   [Shepherd alludes to Reid, *Inquiry* 5.2 (p. 57) on hardness; 6.7 (p. 96) on figure and visible figure; and 4.1 (p. 49) on hearing.]

30   [Shepherd refers to Stewart's description of Reid's work as 'simple and luminous reasoning' in Dugald Stewart, *Philosophical Essays* (Edinburgh: Printed by George Ramsay and Company, for William Creech and Archibald Constable and Company, 1810), Note F (p. 550).]

31   See the 'Essay on Cause and Effect', p. 42. [See p. 36 in this volume.]

the mind'; what the ancients perhaps called species or phan-
tasms; what the moderns call images, ideas, &c. And they all, as
I think, err in this, in considering them as *first* formed, and *then*
contemplated, and taken notice of afterwards. Whereas, the
sensible qualities of things are only formed by being taken
notice of. This is what Berkeley means when he says, 'what are
objects but the things we perceive by sense';[32] and so far I perfectly agree with him. But then he has omitted the consideration
of that circumstance, which is necessary to our belief in the
existence of objects independent of ourselves; *and that is the*
quick suggestions of the understanding; the reasoning, that as
sensation does not itself form the essence of those existences
which CAUSE PARTICULAR KINDS OF SENSATIONS; therefore there must be existences without it; that sensation not
causing the *variety* of its own perceptions, therefore there must
be *variety* without it; that *various* existences must be ready in
order to be perceived, and that these must lie under *various*
positions in relation to each other, as well as to the mind; that
sensation is but as a thin gauze, through which things are seen
in their native proportions, although it imparts to them a
similarity of colouring.

Nor let it be thought that children and peasants, &c. are not
capable of such observations; nature translates these operations
of mind into easier language than I have used, and mixes them
from a very early age, as joint powers with the senses; by which
the practised senses may perceive, (as I have explained above),
that objects are not *only* inward sensible qualities, but exist
unperceived continuously, outwardly, and independently *under*
the imagination of their appearances to the senses;—thus forming
that complete whole, which is termed the perception of outward and inward existence. If it be possible indeed that in
nature the causes for sensation in general, should be mixed up
with those particular kinds of them which yet need the aid of
the organs of sense and of motion for their exhibition, then
indeed, when *that we call ourselves* shall fail, the *external universe*
shall also fail; and as such a proposition is wholly without proof,
so is it beyond the utmost stretch of imagination to conceive:
whilst by keeping these causes separate and independent of

---

[32] [Shepherd quotes Berkeley, *Principles* 4 (p. 84).]

each other, the understanding, the senses, and the imagination, the notions from infancy to age, and those of all men, without one dissenting voice agree, — philosophy and ignorance equally agree, — that all objects are to be considered as outward of, and distinct from each other, and that they may indifferently be changed, without effecting the destruction of the whole mass.

Chapter 3: The Notion of the Independency of External Objects, How Gained?

1. *The same evidence for the independency as for the exteriority of objects.*
2. *Change of qualities proves them to be independent of the senses.*
3. *Some objects appear both like ourselves and different from us, &c.*

1. But it is time to enter upon the third and last member of our question. Whence is it that we consider objects as independent of the mind, when we can only know them by our sensations, which sensations are beings dependent upon the mind's capacity?

I answer, first, That those circumstances which go to prove that there must be truly *outward* causes, for particular sensations, prove them to be independent causes of those sensations. For such causes or objects as are entirely exterior to the cause or capacity for sensation in general, must be independent of such capacity.

But, *secondly*, those objects which are in relation to the five organs of sense and to motion, are considered *independent* of each individual capacity for sensation, because such *alter their qualities*, and seem some of them to suffer pleasure and pain without *our observation* of the change of qualities, and without *our consciousness* of these sensations. If we endeavour to regain a thought by reflection which has been out of the mind, such thought never exhibits any quality which renders it probable *to have* existed in an unobserved state. — But with respect to those objects which are 'ready to appear to the senses', we observe they have gone through *changes of qualities*, the process of which was not observed by us, and which changes therefore, must be independent of any part of ourselves; and not being perceived, cannot be caused by our perception, and must therefore, be wholly independent of it.

Thirdly, Objects are reckoned *independent* of ourselves, because they appear *like ourselves* plus or minus the varieties of qualities;[33] and *we to ourselves* are independent of others, and are minds, beings, capable of sensations.

And this I consider as the chief ground of all our belief in a plurality of minds, as well as other objects from infancy; for *similar sensations are similar objects,* and the *varieties* make the *varieties*; and we, in the *sensation of ourselves perceive continuous* existence, that *might exist independent of others*: then we have sensations of other objects like ourselves but have not *conscious continuous sensation of their existence.* We do not *feel their pleasure and pain,* but they give symptoms of feeling *like ourselves* conscious continuous existence, pleasure and pain, &c. Therefore, we look upon them as masses of qualities *like ourselves,* other human beings in existence, *and so on,* according to the varieties of sensation, i.e. *various causes,* equal to, and commensurate with various *effects.*

If it should be objected, that lost thoughts which reflection recovers, are not considered as independent beings; I answer, *thoughts* recovered by reflection, are *perceived to be* IN the mind at the moment they are seeking for; and by following a train of associations, we only clear away any confusion respecting them, and they never indicate by any circumstance whatever, that they continue to exist when *not perceived by the mind;*— therefore, they are *not like ourselves,* but seem to be only relations or accidents of others of our thoughts which are objects within ourselves: So the organs of sense modify objects *continuously existent, ready to appear* upon the irregular calls of these organs, and which are *outward* from the body, and whose

---

[33] Bishop Berkeley has this idea when applied to the existence of other minds than our own. The reasoning is equally forcible when applied to any kinds of beings and their qualities. This shall be further taken notice of elsewhere. See Essay 1st. of the shorter essays. [See pp. 168–78 in this volume.]

   I find an unexpected coincidence of thought here with Mr. Mill in his pamphlet on Education. [Shepherd refers to James Mill's article 'Education', which appeared in the 1824 *Supplement to the Fourth, Fifth, and Sixth Editions of the Encyclopedia Britannica*.]

causes are *independent* of the cause for sensation in general: — But *reflection helps to form clearer ideas of confused thoughts,* which are NOT *'ready to appear upon irregular calls of the organs of sense'*, are *not exterior* to the body, require *not motion* to be apprehended as tangible, and whose *causes* seem interwoven with the general cause for the associations of our ideas; which associations and their causes, are dependent upon the whole *being* deemed ourselves, ceasing in sound sleep, and reviving with the waking hour. Thus the instruments of the five organs of *sense* relate to outward, independent, continually existing beings; but *reflection* relates to inward, dependent, interrupted beings.

Fourthly, We gain the notion of the independency of objects, from the observation of one object affecting many minds in a manner which renders it impossible there should be as many objects as minds. If five men see a pond, and can only walk round one pond, then there is one pond seen five times over, not five ponds; so the pond whatever it may be when *unperceived*, must at least in its unperceived state, be independent of, and I may add external to *all the minds*; for if the pond were *only* in the mind, there would be five ponds, and every person who perceived a pond would create another pond, and yet this multitude of ponds in perception, would in many respects but merit the definition due to *one pond*. Thus there would be such a contradiction among the 'ideas and sensations', that the mind must come to the belief of only *one pond*, seen by five persons; that is, in other words, an *independent cause* for particular sensations. This objection to his doctrine Berkeley answers, in a very unsatisfactory, hesitating manner in his dialogues.

Fifthly, The relations of abstract ideas are upon the same footing as outward objects with respect to their remaining when unperceived, independent for their existence, of the existence of the mind itself. This continuance of the relations of ideas, ready to be perceived when called upon by the intellect, and independent of its powers for either forming, or perceiving them, although contained in the juxtaposition of the simple ideas themselves, (whether perceived or not, or whether called for or not), is what must ever render the pure idealists, most inconsistent in their doctrine. Because the very position, 'We know nothing but our perceptions', is, if only a truth when perceived, of no force as an *axiom* that is to govern our understanding when not adverted to; when not a sensation or perception, it would be nought, — leaving thereby all objects of the understanding and the senses equally unproved as to their existence; and therefore still liable to be disputed and argued upon according to the different impressions they make in a perpetual circle, without the mind ever being able to come to any settled determination concerning them. — For we must observe concerning abstract propositions, that we gain the notion of their truth being independent of the immediate perception of them by observing, that our discovery of their truth does not *cause* them; they are discovered, and perceived, because the relations exist ready to be perceived: *It is their existence enables them to be perceived, not the perception of them which enables them to exist*; and whenever the relations are as clear as are the original simple impressions, their existence is upon the same footing of certainty, and is demonstratively equal with them.

It is such a perception of the relation of ideas as this, which affords us the abstract notion of existence in general whether sentient, or insentient; — for we knowing that each sensation as it springs up passes as shortly away, and being equally convinced that it cannot have *begun its own existence*, but must have been a change of some existence which already is; and yet that each particular sensation is not always determined to the mind; we judge reasonably *there must needs be some existence which is neither* any sensation in particular, nor yet a mere capacity for sensation in general, in order to be the cause of each particular sensation. Therefore, by such comparison of ideas we gain the notion of indefinite unknown existence; whether as a capacity for sensation in general, (not yet under a state of sensation), or as varieties of qualities capable of exciting that capacity, through the organs of sense. *Indefinite existence, as contrary to the* NON EXISTENCE of which we have the notion by our ideas successively passing away, thence becomes the *genus*, of which each class of the sensations we experience is the *species* or *variety*.

This is an observation which to my mind completely answers the difficulty some at present make, when they say; 'that sensation is the only existence of which we have experience, and therefore we cannot separate any existence from the *idea* of *sensation*'. For we can always separate or abstract the *most general quality of an object from the rest*, whether that quality be *supposed* among them by the *imagination, known* to be among them by the *senses*, or *concluded* to be among them by *reason*, as a result from their mutual bearings.

By such means it is, that the idea of *independency* is generated: an idea, which as a new and superinduced sensation, stands for the thing signified by it; and for which we have formed the *word independency*; and by such means it is, that the curious workmanship of nature has enabled us from thoughts which are necessarily interrupted, inward, and dependent beings, to gain the knowledge of continued, external, and independent existences.

Thus, I hope, I have answered satisfactorily the original question,[34] by shewing that in the sum of our combined sensations (viz. the *perception* of our simple impressions, and their relations), there is contained the knowledge and proof of the existence of 'body' and of the external universe.

Chapter 4: Objection Arising to the Foregoing Doctrine from the Phenomena of Dreams, Further Considered and Answered

Section 1

The phenomena of dreams do not afford a valid argument against the proof of independent existences, external to mind.

If the phenomena of dreams and madness be objected to the foregoing theory, on account of their objects being supposed by the mind, to be continuous, external, independent existences, during their exhibition; let it be remembered, that these objects are not capable of fulfilling their definitions, and that the very reason they are considered in a sane and waking state as delusions, is, because the mind perceives that its powers of comparison were not during the dream in a state to observe such an incapacity.

---

[34] 'Why we attribute a CONTINUED existence to objects even when they are not present to the senses'; and, 'Why we suppose them to have an existence distinct from the mind, i.e. EXTERNAL *in their position* and INDEPENDENT in their existence and operation'.

These powers being restored, the mind immediately takes notice that on account of *several relations of ideas,* which had been obliterated presenting themselves, these objects must be incapable of shewing all their qualities;—they will not affect any more minds than one with the notions of their appearance;—those which are objects of food will not satisfy hunger;—of injury, will do no hurt;—of good, will afford no pleasure; &c.—It is when objects fulfil their whole definitions, that they are *real;* and when they do, it does not appear to me possible, but that their *causes,* (or the objects which are necessary for the formation of those sensations, and to which the senses and motion are relative), must be *wholly independent* of mind;—for when similar objects are perceived at the *same time* by more than one mind, they must necessarily be *external* to each. The only difficulty is to gain a demonstration, that in our *perception* of any of the relations of our ideas concerning the existence of *other men,* their absolute existence is included.

I consider however the arguments I have used, approaching as nearly to it as possible if rightly understood. For it is not enough that the *causes for sensation in general,* CONTINUE *to exist and to be* INDEPENDENT *of the* PARTICULAR *causes which excite* PARTICULAR *notions;* because *these latter* might nevertheless be DEPENDENT *on them;* and this is the case in dreams: But the *particular exciting* CAUSES, for *particular* sensations (termed the perception of qualities,) must prove themselves capable of CONTINUING *to exist,* INDEPENDENT of the *other powers of sensation in general.*

Now this condition, men as well as other objects fulfil, by replying to the irregular calls of the senses and motion; and we perceive that such a circumstance *affords a proof* of such *independent* continuous existence; because as the absence of our minds, whether during sleep, or on a journey, &c. makes no difference with respect to '*the readiness of those objects to appear if called for*'; so neither could the *supposition of our death.* And this relation of our sensations is so obvious, that *all* men perceive it, and *act* on it from infancy; and there is no occasion to have recourse to 'instinct' or 'primary *laws* of belief', &c. to account for their faith in outward continued existences.

[…]

Section 2

1. Remark on Bishop Berkeley's conclusion from dreams, shewing a fallacy in his reasoning thereon, as affording a doubt concerning the reality of objects.
2. Application of the doctrine of cause.

I. Bishop Berkeley says, (sec. 18.) 'What happens in dreams, frenzies, and the like, puts it beyond dispute, that it is possible we might be affected with all the ideas we have now, though no bodies existed without resembling them.'[35] [...] I answer to this, that I do *not* consider it as possible for a person to be affected with the *same train of sensations*, and in the *same order* in a dream, or frenzy, as out of them; *precisely* similar *effects must* have precisely similar *causes*, and in any case where not only *resembling* sensible qualities take place, but an *order* occurs which enables them to return regularly;—and the mind is in a state to compare and observe upon the senses, then the argument holds good, which shows *that the* CAUSES *of the sensible qualities exist* INDEPENDENTLY *of the senses and mind, and* CONTINUE *to exist unperceived;—* and neither such an use of the organs of sense, nor such returns upon them, nor such an *order,* nor such comparison of ideas takes place in dreams, and frenzies. In short, the sensible qualities FORM the sensible objects; but it is a *reasoning* arising out of a perception of the relation of these qualities;—of the different position of colours in relation to motion;—of the knowledge of the place where we are, &c. by which external continuous existences are proved; a reasoning which Bishop Berkeley uses in proof of the independent existence of separate minds, and which reasoning and which minds he does not think can belong to dreams and frenzies, &c. It is by unobserved and apparently slight changes of words and their meanings, that so great a writer and reasoner as Berkeley could deceive either himself or others. [...]

[...]

The phenomena of dreams touch upon the difficulty there lies in the mind detecting the presence of exactly similar objects

---

[35] [Shepherd quotes, with slight alterations, Berkeley, *Principles* 18 (p. 89).]

when it perceives only some of their qualities,[36] and is not in a state to unite the ideas of the understanding with the perception of sensible qualities, which union alone renders objects worthy of bearing their names. Hence it is, that if men reasoned as Mr. Hume says they do from sensible qualities merely, they would be *fools* or *madmen*. Young children, very ignorant persons, men in dreams or frenzies consider the conscious sensible *qualities* of things, as effects indicative of similar objects, because they have not present in their minds those notions of the understanding, those ideas of *their methods of formation*, of *the place in which they are*, &c. and which being compared with the consciousness of the sensible qualities, shew whether they are masses of like effects from like ultimate causes, or not.

The true reason why external *resembling* objects cannot be necessary for producing ideas, is because it is *impossible* that the external object, which is allowed *not* to be an idea, can *resemble* an idea, in that particular quality of its *conscious sensation*.

But again, Bishop Berkeley says, — 'Hence, it is evident the supposition of external bodies is not necessary for the producing of ideas.'[37] This is not evident, for the word, '*resembling*' being dropt, alters this inference from being a *just conclusion* from the premises. Objects — external objects; i.e. objects not one with the mind, nor included in any particular state of its sensation, may, and according to my theory, must be necessary for producing those ideas which are exhibited as *changes upon such a state*. Nay the real, plain, matter of fact is, that objects *external to mind are needed even for illusory ideas;* for all *ideas* whatever, and *their causes*, are external to, (i.e. not included in), any *particular given state of sensation, and its cause.*

For any particular given state of sensation, mixed with the consciousness of our own continued existence, and the *idea* of its continually existing cause, forms the compound idea called *self*; but the *particular* causes for *new* ideas, are not contained *in* these, and so are *out*, and *distinct from them*.

And hence it appears that the *essential* difference between the particular causes for *illusions*, and the particular causes for

---

36   See the shorter Essay, 'That Sensible Qualities cannot be Causes'. [See pp. 82–6 in this volume.]

37   [Shepherd quotes, with slight alterations, Berkeley, *Principles* 18 (p. 89).]

realities consists only in the latter *being* CONTINUALLY *existent;*
for both must be *external,* and neither can be *resembling.*

Therefore it is required that objects should be not only
external, but *continually* existent, in order to be in relation to the
organs of sense, and to produce such ideas of sensible qualities,
as in a sane and waking state of mind proceed in a *regular*
'order', and by different laws than the *irregular* fancies of dreams
and frenzies. It may thus be demonstratively proved, that it is
'impossible to be affected with the same train of sensations, in
the same *order* as a sane waking person experiences them, and
yet these be conducted after the same *manner,* and by the same
causes as dreams and frenzies are'. *Like effects* must have *like*
causes; either the organs of sense are not wanted, or they are
wanted for the regular exhibition of qualities; in dreams and
frenzies they are *not* wanted for the formation of the irregular
fancies of sensible qualities; but upon the supposition that the
organs of sense are used, they must be used in relation to some
objects which are correlative to them, and which Bishop
Berkeley clearly shows cannot be *like* the qualities they are the
means of forming.[38] This answer is further supported by the
following considerations.

1. That it is more than probable that such dreams, &c. could
not exist, unless outward objects had acted previously on the
senses.

2. Because we cannot imagine, that to a mere lunatic illusory
call of the organs of sense there could be a regular reply, unless
God were to work a miracle for the purpose, which it is absurd
to suppose.

3. Such an illusive order of ideas in one man's mind, could
not render them capable of appearing to more minds than one,
if more than one were but supposed in the universe.

4. Because physically and physiologically speaking, there is
upon the perception of every lively forcible image, a peculiar
action of the circulation, which is natural and consistent with
health, when arising from what are called outward objects.
Whilst the perceptions last, their proximate causes may be

---

[38]   That they can resemble ideas in some general qualities, which are
independent of the organs of sense. See Recapitulation page 182, and
ch. 7, sec. 5. [See pp. 164 and 156–8 in this volume.]

considered as a set of temporary, but strong excitements; — but when their ultimate causes are removed, the perceptions vanish, and with them the excitements. Now if the desires of the mind which seek their objects irregularly, were during a dream to be answered as vividly, forcibly, and regularly as when awake; some circumstances would be equivalent to the following contradictory action in the system; namely, to an irregular demand of the organs of sense, and yet the capacity for a *constant* ready reply to them; that is, a quiet, healthy action of the system, and an intranquil, inflamed action, both in unison together.

In other words, it does not seem possible and consistent with health, that the circulation should be capable of carrying on such an action of the system, as should be equal to render life a waking dream; i.e. that within its own powers it should be capable of acting regularly, as well as vividly; and of performing without disturbance the stimulus, of which outward objects are supposed the occasion.

5. Because it appears impossible in the way of *dreams* and *frenzies*, that 'ALL' the ideas we have, and all the 'ORDER' of them, could take place; *the appetites of hunger and thirst not being capable of satisfaction in this way*: — at any rate, the ideal theory, and its contrary, are always understood, to be argued upon the supposition, that the organs of sense *and motion* are truly used, and that they afford by means of their conscious use, the evidence termed, *perception by sense*.[39]

It is not sufficient therefore for the exhibition of the phenomena of waking life, that there should merely exist some irregular sensible qualities, resembling those which may result from the action of the organs of sense and motion. Their action must be truly used; there must be the *true* and *unperceived* mechanical action of the five organs of sense; and there must be a mechanical, unperceived passing of the sentient principle, the self from place to place; and this action of the organs, and this motion must be in relation to those things *which fulfil their whole definitions*. And it is of no consequence what place, space, motion, and external things are when unperceived; they are conditions necessary to a result — therefore the real action of the

---

[39] See p. 54, 55. [See pp. 118–9 in this volume.]

organs, and the true motion of an individual mind must create a change of *self*, in relation to objects which *continue* to exist as the exciting causes for certain sensations or perceptions *in particular*; independent of, and distant from, the powers of sensation in *general*.

The detection of such an action between the organs of sense and the objects of nature, arises from the conscious use of the organs *mixed with the powers of the understanding*; for a stream of conscious life, however many, and separate and independent causes may be necessary in order to supply it, yet would appear merely as the idea of self; such causes would properly and truly determine an individual self, and the consciousness of self as their single combined effect. But whatever conscious applications were made to any other existence, power, or quality in nature, as necessary regularly to introduce new ideas and sensations upon this conscious self, would prove, that such qualities, powers, and beings, were wholly unnecessary to the existence of, and therefore no part of self. The five organs of sense, and motion, are such means of application, and therefore, the use of them, and regular returns upon them, afford the criterion of the presence of other exterior and continuous objects than self; and is the only way in which the phrase 'evidence of sense', can with propriety be used. Motion is thus a sort of sense; for motion will ever appear from infancy upwards to be an action in relation to that space which is outward; i.e. an *existence* not included in the perceiving mind: the child will consider its arms and legs as part of self; but the *place* in which he moves, the capacity of nature which allows him to move, which he by consciousness knows is not *always in him*, but is always ready to return upon the use of his arms and legs, he *rightly reasons or perceives is no part of himself*, his mind, or conscious existence; but yet must necessarily be *always existing* in order to be ever ready to respond to his motions, and to enable him to use his members without resistance.[40] I say, the

---

[40] Since writing this essay, I find that Mr. Destutt de Tracy has many ideas which I am happy unconsciously to have hit upon; but his argument is more confined than mine; — for whereas he considers *body* to be known as a result of that sensation of mind called a *judgment*, from *the comparison of the ideas of* WILL, and RESISTANCE TO WILL; so I enlarge the number of such sorts of *judgments*, by *the comparison of many other ideas,*

infant perceives this *relation* amidst his '*ideas and sensations*', though he cannot analyse or express it, any more than some others who are far removed from infancy.

Therefore, it is the *unperceived* action or *use* of the organs of sense which relates to exterior and continually existing objects, and is the means of determining their qualities to the sentient principle; and it is the consciousness of their use which forms an argument by which men justly infer such permanent exist-ences, and renders valid the phrase, 'perception by *sense*'; for the conscious use of the organs of sense is rightly to be con-sidered as the effect of their unperceived mechanical action, and this action as in relation to the appropriate objects which affect them:[41] Therefore when the mind is conscious of the use of the eyes, the hands, &c., and of *regular* replies to their use, — *it knows* that there are other external continuous existences than itself present; and thus the immediate action of the under-standing uniting with the conscious use of the organs of sense, *together* form 'THE PERCEPTION BY SENSE', and *that of a different* 'ORDER' *of beings from those of dreams and frenzies.*

If the organs of sense (and motion) were not truly used, Berkeley's own theory would fall to the ground, because they are, according to him, '*necessary for the spirit to work on by set*

---

which I think it is clear are made from the earliest infancy, and even perhaps by the fetus before birth. Added to this, none of the notions are the result of any circumstance which proves the *continuity*, and *independency* of existences, as well as their *exteriority*. The former quality must be blended with the other two, in order to the formation of REALITIES. [Shepherd refers to Antoine Destutt de Tracy, *Eléments d'idéologie, Première partie: Idéologie proprement dite* (Paris: Lévi, 1824), pp. 106–108; hereafter cited as *Eléments*.]

Condillac and De Gerando fall into the same mistake; none of these show any thing beyond the action of such accidental circumstances as determine *will* and its *sense of resistance* — even in dreams. [Shepherd alludes to Condillac, *Traité*, and Joseph Marie, baron de Gérando, *Des signes et de l'art de penser considérés dans leurs rapports mutuels* (Paris: Goujons fils, 1800).]

These authors contain therefore no efficient answer to Berkeley.

41   p. 54, 55, and 'Essay on the Nature of Five Organs of Sense'. [See pp. 118–9 and 179–87 in this volume.]

rules and methods'.[42] But if the *order* could go on as in dreams, they could not be needed.

'*In the manner of dreams and frenzies*', therefore, there is no use for organs of sense, *neither are they used*. There exists, indeed, some sensible appearances upon the mind, as if the senses had been in use; but in that state there is a deficiency of the ideas of the understanding, so that images of sense, appear together confusedly *without order* in the mind, which is not in a state to perceive that they can be but fancies.

But in a waking and sane state of mind, the harmony of its ideas, their relations and conclusions, force themselves upon it with a superior and convincing evidence; which in ordinary life is not weakened by those sceptical suggestions, which a consideration of the strength of the delusion in dreams, prompts to the more curious enquirer. A scepticism only to be corrected by the reflection, that it is not justified by reason, or by that comparison and relation of our ideas, which of whatever difficulty in the performance, can but remain the only method in our power of finding truth, or of forming any proposition whatever.

Section 3

Remarks on Dr. Reid's neglect of the consideration of the phenomena of dreams in notions of extension, &c.

Now on the other hand to return to Dr. Reid,[43] when he asks, 'if extension, figure, and motion, are *ideas of sensation*', (saying he gives up the material world, if the question be answered in the affirmative), he forgets that in a vivid dream these ideas may take place as perfectly as when the mind is awake; — he forgets that every perception of sensible qualities whatever must be a *species*, of which *sensation is the genus*, and can only be the attribute of a sentient being. By an illusion arising from the association of ideas, he joined the notions of the sensations of the sensible primary qualities, (of our sense or consciousness of extension, figure, and motion), with the idea of their continually

---

42 [Shepherd alludes to Berkeley's claim that the 'laws of nature' are a 'set of rules or established methods, wherein the mind we depend on excites in us the ideas of sense' (Berkeley, *Principles* 30 [p. 94]).]

43 See Reid's Inquiry, ch. 5, sec. 7. [Shepherd paraphrases Reid, *Inquiry* 5.7 (p. 70).]

existing external causes, as existing together outwardly. For although he explains himself in some places as conceiving external objects not to be like sensations;—yet he still keeps the notion by saying, that *perceptions, or conceptions are not sensations; and that he knows the* EXTERNAL NATURE *of a primary quality, as well as its inward sensation;* as for instance, in *extension,* where the sensation of *moving along a surface,* is unlike '*the hard cohesion of parts sticking together*'. Now *parts, hardness,* and *sticking,* are three '"IDEAS OF SENSATION' also, and can never explain the nature of the external quality, any more than does the *moving along a surface.*

Thus he considers extension, figure, motion, and solidity, to be qualities of bodies, which are not sensations; of whose real nature when *unperceived,* we have a distinct and clear conception:—Now, there are perceptions of sensible qualities; and perceptions of their relations by reasoning, yet both are but species of sensations. The perceptions of sense, neither immediately, nor mediately as signs of conceived qualities, can ever tell us of their positive nature when unfelt, whether they be primary or secondary. *The perceptions of reason,* will tell us, that there must necessarily be exterior objects, and that these must be as various as the sensations they create. But this notion was certainly *not that,* under which Reid contemplated extension, figure, and motion; for he never hints at it. No; he truly thought the senses could suggest the conception of the nature of the real essential primary qualities of matter, without such conceptions becoming sensations, whilst the understanding was satisfied it was legitimate so to do, because 'instinct' compelled the mind to such a conception, and resolved the notion into a '*primary law of human belief*', which could not be disputed without disputing a first principle.[44]—Yet the material world,

---

[44] Against such a doctrine as this, there are few perhaps who might not find a conclusive argument, derived from the experience that every quality whatever (however considered in a waking state as belonging to external things), equally appears in dreams. There will arise extension, figure, motion, hardness, and softness; heat, and cold; colour, and sound: WILL, and the *resistance to* WILL, whether by the resistance of solidity, or the wills of other men.

It is this observation which shews that no conclusive evidence can arise from the arguments of M. de Condillac, and M. Destutt de Tracy,

the universe need not be annihilated, although primary qualities (*after* the senses have taken notice of them) should be 'ideas
of sensation'; as long as the whole 'furniture of heaven and
earth' (whatever that furniture may be unperceived), fits out all
its variety of *causes* and of unperceived objects, to coalesce with
the organs of sense and with the powers of sensation in order to
its production.

Thus, what Dr. Reid calls *common sense*, and considers
erroneously to be a *sense* or *instinct*, is no more than an *observation of the simplest relations of our ideas.* — It is but a *simple inference of the understanding,* after the observation that the use of
any organ of sense is needful to let new ideas into the mind,
that the mind itself was not the object of those new ideas, and that
necessarily a *third* object must be the occasion of them. Therefore, *together with the perception of* THE CONSCIOUS SENSE,
(which takes notice when it is affected), there is *the perception of*
THE UNDERSTANDING, which observing that the sense *not*
being affected by what is properly termed *our mind,* or the mere
capacity for sensation in general, the things which are affecting
it, must necessarily be some other beings, *extraneous* to both: but
this inference which by habit immediately accompanies the
conscious use of the senses, is *knowledge* rather than *instinct.*

Now those beings which do not yield any signs of mind or
capacities of sensation, but exhibit upon our minds solid
extension and other qualities in particular, are termed *material
things;* — whilst such beings as yield the notion of their possessing life and understanding, are termed *immaterial things.* As far
as these conclusions go, philosophy or the scrutiny of the most
rigid analysis will support '*common sense*', *or the simple relations
arising from our original impressions;* — but since added to these
conclusions, ordinary understandings conceive by a very
natural association of thought, that *the ideas of sensible qualities
after* the organs of sense have combined with exterior objects to
their formation, are the *very external material objects themselves*; it
is the business of an analytical philosophy, which intends to
shew the entire method of the generation of our notions, to

De Gerando, &c. for the reality of an *independent, continually existing*
universe. [See pp. 137–8 n40.]

break up this association. For an association of ideas merely, will never *prove* the existence of objects. A notion the fallacy of which some philosophers seem not to be sufficiently aware of.

Section 4

Dreams considered in connexion with the doctrine discussed in 'the Essay on the relation of cause and effect'; viz. How the mind may form a judgment antecedently to trial of future effects from present appearances?

[...]

...the demonstrative conclusions of the foregoing arguments [are], namely,

1st. That things must continually exist in order to be ready constantly to appear.

2ndly, That the causes for particular kinds of sensations, must be external to the causes for its general essence or power.

3rdly, That what is termed the mind is a continually existing essence, capacity, or power in general.

4thly, That what is deemed *in* the mind, is any particular state of sensation at any given period.

5thly, That the causes of things not in any given state of the mind, and yet capable of exhibiting certain qualities upon it, are out of it, whether fitted to create ideas of sensible qualities, or any other ideas.

6thly, That *consideration* is the appropriate method to regain the ideas of memory, &c. but

7thly, That the *organs* of sense are the instruments by which to regain the ideas of *sensible qualities*.

8thly, That of all those things which are *out* of any particular state of mind, those which regularly exhibit sensible qualities upon the use of the organs of sense prove themselves *continually* existing, by such exhibitions.

9thly, That in dreams, &c. there are no such regular returns upon the organs of sense; therefore, though the proximate causes of sensible qualities exhibit their effects, yet there is wanting the proof of the *continual* existence of such causes, by which means they are discovered to be illusions, or objects, different from those for which their names were formed.

10thly, That the independency which the causes of the objects of sense have of the capacity to general sensation, is proved by their affecting changes of qualities, of which the mind has no conscience. – But I shall finish this long discussion by remarking that this, and similar essays are not intended to prove, that there is but *one method* which God and Nature could employ, to arrive at the same ends; but rather to analyse the complex operations of our minds, with such care and nicety, as may show what possibly consistent method has been used in the generation of our belief of external nature; and afterwards to examine if reason will support the notions, which have been formed concerning it. I shall therefore now proceed to draw that inference from the whole doctrine, which was originally the foundation of the observations in this treatise; and which although so long deferred, must at length claim that share of our notice its importance demands.

Chapter 5: On the Nature of Objects When Acting as Causes

The action of cause to be considered as external to mind. – Remark on the vague and popular use of the word Cause. – Sensible qualities not the causes of other sensible qualities. – Two kinds of necessary connexion.

I resume the subject therefore by calling upon the reader's attention to observe, that objects, when contemplated singly as the efficient causes of nature, are to be considered in their outward unperceived state, and as yet unconjoined with each other.

2. That although numbers of objects may be needful towards any result, yet in a popular way, each may be called the cause of an event, when each is absolutely necessary in order to that result. Philosophy does not get rid of an incomplete manner of thinking on this subject, and thus talks of cause and effect *following* each other, &c. &c.; whereas it is the *union* of all the objects absolutely necessary to any given end, which forms a *new object*, whose *new qualities* are the *effects*, or *properties* of those objects when uncombined; and which must be synchronous with the existence of the newly-formed object; and only subsequent to the existence of the previous objects, when in their uncombined state. – But the entire union of the objects, is

always considered, and is the *proximate cause* of any event; and therefore is one with it.

Now all the exterior and uncombined objects, whose junction is necessary to an event, may be considered as one grand compound object; and may, under that idea, be termed and spoken of in the singular number: and when contemplated previously to their union may also be considered to be prior in the order of time, as the cause of a future object.[45]

In all our reasonings, the word *cause* is rendered ambiguous, by applying it equally to a *part of what is necessary to an end*, as well as to the *whole* of what is necessary; and to existing objects *united* to that end, as well as disunited to it; a fruitful source of much unsound reasoning in some of the best authors.

3. The ideas and sensations of the sensible qualities of things *can never be the causes of other sensible qualities of things.*[46] It is not the sensible qualities of fire which burn, of bread which nourish; it is not the *idea* or *conception* of the *cohesion of parts* which *cause* the sensation of hardness; — it is a certain number of amassed, unknown, external qualities, which determine to the senses different qualities as conjoined effects — 'The sensation of hardness is not a natural sign of an external quality of firm cohesion of parts unlike a sensation.'[47] — It is a sign only of another coexistent *effect* with itself determined from the same unknown, external object. This impossibility of sensible qualities, being the *productive principle* of sensible qualities, lies at the root of all Mr. Hume's controversy concerning the manner of causation;[48] for he, observing that such ideas could only *follow*

---

45   This I do presently, in speaking of identity.
46   See Essay VI. [See pp. 82–6 in this volume.]
47   See Reid's Inquiry into the Human Mind, c. 5, sec. 5. 'Let a man press his hand against the table', &c. [Shepherd refers to Reid, *Inquiry* 5.5 (pp. 62–5). Shepherd's errata specify 'In the note after "mind" read "Vol. 2, ch. 4"', which is puzzling, since Reid's *Inquiry* was not published as two volumes, and *Inquiry* chapter 4 concerns hearing, not touch or hardness.]
48   It is this view of things which explains the reason of all the difficulty, inconsistency, irresolution, and unsatisfactory discussions upon *cause*, *laws* of nature, &c. in the writings of Stewart, Reid, and others — Even Mr. Prevost, who clearly perceives Stewart's ambiguity in assigning the same meaning to the word *cause*, as to other antecedents, fails to perceive wherein lies the true nature of *power*; wherein consists that

one another, resolved causation into the observation of the customary *antecedency* and *subsequency* of sensible qualities. But objects, when spoken of and considered as causes, should always be considered as those masses of unknown qualities in nature, exterior to the organs of sense, whose determination of sensible qualities to the senses forms *one class of their effects*; whereas philosophers, (with the exception of Berkeley), and mankind in general, look upon the masses of sensible qualities AFTER determination to the senses as the *causes*, the *antecedents*, the *productive principles* of *other* masses of sensible qualities, which are their *effects* or *subsequents*; a notion naturally arising from the powerful style of the associations in the mind, and which our Maker has ordained for practical purposes;—but *monstrous* when held as an abstract truth in analytical science.

In a loose and popular way, men undoubtedly conceive the sensible qualities of a loaf of bread for instance, which are determined to the eye and the touch, (through intimate association), as existing outwardly, along with the natural substance or particles of bread; and consider, that *that whole* will nourish them; but this notion is very different from conceiving that *whiteness* and *solidity* will nourish; they never do thus think; they never consider the sensible qualities *alone* as the true causes of nourishment; and if allowed to think and explain themselves upon the subject, would show that they supposed the same mass which outwardly determined by its action on the eye a particular colour, and to the touch a certain consistency, would, on meeting with the stomach, satisfy hunger:—In short, concomitant or 'successive sensible qualities', are considered by all men when they come to analyse their notions, (and ought to

---

manner of action between objects, by which there arises 'the producing principle' of other objects. See Stewart's Philosophy of the Human Mind, c. 4, sec. 1, to p. 333. Note O, to ditto, vol. 2, Appendix to ditto, art. 2. Reid's Inquiry, c. 6, sec. 24. [Shepherd refers to Dugald Stewart, *Elements of the Philosophy of the Human Mind*, Vol. 2, 2nd ed. (Edinburgh: Archibald Constable and Co., 1816), chapter 4, section 1 (pp. 325–33), Note O (pp. 556–9), and Appendix article 2 (pp. 592–5), hereafter cited as *Elements* Vol. 2; and to Reid, *Inquiry* 6.24 (pp. 190–202). Pierre Prévost (1751–1839) was a Swiss physics professor; Stewart discusses his views in the Appendix to his *Elements* (pp. 592–5).]

be so held by philosophers), as concomitant or *successive* EFFECTS, *arising from the different actions of an external independent object, meeting either at the same time, or successively, with different instruments of sense with which it unites*—Thus, the *antecedency* and *subsequency* of certain respective aggregates of sensible qualities, must *necessarily* be INVARIABLE in like circumstances; *for they are successive and similar effects*, from successive and similar causes, instead of the *succession* itself forming essential *cause and effect*. *Whiteness, consistency*, and *nourishment*, are as many *invariable* and successive *effects*, arising from an unknown object, exterior to the instruments of sense, and independent of mind; which, *formed* after a certain fashion, and meeting successively with the eye, the touch, and the stomach, determines its successive sensible qualities.[49]

Thus it is in like manner throughout all nature;—and such a view of the subject would cure the error, which has of late crept into the works of science; namely, the considering conjoined or successive effects from a common cause, as possessing the nature of the connection of cause and effect.

'When things are found together, an ultimate law of nature is[50] supposed to be found', and an enquiry after *cause* as a *productive principle*, proves an ignorance of that *new and improved* light which the labours of Mr. Hume, Dr. Browne, and others, have thrown upon the doctrine of causation. Whereas, causes, or objects, previous to their union with the instruments of sense and the powers of sensation, from whose junction are *created* the very sensible qualities themselves, must be exterior to, and independent of both; whilst the regular *successions of sensible qualities*, are in their turn entirely dependent upon the regular successions of such junctions.

4. The necessary connection therefore of cause and effect, arises from the obligation, that like qualities should arise from the junction, separation, admixture, &c. of like aggregates of external qualities. But the necessary connection of *invariable*

---

49   See Locke.

50   See Lawrence's Lectures, from p. 80 to 84. [Shepherd refers to William Lawrence, *Lectures on Physiology, Zoology, and the Natural History of Man, Delivered at the Royal College of Surgeons* (London: Printed for J. Callow, 1819), pp. 80–4.]

antecedency and *subsequency* of successive aggregates of sensible qualities, arises from the necessity there is, that there should be invariable *sequences of effects,* when one *common cause* (or exterior object) mixes successively with different organs of sense, or various parts of the human frame, &c.

Of this obvious and important distinction, between these *two kinds of necessary connection,* the authors alluded to take no notice.

But I must now advert to an observation of another description, it being not only necessary for the sake of clearness, but also immediately relevant in this place, where we are speaking of the different notions we form of objects; i.e. when we consider them as masses of unknown, exterior qualities.

I allude to the proper definition and use of the word *idea*—upon which the whole of the foregoing treatise has an influence;[51] and the understanding of which will greatly facilitate the comprehension of the mystery intended to be unfolded to whoever has sufficient zeal, curiosity, and patience, to undertake a second perusal of these pages.

Chapter 6: On the Use of the Word Idea in this Treatise, and Cursory Observations on Its Nature and Proper Use in General, &c.

Section 1

The word idea is used as signifying a distinct class of sensations; as a sign in relation to continuous existences not present to the mind; — Berkeley's ambiguous use of the word. — Objects in the mind compounded of sensations, (by means of the organs of sense), and Ideas the

---

51 M. de Condillac most justly observes that 'there is a great difficulty in finding a fit place for important definitions—If they are entered upon too early, it is before their analysis proves their propriety—If too late, the just views they may include, are wanted in vain for their purpose.' —This is precisely the case in which I find myself with respect to the definition of the word *idea*. [Shepherd may be referring to an 1809 translation of Condillac's *Logic* where he asks, 'If definitions confine themselves to shewing us things, what does it matter whether we are shewn them before, or only after we know them? It seems to me the essential point is to know them' (Joseph Neef, trans., *The Logic of Condillac* [Philadelphia, 1809], p. 104).]

result of their relations perceived by the understanding. – Evidence for the existence of the different parts of the same object unequal. – Objects of memory how compounded. – The continuous existence of an individual mind, or self, an inference from the relations which exist between the idea of remembered existence, and the sensation of present existence. – The idea of existence in general, how found as an abstraction from each sensation in particular.

I use the word *idea,* as signifying a distinct class of sensations, being the result of that reasoning or observation which shows that under certain conditions, there must needs be an existence when we cannot perceive it. In such is included the evidence for *memory of the past*; of such is compounded *expectation of the future.* Thus we have an *idea* of continual, unperceived, independent existence; – but only have a *consciousness* or *sensation* of dependent, interrupted, and perceived existence; whenever I have used it in any other sense, it is in a popular manner signifying notion or object of thought, &c.

Berkeley used the word *idea* ambiguously for the perception of combined sensible qualities called an object; and for a result of reasoning which yielded him an *idea* that there must be *causes* for his perceptions; which causes he considered *the actions of a spirit.* Thus the word *idea* has been indiscriminately used both by him and others, for the consciousness of the sensible qualities, which arise from the use of the organs of sense, in relation to external beings, and for the conclusions of the understanding, after surveying the various relations and circumstances, attendant on these sensible qualities. Now objects in our conscious apprehensions are compounded of each of these kinds of ideas; or rather of *sensations* of *sensible qualities,* and *sensations* of *ideas.* – They are not only blue or red, sweet or sour, hard or soft, beautiful or ugly, warm or cold, loud or low; but the ideas of their *causes* are included in their *names* as *continually existing,* and *that* even when the organs of sense are shut.

Had I not been fearful of interrupting the main and important object of this Essay, by diverting, and perhaps engrossing the reader's attention in entering on the scholastic and unsettled dispute concerning the meaning of the word *idea,* I should have followed the suggestions of a strict philosophy, by more fully developing the notion, that *all consciousnesses whatever* ought to be ranked under the one generic term, *sensation*; and that these should be divided *into the sensations of present sensible qualities*;

sensations of the ideas of memory, sensations of the ideas of imagination, sensations of the ideas of reason, &c.

Thus simple sensation has many varieties of kinds. When it refers to no other existence than itself, it should be considered as *sensation* properly and immediately. In this sense we have *the sensation of an idea*; but then *idea* refers to an existence always considered independent of sensation; which idea is only its *sign, representative*, IMAGE, or whatever name it may please philosophy to term it. Therefore our sensations include the notion of existences, which *have existed, may exist, will exist, must needs exist*, but whose qualities are not presently determined upon the mind.[52]

Objects of memory are compounded of the fainter *sensations* of sensible qualities, mixed with the *idea* that the causes of the original impressions are removed; (the which *idea* is the result either of observation or reasoning); these again are united with the perception of the lapse of time, or of our own continuous existence going on between the original moment of the impressions, and the existence of the PRESENT faint sensible qualities. Therefore the *objects* of memory are, *masses of sensible qualities plus* the *idea* of past time, *plus* the *idea* of having been caused by causes now removed. And thus the *idea* of TIME is not itself a mere sensible quality; for although the present moment be but a sensation of immediate existence; yet the past moment is only *remembered* in the present; and the memory of it is its *idea*, and not the very sensation itself: and this *memory* of past existence, and this *sensation* of present existence, includes in their union a *corollary*, which is the result of a relation that exists between the *idea* of remembered existence, and the

---

[52] A strict Idealist who really will not admit the knowledge of any thing but his own sensations, and thus refuses to believe in insentient qualities, ought, if consistent, to reject memory of the past and expectation of the future, and to admit nothing but each sensation as it rises as an existence; for the existences (i.e. the sensations) which are *past*, and to *come*, are as much and entirely exterior to, and independent of present sensations, as any insentient existence whatever can be of sensation in general. Both may be known by receiving the evidence arising from the comparison *of ideas*, but they must stand or fall together. — I insert this note in consequence of a late conversation with a modern Idealist, who carries the notion so far as to assert, that there is no *evidence* for any existing sensations but his own.

sensation of present existence; namely, that there 'MUST NEEDS BE' *a continued capacity in nature, fitted to* UNITE MEMORY TO SENSE, *and fitted to continue existence, which itself is neither memory nor sense;* for each particular memory, and each particular sense passes away—but the powers of memory and sensation in general *continue* to exist, of which each particular memory and sense arises as a change, and '*a change could not* BEGIN *of itself*'.[53]—'Thus the notion of TIME is an idea the *result of reasoning;* but TIME itself is a capacity in nature fitted to the *continuance* of any existence.'

Again, *ideas of imagination* are faint images of sensible qualities *unmixed with any notions concerning time;* whose causes are considered as at present removed from their operation on the senses; and variously compounded by the influence of fancy, or rendered more or less *vivacious* by its power.

Thus the objects of memory and imagination differ as to the *nature of their* COMPONENT PARTS, and not *merely* as to the comparatively higher *vivacity* of those of imagination:—A *puerile* notion, on which however Mr. Hume has reared the whole fallacy of his system with respect to that BELIEF by which expectation of similar future effects arises upon the presence of similar causes.—He argues, that because what are called *real* things yield *vivacious* images, therefore the mind considers all vivacious images as *real;* and thus BELIEVES in those future qualities of things, which are *associated* in a *lively* manner by *memory with present impressions.*

---

[53]   It is this primeval truth, 'That no quality can *begin* its own existence', which is the key to every difficulty that concerns the sources of our belief or knowledge.

M. de Condillac's system, (which I have read since writing these papers), notwithstanding its extreme beauty of conception, and close reasoning in general, falls in my judgment very early to the ground; for he supposes *the statue* 'to generate the *idea* of SELF by the perception of the *succession* of faint and strong scent only'. This is a most important oversight—*Self* is always considered as a *continuity,* and is generated by the sense of continuous life, and the idea of its continued object which is the subject matter of all the changes.—So well was M. de Condillac aware that this notion was necessary to prove exteriority, that he shifts his *ground* in the chapter upon touch. [Shepherd paraphrases Condillac, *Traité,* pp. 122–6.]

Berkeley has also this fallacy in answering the objection made to his doctrine when his adversary advances, that *mere ideas* cannot be real things, namely, 'That the superior order and *vivacity* of some ideas above others make *the whole distinction between what the vulgar deem real, or illusory objects.*'[54]

Now *vivacity* being one of the qualities usually accompanying the objects which impress the sense, it must necessarily belong to such, as a component part of their whole *effects*, and therefore, other things being equal which influence the judgment, *vivacity* of sensible qualities, will as one of their *effects* be ever referred to such objects; and the remainder of their qualities will be *expected* to be fulfilled in consequence. BELIEF, therefore, (in this case), and expectation in consequence, arises, 1st. From the necessity that like *effects* should have like causes; and 2ndly, From the *probability* that such should be conjoined with such apparent causes as those with which nature usually unites them; and therefore will fulfil the remainder of the definitions, which the complex exterior objects bear: and this trust in the regularity of nature in forming her compound objects alike, is on account of *regularity* itself being an *effect* which must have its *equal cause*. So little is merely a *vivacity of image* trusted to in a sane and waking state of mind, as indicative of the real presence of the exterior objects which influence the sense, that the mind, in many cases, perceiving surrounding circumstances *differ, justly doubts upon this matter.*

Then thirdly, *the ideas which are the result of reasoning testify, as mere signs, the existences of things, which are not sensations.*

Now objects in the mind are aggregates of the *sensations* of sensible qualities, and of the *sensations* of the IDEAS of memory, reason, imagination, expectation, &c. variously compounded: And hence there arises a reason why the evidence of the *certain existence* of different parts of the same object must *necessarily* be UNEQUAL. For the sensible qualities have an immediate incontrovertible evidence, from the consciousness of their immediate presence. — They are felt — and the *feelings* are themselves the very existences. — But the evidence from memory, and reason, can never rise higher than memory and reason are capable of testifying.

---

54 [Shepherd paraphrases Berkeley, *Principles* 33 (p. 95).]

These sensible qualities equally exist in an hallucination of mind, as in its sane state, and however incongruous they appear they do and must exist; but if a conclusion be drawn amiss in reasoning, if the memory be treacherous, or the judgment erroneous, then in such cases, these false ideas being mixed up and associated even with the most clear and orderly set of sensible qualities, would render the *evidence* for the existence of such an *object*, (or aggregate of various qualities), *ambiguous and unequal.* Thus it cannot be denied but that the *whole* objects present to our consciousness, contain *parts of* UNEQUAL *evidence as to their existence*; some of which sometimes failing, yield a just ground of scepticism;—a scepticism, which however, should never rise higher nor extend further than the *irregularity* of nature justifies; for *as is the effect, so is the cause*—the balance of regularity, and irregularity, we hold in our hands; these are *effects*, and their causes must hitherto have been equal to them, and unless some interference is observed, or supposed possible, should reasonably beget in the mind a *proportional* reliance for the future. But if in any instance whatever, there had been hitherto perfect regularity, yet it would not thence follow there were an equal demonstration for the future; and *that* because we are ignorant of the *cause* for the regularity; and cases might be supposed in future to occur, where a difference would be absolutely necessary in the *apparent course of nature*, or *providence* to take place. We have very strong evidence which goes to prove that single varieties, to otherwise universal experience, have taken place with respect to both kinds. That is, there have been *single exceptions* to universal experience, *which seem to have had no precise end in view*, nor *to have contributed to any end whatever*; AND THERE SEEMS TO HAVE BEEN OTHERS WHICH HAVE BEEN MADE USE OF, AS MEANS TO AN END, AND WHERE MOST MATERIAL EVENTS HAVE ENSUED IN CONSEQUENCE.

The former kind, when well attested, men seem not to find any difficulty in believing;—of the latter they are infinitely more incredulous and jealous in receiving the testimony.— Indeed, it must be allowed that a *marvellous event* becomes a very different object of attention when it presents itself to our notice, not merely as singular of its kind, and one whose causes are not obvious, but, also as one which by its *manner of production*, forces the mind upon the *inference*, that as the apparently immediate cause is inadequate, therefore certain other alledged causes both adequate and necessary are the true ones.[55] In each of these cases there are true *miracles*; i.e. *marvellous events*, singular exceptions to nature's course; but the latter only affords what ought to be termed *miraculous evidence* to a doctrine; or in other words *a similarity in the course of nature, with respect to the necessity and action of efficient cause, but a variety from its apparent regularity, in order to be used as a means towards a specific end.*

This difference between the *singularity* of an event and its *intention*; between an insulated and surprising *fact*, and the object to be gained by it, is not shown (that I know of) by writers on this head. That there are such facts without any doctrine being in question, which are attested and reasonably believed in (and that *'with full assurance of faith'*[56]), at once dissolves the whole fabric of Hume's *argument* on the matter; and that whether a doctrine be *true* or *false*, — whether there be religious miracles or not: because he points his force against the absurdity of admitting evidence which testifies to the occurrence of an event, DIFFERENT *from the course of experience;* OUT *of the order of the apparent train of cause and effect,* and which he terms the *course of nature.* Whereas men very well know that nature, whatever her apparent course may be, still keeps them *'at a great distance from all her secrets';*[57] from the knowledge of the precisely *efficient cause* acting in any particular case, and therefore, that there is nothing contrary to her *real* course (by means of some secret efficient cause) that singular varieties should take place; and for this reason they conceive that evidence ought to be admitted on the subject. The examination, reception, or rejection of evidence on it, tries the intellects of men much in the same way as other things do, but their hearts still more when it concerns the subject of religion.

It thence follows that a regularity with respect to certain events in one country, does not *prove* there must be the same regularity in another. Nor does that which is a regular

---

55   See further, the Essay on Miracles. [See pp. 219–26 in this volume.]
56   [Heb. 10:22.]
57   [Shepherd quotes Hume, *Enquiry* 4.16 (p. 113).]

appearance at one age of the world, *prove* the same must exist in all ages of the world.

Nor do the usual actions of God's providence which are most wise in order to our reliance on his modes of operation, *prove* that he will never alter his action, if he should intend to convince us in any case of his immediate presence. But to return to the more immediate object of this chapter, it follows from the reasoning adduced in it, that both Mr. Hume and Dr. Reid are wrong in their notions arising from the observation '*that the real table can suffer no alteration, as we recede further from it, although it appears to diminish*'.[58] Mr. Hume hence argues, that we cannot see a *real* table, but the *image* or IDEA of a table only; and that thus 'we can *have no absolute communication by the senses with external objects*'.

And Dr. Reid answers, '*that we have such communication, because a real table would by the laws of optics, thus diminish upon the sight*'. Now the truth is, that no real table is formed, no image of a table is formed, unless the whole united mass of the unknown objects in nature exterior to, and independent of the instruments of sense (not *yet worthy of the name of* 'TABLE') unite with the mechanical action of these, and by their means with the sentient principle, in order to *create* in such an union that object which alone can properly be termed 'TABLE'. Yet *after* experience, *the* OUTWARD OBJECTS, the CONTINUALLY EXISTING PARTS of the whole causes necessary to the creation of a *table*, must be named by the name by which the whole is named; for there is no other name whereby they can be called, nor any other *ideas* by which the *memory* of them can be introduced into the mind, save by the appearance of 'the faint images of those sensible qualities' which their presence originally created.[59]

---

[58] See Reid 'on the Intellectual Powers', for Hume's objection, and Reid's answer. [Shepherd paraphrases a passage from Hume, *Enquiry* 12.9, that Reid quotes and then rebuts; see Reid, *Essays* 2.14 (p. 178 and pp. 180–2).]

[59] See p. 137. [See p. 149 in this volume.]

Chapter 7: Application of the Doctrine Contained in the Preceding Essay to the Evidence of Our Belief in Several Opinions

[...]

Section 4

Cursory observations on instincts and prophetic vision.

Instincts[60] give notions of *real* beings, if the objects to which they point fulfil their whole qualities. It is consistent with the previous doctrine, that instinct be an action of the brain excited independent of impression, in the first instance from external objects, but afterwards capable of being kept up by their means. For as the brain is the exponent of the soul, so any of its actions whatever, being either the effect of an impression from an outward object, or brought about by any other cause adequate to a given action, would equally give rise to the idea of the corresponding object; as in dreams, &c. But in dreams the objects do not fulfil the whole qualities expected of them, from the first impressions made upon the mind: in instincts it is otherwise — for after the first impressions begin to fade, the images can be renewed by the acquaintance made with those external objects, which are not only capable of fulfilling the first expectation formed of them, but also of affording a regular and constant reply to the demands of the organs of sense.

In like manner, prophecy is also true prophecy, if a lively action of the brain, does through any cause whatever which produces it, testify the future existence of such things as do really happen afterwards, in such fulness, and order, and perfection as renders it improbable that the coincidence of the prophecy and the events which arrive, could take place by chance. The probable evidence before the accomplishment of a prophecy that it will be accomplished, must arise from a number of collateral circumstances, which, after accomplishment, have much to do in rendering it of interest, veracity, and importance.

---

[60]   As for instance, the instincts of birds give them notions of the materials requisite for making their nest previously to a first formation.

Section 5

On the knowledge of the nature of unperceived objects.

With respect to the nature of unperceived objects I shall take notice, that we can form some ideas of their *natures* by *subtracting from them* EQUALLY that which is common to all, viz. the action of the instruments of *sense and the mind.* For although it be true that nothing can be like any sensation, but a sensation; yet it does not follow, but that there may be qualities connected with our sensations, and arising out of them, which we perceive have not sensation for their essence, and so may belong to insentient natures. Now it is by separating the idea of sensation in general from the ideas of particular sensations,[61] that we gain the notion of existence which need not necessarily be sentient;[62] for as the capacity for sensation in general, or *mind*, cannot be contained in any one sensation in particular, so it cannot in all; and therefore in like manner, as there is one eye, but many colours and figures, so there must be one *capacity*, but many sensations — one *continually* existing power, of which these are but the changes.[63]

Again, as variety does not depend upon sensation as its *essence*, so we perceive that *variety* may take place among any supposed existences whatever; and not only so, but that the quality itself of *variety* when unperceived, will be *like* perceived variety, in as far as it is *variety*; and that such a quality must necessarily exist amidst that set of wonderful objects which is neither contained in the uniform capacity called mind, or the uniform action of the organs of sense, and which therefore we justly consider as forming AN UNIVERSE *independent* of both.

Thus the *ocean* must be *vast*, in comparison of a drop of water, when both are unperceived. *Time,* in union with the powers of sensation, may be measured by a succession of ideas in the fancy; but *time* in *nature*, and *unperceived*, measures, and

---

61   See the short essay, That sensible qualities cannot be causes. [See pp. 82–6 in this volume.]

62   See the note page 42 of the essay on cause and effect, and pp. 42, 83, 84, 182 of this essay. [See pp. 36, 113, 130, and 164–5 in this volume.]

63   It is supposed here that the reader has acquiesced in the Doctrine of the foregoing Essay, 'That qualities cannot *begin* their own existence', and that the *union* of qualities or objects is necessary to form new existences.

is not measured by, the succession of events, whether sensations or not; as the revolution of seasons; the birth and fall of empires; the change of harmony to chaos, or of chaos to harmony. — Again, subtract the organs of sense, from the most minute divisions of matter, and they are only little in comparison with what is large; and the question concerning the infinite divisibility of matter, resolves itself into the impossibility of the imagination conceiving and *not* conceiving of a thing at the same time — for the conditions of the problem are, that something is to be imagined too small for the imagination to conceive; and to imagine it under the forms of an extension, which extension is not conceivable when unperceived either by the senses, or the imagination; whereas we know not what extension unperceived is, although I am willing to concede a *mite* cannot be the *same as the globe*, not only with respect to that condition of being which, *when exhibited upon the eye or touch*, yields the *notion of extension*, but which, when subjected to calculation, manifests that in its unknown state, it must be liable to *that variety*, which *when perceived*, is called *size* or *figure*, and becomes altered in its dimensions: still when that *unknown being matter* is in its unperceived state subject to that condition or state called divisibility, when fancy has done its utmost, and attempted a conception of *inconceivable* subdivisions, perhaps such a portion of matter is a world, and is an unknown quantity of 'something' (as Hume calls it) supporting the means of life to millions of beings under no manner of relation either to our senses or minds.

It is here that it would be proper to show more fully and distinctly than has yet been done, what is the error of Bishop Berkeley's doctrine, concerning the knowledge we have of external objects, and to call upon that which has been laid down in these pages, to point out where the fallacy lies in his reasoning, which at once is considered as unanswerable, and nevertheless at variance with the common experience of life.[64] But it is impossible to place his curious system in a proper light, or render the argument against it apparent, without some extracts from his Essay on the Principles of Human Knowledge. I would

---

[64] Mr. Hume calls it a doctrine which equally fails to enforce conviction, or to suggest an answer to its fallacy.

rather do this in a detached manner, than introduce it here, and then take the opportunity of showing a little more at length than would now be convenient, the manner in which the fore-going doctrine enables me distinctly to point out, how obvious an answer presents itself to those points of his doctrine, which from a lapse in the reasoning fail to produce conviction; and how truly consistent, and philosophical, and accordant with experience, is the rest of his matter, however much it may vary from commonly received notions. I shall therefore throw these paragraphs, with the observations annexed to them, in a short and distinct essay; and shall conclude, for the present, this subtle, complicated, and, I fear, fatiguing subject, with a concise summary of the doctrine.

Chapter 8: Recapitulation

The perception of independent, external, and continued existences, the result of an exercise of the reasoning powers, or a mixture of the ideas of the understanding, with those of sense. – External objects unknown as to the qualities which are capable of affecting the senses. – Known as compounds of simple sensations, mixed with ideas of reason or conceptions of the understanding. – Reply to an objection concerning extension. – There exists, however, one set of exterior qualities, which resemble such as are inward; these are variety – independency – existence – continued existence – identity, &c. – Exteriorly extended objects, cannot be like the idea *of extension. – An appeal to the phenomena of the diorama as an evidence for the truth of these notions. The ideas of this treatise do unintentionally coincide with some mysteries of religion. – Conclusion.*

The perception of external, continually existing, independ-ent objects, is an affair of the understanding; it is a mental vision; the result of some notions previously in the mind, being mixed with each sensation as it arises, and thus enabling it to refer the sensations to certain reasonable causes, without resting merely in the contemplation of the sensations them-selves; by which it comes to pass, that names stand for these compound mixtures; and that the organs of sense are the instru-ments which immediately detect the presence of those things which are external to, and independent both of the organs of sense and the mind.

I consider the chief proposition, thus used as a mean of quick and constant reasoning, applicable to, and immediately associated with, certain exhibited sensations, to be that which comprehends the relation of cause and effect.

By these means, there is the reference of *similar effects to similar causes*, and of *differences of effects, to proportional differences in causes*.

That class of ideas which Dr. Reid terms instinctive, and Mr. D. Stewart considers as composed of simple ideas not *formed* by the senses, but generated upon certain *fit occasions* for their pro-duction, I consider to be the conclusions of a latent reasoning;[65] as the mere results and corollaries, included in the relation of those ideas and sensations already existing in the mind, and which were previously formed by the senses. The idea is very soon learned, *that it is a contradiction to suppose things to* BEGIN *of themselves*; for this idea is occasioned by the impression, (the observation), that the *beginning* of every thing is but a change of that which is already in existence, and so is not the same idea, (the same quality,) as the *beginning of being*, which is independ-ent of previous being and its changes. The two ideas are there-fore *contrary* to each other; and the meanest understanding perceives them to be so, as easily as it perceives that white is not black, &c. *Changes* therefore require beings already in existence, of which they are the affections or qualities; and children, peasants, and brutes know and perceive these relations, though they cannot analyse them.[66] The mind there-fore taking notice of changes, refers them to objects of which they are the qualities.

Thus a very young and ignorant person will soon perceive, that the various sensations of which he is *conscious*, are mere *changes* in relation to some other objects in existence.

Such an one on hearing himself speak, or sing, will not con-sider the sensation of sound apart from its cause, or the *object* of which it is a change, and on hearing another voice than his

---

[65] Since writing the above, I find M. Destutt de Tracy of my opinion. [Shepherd refers to Tracy, *Eléments*.]

[66] M. D. de Tracy considers children as capable of perceiving a relation between two ideas, as of their original perception. [Shepherd refers to Tracy, *Eléments*.]

own, will refer such *variety* in the effect, to a proportional variety in the cause; for here his consciousness tells him, that the sound is not formed by the same means which formed the first sound, yet it appears in many respects a similar effect; therefore, he concludes that in as many respects there are *similar* causes, i.e. similar objects of which there has been sound as a change: and in some respects the effects are diverse, therefore, the causes are equally diverse; i.e. are uttered by another being than himself, thus concluding another being like himself to be present. The same method regards the perception of every sense, and the objects in relation to it; and I consider primary qualities of matter, in this respect, to be upon the same footing as those which are secondary: Objects are therefore, *beings like ourselves*, plus or minus the *differences*; in as much as *they are the proportional causes of the sensations which they create.* Thus we can but virtually touch causes, and that is by reasoning. And as the knowledge of external nature is but an inference from reason, either from the relation of cause and effect, analogies, probabilities, &c. so its absolute independency of each mind, can have no further certainty than such inference, however strong it may be, can afford. Indeed, in one point of view, such complete independency as should suppose the annihilation of any one essence in nature would appear impossible; one change is independent of another change, a man may die, and his child continue to live; but I conceive the frame of nature so completely one whole, and all its changes but such constituent parts of it, that either, on the one hand, it must be wholly impossible for a true annihilation to take place of the essential and permanent existence of any part; or on the other, that if it were possible, the whole must be destroyed together.

Now, although the reference of like effect to like cause be absolute demonstration, yet it may be, that in some instances, we consider *effect partially*; referring some like effects not only to like causes, but to compound objects with which they are usually associated; and which objects will exhibit *other effects*, for which there may not be sufficient proof or likelihood; also the very comparison of what is like, to like, supposes an ability to perfect comparisons, a subject on which we frequently make mistakes. *Independent* existence is then, however, a conclusion of reasoning; an idea in the understanding in relation to the perception of the necessity there should be like cause for like effect, and proportional causes for proportional effects.

Again, as to the CONTINUATION of the existence of *independent objects*, the original causes and capacities for every thing must be concluded as uninterrupted, *as long as effects are renewed at intervals*; it being a contradiction *that such effects should begin their own existences*. Therefore, the perception of the *continued existence* of objects is also in relation to the knowledge of causation, and is an idea gained by the understanding by reference from reason. *Outward existence, is the perception of a continued independent existence in relation to motion, from our own minds taken as a centre whence we set out*; the which motion is a sort of sense, whose sensible quality merely, could not *immediately* yield the notion of *unperceived* exteriority, unless mixed with the powers of the understanding, which refer its *sensible quality* to an *unperceived cause*, in the way that has been described to be the case both with respect to itself, and to the other senses; by which means they are considered to interact with those things known by consciousness not to be minds. For motion is when unperceived a capacity or quality of being, in relation to those various objects which are *proved to be continually existing* by their regular reply to its action.[67]

And when motion is considered in relation to empty space merely, it is also perceived to be in relation to a mode of existence, proved by the same process of the understanding to be *continually existing*. For as the exteriority of space, or distance between objects, replies regularly to the sense and use of motion, so must it be regarded as a *common quality to all* objects, having its own *unperceived essence*. Although, therefore, the instruments of sense, and motion, can only *after* their action form *sensible qualities*, 'ideas of sensation', yet their use *immediately* gives notice of outward, insentient, and unperceived existences; — because the understanding being supposed correct in the notion that such '*must needs exist*', in the manner explained at large in this treatise, informs the mind that it is with these continuous *unperceived* existences, that the organs of sense and motion themselves also as unperceived existences

---

67 See this Essay, p. 83, 84, and from p. 102 to 107; 'It is not sufficient therefore'; also Essay VI. [See pp. 130, 136-8, and 82-6 in this volume.]

interact *in order to the perception of their sensible qualities* when the whole union touches the sentient capacity.[68] But it is motion, as first in order, and first in proof, which is impowered to detect the OUTWARDNESS of objects:[69] because those things which return upon the application of motion to the sense of touch, are by that *necessity* of motion in order to apprehend their tangibility *justly defined as distant* from the mind which apprehends them,[70] for every distinct quality may be named as we please according to its variety of appearance. But it is these distant continuous existences, which exhibit their qualities, one quality, that by the ear is perceived as sound; another, by the palate as taste; a third, by the nostrils, as smell; a fourth and fifth, by the eye, as figure and colour. Nevertheless these distant independent beings in relation to motion, are wholly unknown as to their *unperceived* qualities, which yet we immediately *perceive must exist by means of the sensible qualities* they excite, and which are associated with the *ideas* of their causes. It is not, therefore, colour only, but all sensible qualities whatever, which are carried *out* by an act of the mind, and considered as

---

[68]   See pp. 54, 55, &c. [See pp. 118–9 in this volume.]

[69]   It is here I differ with several French authors whose works I have met with since writing this treatise, with M. Destutt de Tracy, Condillac, de Gerando, &c.

 The sense of the resistance of solidity to the sense of voluntary motion, no more proves the exteriority, independency, and continuity of objects, than the reply of colour to the use of the eye. The will is no more self, than is the eye, or the hand. The five organs of sense in their conscious use, afford by the phenomena which take place in consequence, an equal proof of these attributes belonging to those constituent parts of the whole causes of our sensations, which are by consciousness known not to be contained in the mere possession of the mind itself, and in the motions of the five instruments of sense. *For these latter* can exist and act without certain given ideas, therefore the REMAINING NECESSARY PARTS of the whole cause of such ideas, are *independent* and *separate* from them. Such also *regularly* reply to *irregular* applications, in relation to them, therefore, *continue* in their existence. This is the argument, and it applies, *equally to each of the five organs of sense,* as much as to the sense of touch. The touch would not prove this point, without a mixture of reasoning: and which reasoning would be sufficient to draw the same result from the phenomena of the other senses.

 See Destutt de Tracy Ideologie, p. 114, duod. [Shepherd refers to Tracy, *Eléments*.]

[70]   See p. 57, &c. of this Essay. [See pp. 119–20 in this volume.]

proportionally distant from the mind, as is the quantity of motion required to attain them in their *tangible* form, and as immediately coalescing, and inhering in and with those independent objects.[71] Infants very soon perceive motion to be in respect to existences, which are not included in the idea of themselves; and which they also very soon conceive to *continue* to exist unperceived, as they are '*ever ready to appear' upon the caprice of their action*; that is to say, the influence of *thought* or *conception of ideas*, is soon mixed with *simple sensation*, forming thereby those complex beings called outward objects; (I may say, those perplexing beings, at once ideas of the mind and existences independent of it!) Now the understanding perceiving that independent continued existences, are not the same beings as those which are included in our own sentient natures; that they are not *merely* sound, colour, &c. *places* them beyond, (that is, considers them as existing under a capacity of being independent of) every source of our own sensibility; viz. out of *the limit of the definition of our bodies and minds*; associating with the *ideas* of their distances their whole sensible qualities.

I now repeat this reasoning is also applicable to the primary as well as the secondary qualities. For what are 'parts in cohesion or extension',[72] when separated from that external independent existence which the understanding allots to the unperceived unknown *causes* of these ideas in the mind, and from their relation to motion, (which when unperceived is also unknown as to its nature), but '*ideas of sensation*' exhibitions of colour and of touch, &c.

Nor will it be a reasonable objection to say (as Dr. Reid does) 'an idea cannot be extended and solid',[73] for the proposition concerning the perception of external qualities, intends to assert, that the idea of *extension* as a sensation *independent of its cause* is not an extended or solid idea, any more than the idea of a colour is a coloured idea; or of a sound a noisy idea.

---

[71]   See Essay 4th, on the union of colour and extension. [See pp. 189–200 in this volume.]

[72]   See Reid's Inquiry. [Shepherd quotes Reid, *Inquiry* 5.4 (p. 61).]

[73]   [This may be a paraphrase of Reid's claim, which he ascribes to Berkeley but endorses, that 'an idea cannot be in a subject that is extended and solid' (Reid, *Inquiry* 7 [p. 217]).]

For although the qualities are understood to be created by their exterior causes, yet these qualities are but effects;—a certain *'idea of sensation'* is not coloured, it is colour—does not emit a sound, it is sound—does not exhibit extension, it is extension, and so of the rest. They are all simple sensations, created by causes which the understanding concludes to be external and independent of self; and are in relation to motion and the five senses, for the exhibition of their appropriate effects, and having corresponding proportions among themselves. Parts, therefore, are unknown powers, save that they exist in relation to motion, to touch, and other affections, the which when unperceived are still also unknown powers, *save in their existences, their mutual relations, and their proportional varieties.* For there exists *one* set of exterior qualities, *which we may know of, as resembling such as are inward.*[74] They are the same as those, which affect the sensations, and which the understanding can apply to every kind of existence, sentient or insentient. Such is that of *variety;* we perceive variety amidst our sensations; but other existences might also be various; and being so, we intimately and *immediately* know what variety means. The same of *independency;* one sensation may be independent of another, so may any other existence, and we know what quality it is we speak of, when we predicate independency of unperceived existences.

Existence is upon the same footing also; existence of a sensation is in the very exhibition and conscious feeling of a quality. But the idea of existence *in general* is the very being of any quality whatever, as barely contrary to non-existence.[75] This *idea* of existence is gained by comparing the consciousness of successive sensations *with the idea*[76] *of non-existence;* which idea is also generated by the means of their successive *disappearance.* Thus, the idea of existence is a more *general idea* than that of *the idea of sensation,* for as each sensation in particular successively ceases to exist, so they all must; and as they do not begin their own existences, so they are but changes of *something* which is neither *any one,* nor *yet the whole* of our sensations: therefore,

---

[74] See p. 162. [See p. 156 in this volume.]
[75] See p. 42, 162, 163, Essay VI. [See pp. 113, 156, and 82–6 in this volume.]
[76] See p. 50, concerning negative *ideas.* [See p. 116 in this volume.]

sensation is not necessarily existent, but existence is something which is not included in any consciousness, and is the general quality of which sensation is the accident, or exponent; instead of sensation being a mere synonymy with existence, as I have heard contended.

Therefore an unperceived quality may exist unfelt, and in that quality of existence, can be conceived of when unperceived, as similar to perceived existence: Also in a more popular and practical way, we judge that another mind might not perceive our sensations, nor we the sensations belonging to another, yet that both would equally exist in relation to each unperceivedly. *Continued* existence is likewise subject to a similar observation, and signifies that no interval of time, interrupts the existence of a particular quality; such an affection may belong to unperceived as to perceived existences.

Identity, or the continued sameness of a quality, may be predicated of an unperceived quality, and there may be other affections liable to similar reasoning, which at present do not occur to my mind, unless it be the relation of cause and effect, which may equally exist among insentient as sentient natures. The reason why these unperceived qualities, may *resemble* those which are perceived, and not any of the primary or secondary qualities of bodies (relating to the five organs of sense) be resembling in their perceived and unperceived state, is because the external qualities which are in relation to the senses and mind, require their aid to *modify* them; and that which is *altered* cannot be the *same* as when existing *previous to alteration.*

Unperceived, unconscious, extended parts, (whatever parts unperceived may be), cannot be *like* the idea of extension. But among sensations themselves, *after* their determination upon the mind, there may exist relations which the senses have nothing to do with, have *not* altered, and which may be applicable to any existence whatever: — Putting all these things together; the colouring of a scene in nature or art, is in relation to real or supposed motion — and motion is conceived in relation to existences independent of self; therefore colouring will always be seen as though it were outward, and therefore conceived of as thus by the imagination. The organs of sense convey sentient existences internally to the inmost recesses of the soul: the understanding reacts upon them, and places all things without it in similar proportions. If this proposition were not capable of proof by abstract reasoning, the exhibition of the Diorama now before the public (of a scene of natural size from nature, and another from art),[77] would be enough to prove that colouring is placed in proportion to the position of *things among themselves*; and such positions are as the capacities of distance, and the powers of motion *in relation to us,* as well as *among themselves*: The scene, independent of the understanding, is a scene of mental sensation; for when the mind is for a moment deluded, (of which I speak from experience, knowing that this extraordinary facsimile of nature and art has the power of effecting a complete delusion), and forgets the *place* in which it is — the relation of place being forgotten, the scenes are conceived of as *real*; i.e. the colouring is symptomatic as a quality of beings, which will fulfil the remainder of the qualities belonging to their definitions upon trial, and thus be equal to their whole definitions. But when we recollect where we are, the mind perceives these thoughts to be illusory, and the colouring is not then conceived to be a quality of such objects as will fulfil their whole definitions. I shall conclude with saying, that as we never can experience the fulfilment of that part of the definition of external objects, viz. their existence after our own ceases; so although it be an inference of high probability, yet it is short of strict demonstration. We can indeed by referring like effects to like causes, and proportional effects to proportional causes, demonstrate thus far; but we never experience this further complete independency of outward object as an effect. All we can do is to refer compound similar and various effects, to compound similar and various causes; which occasions an inference that such causes are like ourselves, plus or minus the varieties,

---

77   [The first Diorama opened in Paris in 1822; it was a rotating theater in which viewers could observe various illuminated paintings of landscapes and building interiors that realistically shifted in appearance (as if the sun were setting, for example). A similar Diorama opened in Regent's Park, London, in 1823. As a contemporaneous article in *The Times* of London reported, 'Even after the spectator is advised that he is looking at a flat surface, the illusion is so strong that it is almost impossible to believe the fact' ('Diorama', *The Times* [London: 4 October 1823], p. 3). For an authoritative account of the nineteenth-century diorama, see Laurent Mannoni, *The Great Art of Light and Shadow: Archeology of the Cinema,* trans. and ed. Richard Crangle (Exeter: University of Exeter Press, 2000), pp. 185–91].

and we finding ourselves independent of them, are led to conclude they will in like manner be independent of us.

This statement of the matter immediately touches upon the
difficulty there is in the detection of like compound objects
being present to us. However, the reasoning on the point is
nearly demonstrative, and practically is entirely so — for when
we get at objects like ourselves, which must exist as causes of
the effects we experience, nothing is perceived capable of
making such a difference, as should prevent them from existing
independent of us were we no more — yet things are real, if even
this last test of independency remain without proof; for *they* are
real which fulfil the definitions for which their names were first
formed. The being true to expectations formed of their qualities,
is the very criterion of reality; and even upon the supposition of
a total independency being out of contemplation, still all
existing things would be in relation to our senses, and to
motion; and be independent of our thoughts and actions. Nor
let it be thought that infants, peasants, and brutes, do not
reason; all of these are capable of perceiving certain relations,
included in the impressions made upon them, and of drawing
them as occasion requires into practical results.[78]

With respect to the nature of God, (in which all men are so
much and justly interested) his essential existence, his continued existence is demonstrated, by the abstract argument
used in this treatise. Whatever variety and changes of beings
there are, all changes must finally be pushed back to that
essence who *began not,* and in whom all dependent beings
originally resided, and were put forth as out goings of himself
in all those varieties of attitudes which his wisdom and
benevolence thought fit.

And I shall not shrink from saying, that such thoughts as
these, do unintentionally render the mysteries of religion easier
to the comprehension than otherwise they would appear; for
shall we limit the capacities and attributes of Divinity, in his
unknown, unperceived state, by our meagre perceptions? May
he not to every world that hath come forth from him, offer a
protection, and an interference, in proportion to, and in relation

---

[78]   M. de Tracy says, 'Un enfant apperçoit un rapport comme il apperçoit
un couleur.' [See p. 87 n72.]

to its wants? May not some confined manifestations, of the universal essence, *be sent* to different worlds adapted to their capacity for moral improvement, to the motives which may act upon them, and the uses which result from such a manifestation of his presence, in the way either of action or *passion*? Again shall all things swarm with life, and the principle which divides animate from inanimate nature be still undiscovered, and yet no emanation from the essential deity, brood over the face of the deep, or breathe into man the breath of life? or finally, shall God be either limited, or divisible, by senses that cannot detect his presence, although known by the understanding that he 'needs must exist', and be in all times and places 'ready to appear' to his creation, as the continually existing cause for its support, its life, its hope, its confidence, and its joy!

Selection D

(Excerpted from *Essays on the Perception of an External Universe* [1827], pp. 195–270.)

Essay 1: Consideration of the Erroneous Reasoning Contained in Bishop Berkeley's Principles of Human Knowledge

Section 1

'When several ideas', says Bishop Berkeley (section 1st), '(imprinted on the senses) are observed to accompany each other, they come to be marked by one name; and so to be reputed as one thing, thus a certain colour, taste, smell, figure, and consistence, are accounted one distinct thing, signified by the name of apple; other collection of ideas form a stone, a tree, a book, &c.'[79] (Section 3rd, p. 25), 'For what are objects but the things we perceive by sense? and what do we perceive but our own ideas or sensations?[80] for, (section 5th), light and colours, heat and cold, extension and figure, in a word, the things we see and feel, what are they but so many sensations, notions,

---

[79]   [Shepherd paraphrases Berkeley, *Principles* 1 (p. 83).]
[80]   [Shepherd quotes, with slight alterations, Berkeley, *Principles* 4 (p. 84).]

ideas, impressions on the sense? and is it possible to separate even in thought any of these from perception.'[81]

Sec. 9, p. 27. 'Some make a distinction between primary and secondary qualities; but extension, figure, and motion, are ONLY *ideas* existing in the mind. And an idea can be like nothing but an idea, for neither these nor their archetypes, can exist in an unperceiving substance.'[82] (Section 15th.) 'It is impossible, therefore, that any colour or extension at all, or sensible quality whatever, should exist in an unthinking subject without the mind, or indeed, that there should be any such thing as an outward object.'[83]

Thus far Bishop Berkeley, on *objects* being *only ideas*, or sensations of sensible qualities, and these ideas as comprehending the primary as well as secondary qualities. Many, I conceive, will think, from what I have said in the foregoing pages, that there is no material difference between my doctrine, and his. But a careful investigation of both, will show there is a very considerable one. For although, I agree with him, 1st. That nothing can be like a *sensation*, or *idea*, or *perception*, but a *sensation, idea,* and *perception*; 2ndly. That the primary qualities, *after* the impressions they make on the senses, are sensations, or ideas, or perceptions; as well as the secondary ones. Yet I do not agree with him, in stating, that *objects* are nothing but what we perceive by sense, or that a complete enumeration is made of *all* the ideas which constitute an apple, a stone, a tree, or a book; in the summing up of their *sensible qualities*. For I have made it clear, I trust, by the foregoing argument, *that an object perceived* by the mind is a compound being, consisting of a certain collection of sensible qualities, 'mixed with an *idea* the *result of reasoning*' of such qualities being formed by a 'continually existing outward and independent set of as various and appropriate causes'; therefore that there must be '*an outward object*', existing as a cause to excite the inward feeling. The logical error, therefore, of Bishop Berkeley on this part of the subject, is an *incomplete definition*; for no definition is good which does not

---

81   [Shepherd quotes, with slight alterations, Berkeley, *Principles* 5 (p. 84).]

82   [Shepherd paraphrases and adds emphasis to Berkeley, *Principles* 9 (p. 86).]

83   [Shepherd quotes, with slight alterations, Berkeley, *Principles* 15 (p. 88).]

take notice of *all* the ideas, under the term; and in every object
of sense which the mind perceives, the knowledge of its *genus*,
as a general effect arising from a *general* cause independent of
mind, *is mixed with the sensations or ideas resulting from its special
qualities affecting the same.* The notion of this *genus* is omitted in
Dr. Berkeley's *definition of an* OBJECT, by the limiting words *but*
and *only.*

2. Bishop Berkeley is guilty of an ambiguity, when he speaks
'of ideas being *imprinted on the senses*', 'of our perceiving' (*by
sense*) 'our *own ideas and sensations*', for he appears to speak of
the '*senses* on which objects are imprinted', as if he intended by
them those five organs of sense, viz. the eye, the ear, &c.
vulgarly called the senses, but which, in truth, have no sense or
feeling in themselves as independent of mind: but are
mechanical instruments; which as powers modify exterior
existences, ere they reach the sentient capacity; the which
capacity as a general power or feeling becomes modified
thereby; for undoubtedly, the senses as organs cannot perceive
what the senses as organs are required to form.[84]

When he speaks of 'ideas being imprinted on the senses', *the
phrase contains* the very doctrine he is controverting.

The *ideas* of colours cannot be imprinted on the *eye*; nor
those of sound on the *ear*; nor those of extension on the *touch*;
for there are no such IDEAS, until *after* the eye, as an instrument, has been affected by *some sorts of outward objects*, fitted to
convey to the sentient principle, a sensation of colour, and so of
the rest. Therefore the objects *perceived* by the organs of sense
cannot be our ideas, and sensations. Indeed, he does not take
notice that he uses the notion of *perception* (which is that upon
which the whole argument depends) in two different methods,
or meanings. For the term perception, when applied to those
objects for whose observation the organs of sense are required,
and by which certain qualities are determined upon the perceiving mind, is used as the *notice* the mind takes of the
presence of certain qualities *in consequence of the conscious use of
the organs of sense*, the use and action of which must, therefore,
be in relation to *some* objects which are not the mind; but when
applied to the 'ideas and sensations of sensible qualities',

---

[84]   Dr. Reid on visible figure, &c. is guilty of a like error.

perception is *only* used as the mental consciousness of those qualities, leaving out the conscious use of the organs of sense, and the ideas of the outward objects which must necessarily have acted on them.

Nor is this reasoning I am using, the mere turning of an expression, for in this sentence '*what are objects* but the things *we perceive by sense?*' and 'what do we *perceive* but our ideas and sensations?' there is an offence against one of the plainest and most useful of logical rules; for the argument if placed in a regular syllogism, will be seen to contain a middle term of two different and particular significations from which, therefore, nothing can be concluded.

Let the question be, 'Are *objects, ideas* and *sensations* only?' and the middle term, '*The things we perceive*', – be united with the predicate for the major proposition, and then be altered to – 'the things *we perceive by sense*', when joined to the *subject*, for the minor; it will be seen that an inconclusive syllogism is thence formed. – For if the major proposition stands, 'Our ideas and sensations, are the only things we *perceive*', and the minor, 'Objects are the things we perceive by sense', the conclusion, viz. 'Therefore *objects* are only our ideas and sensations', does not logically follow, because the middle term would then consist of '*two different parts, or kinds*, of the same *universal* idea', i.e. the idea of perception in general; '*and this will never* serve to show whether the subject and predicate agree, or disagree'.[85] *For in the general conscious perception of sensible qualities, are included the knowledge that the organs of sense are used, as mechanical instruments acted upon by certain causes, and the* IDEAS *of these causes.* And this conscious use of the mechanical action of the five senses in relation to other beings than the mind, *is a very different part, or kind of the universal idea of perception,* from the *mental consciousness of* PARTICULAR SENSIBLE QUALITIES *only*; which is also another part, or kind of the general notion of perception; *which general* notion *includes every species of consciousness whatever.* The consciousness whether the organs of sense be used or not, in perceiving objects,[86] is the great

---

[85]   Watts's Logic. [Shepherd refers to Isaac Watts' *Logic, or, the Right Use of Reason in the Enquiry After Truth* (London, 1824), p. 247. See p. 52 n24.]

[86]   See p. 220, &c. [See pp. 179–87 in this volume.]

criterion of a sane, or insane state of mind, of its waking or sleeping condition; the consciousness that the organs of sense are used, makes all the difference between objects of sense, or objects of memory, reason, or imagination. *By the quick and practical use of the senses subsequent to infancy, the associations of ideas, resulting from reason and experience, are so interwoven and so immediate with the consciousness of their use, that they ought always to be considered as forming a component part of the whole ideas which lie under the terms,* THE OBJECTS OF SENSE. The *objects of sense,* therefore, (under the conscious use of the organs of sense), are known, (according to the reasoning used in the foregoing chapters of this essay), to be *the continued, exterior,* and *independent existences* of external nature, exciting ideas, and determining sensations in the mind of a sentient being; but not ONLY to be *ideas and sensations.*

In the sentence already commented on, and which contains the sum of Dr. Berkeley's doctrine — the word *object,* as well as the phrase *'perception by sense',* is of ambiguous application; — for in his use of the word *object,* he begs the question; meaning thereby a collection of sensible qualities, formed by the senses and apprehended by the mind; whereas the adversary means by that word, a set of qualities exterior to the mind, and to which the organs of sense are in relation as mechanical instruments, and of which they take notice as those permanent existences, which the understanding is aware *must needs continue* when unperceived, ere they are transformed by their action into other beings. Objects before the notice of the senses, are not the same things as after their acquaintance with them. All men mean by objects the things which exist previously to their mixture with the action of the organs of sense, and which FROM POWERFUL ASSOCIATION, *they conceive to exist under the forms of their sensible qualities;* — therefore by *feigning* the contrary notion there can arise no convincing argument.

To go on, however, with the argument, (by which I would show that objects of sense are not *only* the ideas of their sensible qualities), I observe that reason discovering these objects to be in their relation to each other, as *various* as the *impressions* they convey; also perceives them to be in *one* respect *like* the ideas they create; i.e. in the same proportions and bearings to each other, *outwardly* as they are inwardly. Therefore among the observations we have of 'our ideas and sensations' of sensible qualities, we do perceive *something else* than these mere '*ideas or sensations*'; for we perceive by *reason*, that those things which must needs be present in order as *causes* to affect the sense, may on account of *their variety*, their *similar distinctness*, and *proportions,* be named, (when considered as existing exterior to the instruments of sense), by the names they bear when inwardly taken notice of.

Now I consider the observation of this latter circumstance as containing a full answer to all the puzzling contradictions of Bishop Berkeley's theory; for although, in a popular manner, men consider things are *outwardly* the *counterpart* of what they perceive *inwardly*; yet this is not the whole reason of the difference they make amidst things: for the soul does truly in a sense *perceive* outward things, *as* they are when existing outwardly, for after *reason* shews that the qualities of things, in a state of *perception,* cannot *be like* them out of a state of perception, yet being conscious that sensation is only a *simple* act, (a power, a quality), *it perceives* by the understanding that the *varieties* of things are in relation to each other *outwardly* in the *same proportion* as are the inward sensations. Thus hard and soft, bitter and sweet, heat and cold, round and square, are therefore *perceived* not ONLY to be sensations, but to be certain unknown qualities of objects independent of the mind *in relation to each other,* and in that *state 'to continue to exist, ready to appear to the senses when called for'.* Popularly, the *sensations these excite, are associated with the notions of the outward objects,* and all their varieties. But when philosophy breaks up this association, she should not take away *more* than what this natural junction of thought has created; Bishop Berkeley does not merely separate what is mixed, but would destroy the whole compound together. This observation, in my opinion, contains a *demonstration* against the Berkelean theory, and restores nature entirely to her rights again. 'Equals taken *from equals* the *remainders are equal.*' Take *sensation,* simple sensation, the power or capacity of feeling merely, from extension, from colour, from sound, and from taste; from heat and cold; from electricity or attraction; from fire, air, water, or earth; from the *perception* of life, or the *idea* of death; from motion or rest. Is there nothing left? Every thing is left that has any variety or difference in it. 'What are objects' (says Bishop Berkeley) 'but the ideas perceived by sense?' They are beings perceived by reason, to be continually, independently, outwardly existing, of the same proportions as are the inward sensations of which they are the effects. Had Bishop Berkeley allowed of the force of a most finished piece of reasoning he uses in respect to the proof of the existence of *other minds* than our own, in behalf also of objects that are not minds, he had not set before the public, some paradoxes, unhappily considered as *unanswerable*. In (sect. 195), he says, 'From what has been said, it is plain that we cannot know the existence of other spirits otherwise than by their operations, or the ideas by them excited in us. I perceive several motions, changes, and combinations of ideas, that inform me there are certain particular agents *like myself*, which accompany them and concur in their production. Hence the knowledge I have of *other spirits* is not immediate as is the knowledge of my ideas, but depending on the intervention of ideas, by me referred to agents or spirits *distinct* from myself, as effects or concomitant signs.'[87]

Now my argument (however ill I may have executed it) intends the whole way to show 'that our knowledge of other objects (of any kind) is not *immediate* as is the knowledge of our ideas', but depends on 'the *intervention* of our ideas', by us referred to 'agents or spirits', (to *unknown proportionate causes* distinct from ourselves), and that the several '*motions, changes,* and *combinations* of ideas, which we perceive, inform us that there are certain particular agents *like ourselves*' (always like ourselves as continuing to *exist*, and *in other qualities, plus* or *minus* ourselves) 'which accompany them, and concur in their production'.

In order, however, to carry the argument a little farther on these matters, let us examine with a greater nicety than we have yet done this proposition;—'figure, extension, and motion are *only* ideas in the perceiving mind',[88]—and let us select one quality, say *figure*, for this examination, in order to simplify the analysis; then the argument which applies to figure, will also apply to the other qualities.

Let the question be; Is figure an *idea only* in the perceiving mind? Now undoubtedly the sense, inward perception, or

---

[87] [Shepherd quotes Berkeley, *Principles* 145 (p. 143); emphases are Shepherd's.]

[88] [Shepherd paraphrases Berkeley, *Principles* 9 (p. 86).]

notion of figure, (or by whatever word shall be designated the conscious sensation of a living being which it has, under the impression of figure), can *only* be in a perceiving mind; and nothing else can be like it but such another sensation: but this *sense of figure*, is not what the word figure, only means when applied to an object which affects either the sense of sight or touch. It is then a relative term—a sign of a compound notion, signifying a particular sensation *caused* by a particular *cause*, which cause is not a sensation. Moreover, the word *is also understood to be applicable to the proportion which that cause (or 'outward continuous object') bears to the other outward beings surrounding it*; (and this without supposing they are the least like our ideas); for let us consider a round figure, for instance, apart from our perception of it; the *line* which bounds this solid substance *outwardly*, (whatever *line* and *solid* may be), and parts it from the surrounding atmosphere, (whatever *parting* or *atmosphere* may be), must still be a *variety*, or *change*, or *difference*, among these outward things, and this difference among outward unknown things, *not like sensations*, is *outward*, and is always meant in that sense by the word, which signifies, *a certain state of continuous existence*, which is independent of mind. The word and notion are *compound*, and each stands for the *cause and effect united*, and not *only* for the *effect*. Philosophers, therefore, ought to be capable of perceiving that figure, extension, and motion, &c. are *not only ideas in the mind*, but are capacities, qualities, beings in nature in relation to each other when exterior to mind.

It is owing to our ideas being the counterparts of the *proportions* of those things, which our reason teaches us must be independent of mind, that Dr. Reid talks of an *intuitive* conception and knowledge of the nature of outward extension, &c. Whereas it is by observing the relations of our ideas which are effects, whose causes must be equal to them, that we have a knowledge of that relation which the independent and permanent objects of the universe must needs bear to each other; if *instinct* only guided us, there would be no more proof of the external world than of a dream, where there is an equal instinct in behalf of what is afterwards acknowledged to be non-existent.

But the perceptions of the relations which our ideas and sensations bear to each other, and the results therein deduced, put the proof of an external and continually existent universe upon the same footing as the existence of the sensations themselves, and form a deduction as demonstrable, and clear, and convincing as any mathematical certainty whatever.

To go on, Bishop Berkeley however allows *that there are causes* for the sensations of sensible qualities; independent of the perceiving mind. But it is in descanting upon their nature that he is again guilty of as fallacious, and inconclusive, and paradoxical reasoning as that which we have just examined; for he uses the very argument of his adversary, (which he has been industriously endeavouring to destroy), as an instrument to prove his own doctrine, and I shall now proceed to shew that he does so.

Section 2

(Section 25th and 26th.) 'We perceive', says Bishop Berkeley, 'a continual succession of ideas; there is therefore *some cause* of these ideas. This *cause* cannot be any quality or idea; for an idea' (section 25th) 'is an *inert* being, and cannot be the *cause* of any thing. It must therefore be a substance', (section 26th), 'and as it has been shown there is no *material* substance, it remains the cause of our ideas, is an incorporeal, active substance or spirit.' (Section 27th.) 'A spirit is one simple, undivided, active being, which hath understanding and will.' (Section 28th.) 'My own will excites in my mind ideas at pleasure, and by the same power they are destroyed. This making and unmaking of ideas, very properly denominates the mind active.' (Section 29th.) 'But the ideas imprinted on sense are not the creatures of my will, there is therefore some other will or spirit which produces them.' (Section 30th.) 'Now there are set rules, or established methods, whereby the mind we depend on excites in us the ideas of sense, and these are called the Laws of Nature.'[89] (Section 156th.) 'By nature is meant the visible series of effects or sensations imprinted on our mind.'[90] The conclusion of the

---

[89] The remaining sections are taken up in answering objections, and are quite immaterial to the subject of these remarks. [The quotations in this paragraph, up to this point, are Shepherd's paraphrases from Berkeley, *Principles* 25–30 (pp. 92–4).]

[90] [Shepherd quotes, with slight alterations, Berkeley, *Principles* 150 (p. 145).]

whole matter is, that there is nothing but two sets of objects, viz. 'spirits' and 'ideas'; 'spirits as causes, and ideas as their effects'. Now it is plain we can know no more of *activity, indivisibility,* and *simplicity,* as applied to a *substance,* called mind, than of *inertness, divisibility,* &c. applied to another sort of substance, called *matter.* These are still only ideas gained in the usual way, rejected when applied to objects of *sense* existing *without the mind,* but made use of by him, when applied to *spirit, existing without the mind.* 'Motion' (Bishop Berkeley distinctly says) 'is *only an idea* existing in the mind.'[91] If so, I ask, what does he know about *activity,* as *absolutely necessary to constitute a* CAUSE, and which CAUSE, he says, *cannot be an* IDEA? because ideas are 'visibly *in*active'. Also, what notion can he have of cause at all, if he knows of '*nothing but ideas*'; and *ideas are not causes,* and what too are the *rules* and *methods* of the working of a spirit, which as rules and methods and laws of nature, cannot themselves be spirit or substance, yet are not allowed to be material beings? And how can the will at pleasure, call upon an idea, when before it begins to call, it must know what it wishes to call, and so must have consciousness of the idea in question, which as an object associated with another idea, can and does truly act as a cause in order to introduce it. But *I* argue as we can distinguish between the capacity for sensation in general, and that for the exciting causes of extension and other qualities in particular, so we have a right to name *this mind,* and *that* body, and that after all the talk of *materialists,* who say, 'matter cannot act on mind', ('they are discordant *beings*; so *all* is matter'); And the immaterialists who say the same things, ('and that *all* is mind', for the same reason); it appears perfectly easy that such causes and capacities, such collections of qualities should intermix, and produce those results, which take place under different forms of sensible objects; and which in my opinion are combined by the junction of the qualities of matter, or unknown powers, or qualities in nature; the senses, or instruments fitted to act along with these; and the *mind,* or *sentient principle* and capacity. Nature in her whole works bears witness such is the case. — Also by keeping strictly in view, that the power of sensation is

---

91   [Shepherd paraphrases Berkeley, *Principles* 14 (p. 88).]

one and *simple*, — and that subtracting it from all the objects with which we are acquainted, the remaining qualities will bear still to be considered as worthy of holding the various names affixed to their appearances upon the sense, and reasoned on as before; — there will be cause and effect, extension and space; time and eternity; variety of figure and colour; heat and cold, merit and demerit; beauty and deformity, &c. &c.

The proportions of all these beings among themselves, the external independent qualities in nature among themselves, corresponding to our perceptions, must be as *various* as they appear to the mind; therefore, there is figure, extension, colour, and all qualities whatever. Nor is it necessary in order to support the idea of Deity, and his constant presence and providence, to have recourse to the ridiculous notion of his *activity* as a 'spirit' upon our senses in order to change our ideas; for whilst the *perception* of sensible qualities *immediately* informs us of our own *sensations*,[92] reason by the intervention of the ideas of their different relations, equally discovers to us insentient existences, as well as that of our own, and other minds; whilst with respect to the being of God, his essential existence, his continued existence, is demonstrated, by the abstract argument used in this treatise. 'Whatever variety and changes of being there are, all changes must finally be pushed back to that essence, who *began not to be*, and in whom all dependent beings originally resided, and were first put forth as out-goings of himself in all those varieties of attitudes, where-with his wisdom and benevolence are able to fit out every variety and gradation of creature.'[93]

Essay 2: Upon the Nature of the Five Organs of Sense, and Their Manner of Action with Regard to External Perception

I would here more fully consider a subject of great importance, upon which I have but briefly touched in the larger essay, '*on external perception*'; namely, *The nature of the five organs of sense, and the manner in which they are used, with regard to the conveyance of the perception of external objects to the mind.* This subject

---

[92]　See p. 14, 'Also the mind', &c. [See pp. 100–103 in this volume.]
[93]　See p. 189. [See p. 167 in this volume.]

appears to me but partially analysed by the authors to which I have there alluded. It is naturally complicated; embraces a vast variety of particulars bearing upon each other; — Each of which in order to be examined aright, must, during the period of its examination, be equally considered as unproved, as well as others which might suffice as proofs, were they not also involved in the uncertainty of the point in question. When this is done, every object whatever of supposed existence, independent of mental consciousness, is found to be upon an equal footing, and must necessarily be put aside, on account of being as yet unacknowledged.

What then remains as given data? Nothing but our sensations, mental consciousnesses, (simple or complex), arbitrarily named, and their relations; and this seems to leave so frightful a void; the analysis of our knowledge into such materials seems so impossible; and the being capable of arriving at any certain evidence for *real* things (as they are called), by a synthesis formed of such, seems likewise so impossible, that the soul starts back with a wise alarm for fear of venturing too far, and beyond the limits whence it may be able to *retread* its steps if such should be the case; yet as I have attempted to question so much, I must in order to be consistent, push my enquiries still further. I must lead on to where this subject points, and endeavour to make that theory, which to my own mind is consistent and luminous, appear so to others.

Now, that our living conscious sensations, that is, those consciousnesses which are sufficiently vivid to form *strong impressions*; and *long enough in duration* to admit of being compared together; with the results of their comparisons as again forming a new class of sensations, (*ideas* of reason), are the only, the original, and immediate materials of our knowledge, is the chief feature of the philosophy I would profess. And I do consider these materials as sufficient for every useful opinion; for the proof of every existence which others refer to '*instincts*', '*primary laws of belief*', '*ultimate facts*', '*immediate knowledge by the senses*', or other means, the which do truly leave the objects of which they testify wholly without any proof whatever; for, '*that*

we are incapable of thinking otherwise than we do',[94] can itself be no
reason that we think rightly. The same instincts, laws of belief,
immediate knowledge by senses, do, in the course of every
twenty-four hours, afford the same kinds of proof for the
independent existence of objects which men admit to be
non-existent without a doubt remaining on the subject; but
when our consciousnesses of sensation, and the results arising
from the comparison of them are reposed in, as being the only
original materials of our knowledge, and as therefore containing the proofs of the existences, with which we are acquainted,
then inasmuch as the original sensations are the beings, the
very beings themselves; so the knowledge of their existence is
in and with themselves, as well as of the existences contained in
their relations.

The ideas of reason are thence upon the same footing as to
certainty, as are those of sensation, and are true demonstrations
of existences. The reason, therefore, for believing in existence,
independent of consciousness, must bear to be examined and
substantiated upon this foundation; i.e. as being the result of
the comparison of *our 'ideas of sensation'*. The ideas of reason
must be the corollaries included in the impressions of sense,
from whatever source they may be supposed to arise; they must
be the conclusions of the judgment when the faculties are in a
state to exert their power. For *independent* existences are, by the
very terms, and supposition of the statement, unconscious; and,
therefore, must be known of as a result derived from the comparison and included in the relations of those which are
conscious.

In this enquiry all writers I have met with, (especially
Bishop Berkeley, who professes idealism), are to be blamed for
an oversight, when they speak of the *senses* in such phrases as
these, *'objects imprinted on the senses'*, 'the perception of external
objects by the senses'; &c. without even considering that the
whole question is begged by this use of the word *senses;* an

---

94   [Shepherd may be alluding to Reid, *Inquiry* 6.20 (p. 169), where he
     writes of his belief in external objects that his 'belief is carried along by
     perception, as irresistibly as [his] body by the earth. And the greatest
     sceptic will find himself to be in the same condition. He may struggle
     hard to disbelieve the informations of his senses, as a man does to swim
     against a torrent; but ah! It is in vain.']

object imprinted on the eye, for instance, must mean, (even in Bishop Berkeley's sense), an object rendered conscious by the use of the eye; but what is the use of the eye itself, other than a conscious sensation, or action, supposed to involve the *knowledge of an object,* EXTERIOR *to,* and INDEPENDENT *of* that mind, to which it serves as an instrument of perception? For unless the whole subject in question is granted, the consciousness of the use of the organs of sense, can but be considered as *some* 'sensations and ideas',[95] which introduce into the mind, OTHER *'sensations and ideas'*. Yet Berkeley evidently considers the use of the organs of sense, as a circumstance distinguished and different from 'ideas and sensations'; because he considers that 'God by set rules and methods, called the laws of nature, works upon and with *the senses,* in order to create ideas of sensation, objects of sense every moment.' He thus makes an essential difference between the two powers in nature, without marking out any *criterion* of distinction by which the mind may recognize any such difference between them; the *senses,* therefore, in his notion of them, are as necessary, to be acted upon *'by these set rules and workings* of a spirit', as they are in order to be worked upon by real *extension,* &c. in the language of the anti-idealists. What then, I again ask, are the *senses* so worked upon? are they *other set rules of the spirit*? If so, one set of rules acts upon another set of rules, in order, for instance, to give us ideas of vision; but one set of rules would seem enough to give us such ideas. It appears, then, that the 'senses' in relation to the actions of a spirit, must at any rate be something extra to the consciousness of their use. They are *something* in Berkeley's sense by which the spirit we depend upon introduces 'ideas in our minds', but they are not as yet sensations in a mind, for it is *by* them sensations and ideas are introduced into the mind. The *consciousness* of the use of the eye could not introduce light; it must be the eye properly so called, whatever that organ when unperceived may be: therefore, the organs of sense are at least, even in Berkeley's sense, *some objects – not themselves 'the set rules of a spirit',* nor yet 'ideas and sensations', but, existences independent of either, which must *needs exist as continuous*

---

95 'Sensations and ideas', is the phrase by which Berkeley always expresses the conscious perception of any sensible qualities whatever.

existences, unknown and unperceived in their qualities, in order to account for the *creation of sensations and ideas in the mind.* And if so, there may be others like them, and every variety which may be unlike them, save in that one quality of existence.

In Mr. Stewart's and Dr. Reid's[96] sense, the 'senses' mean mechanical, extended, figured, solid existences; as means, instruments, and causes, by which we immediately perceive the existence of external objects, and to the use of which there is *instinctively* annexed, the knowledge of the *nature* of their primary qualities, when existing independent of any perception of mind; as well as an *'ultimate law of belief'*, 'without any process of reason',[97] by which there arises the knowledge of their permanent independent existence.

It is evident, the whole question in such a doctrine is again taken as granted. Does the eye, then, tell us what the eye is made of? or, does it acquaint us with what is the nature of touch? Does the ear tell us of its own formation? or, the nostrils prove to us their solidity and extension? This obviously cannot be the case. Let then the organs of sense be set apart they ought, (if the argument is to be logically conducted), and the knowledge of these as external, independent, and continuous existences be involved in the general question. In this sense, how is their existence known?

I suppose Dr. Reid and his friends will tell us, that the touch, as a mere sensation, would be capable of 'suggesting' the exteriority and independency of the other organs of sense: 'That the hand might grasp' the eye 'as a ball, and perceive it at once *hard, figured,* and *extended'*: *'That the feeling is very simple, and hath not the least resemblance to any quality of body'*: yet, that it *'suggests to us three primary qualities perfectly distinct from one*

---

[96]   There may be some slight shade of difference between Mr. Stewart's and Dr. Reid's sentiments on this head, but if so, it is too indistinctly set forth, to enable me exactly to descry its boundary.

[97]   [I have been unable to locate these exact quotations, but the views they express are found in, for example, Stewart's claim that beliefs in an external world and in the uniformity of nature are 'ultimate or elemental laws of thought' (Stewart, *Elements* Vol. 2, chapter 1, section 2 [p. 58]).]

another, as well as from the sensation which indicates them';[98] for 'that although the feeling of touch no more resembles extension than it does justice, or courage, yet that every moment it presents extension to the mind; and that by it we have the notion of a quality of body';[99] (which, however, is not a NOTION but a quality of body).

But when the *eye* is in the hand, what informs the mind by this touch; what suggests the *independent continuous* existence of its extension, figure, and hardness, granting these qualities were proved? (for this is the material part of the question): For when the organs of sense, both by idealists and anti-idealists, are spoken of, it is taken for granted, that as mechanical instruments they are *continued independent existences*; and are neither sensations of mind, nor yet the qualities of bodies.

The power of motion, as a sixth organ of sense, (for so it may be regarded), as the method of overcoming distance, and of becoming acquainted with tangible extension, is equally taken for granted, as existing unperceived, and as an aid to the five organs of sense.

After perceiving these errors in the distinct manner I do, I feel anxious in entering upon a statement which I would fain believe less open to objection. I conceive, however, that the doctrine I have laid down at large in the essay on external perception, must, if understood rightly, be so considered, and I will add thus further to it.

Philosophically, the organs of sense must be considered as *un*known existences in their unperceived state, yet as yielding their own peculiar and appropriate sensations or ideas to the mind; their *continued, independent* existence is found as a result, or perceived by the understanding as a relation of its simple sensations; for the *mind* perceiving, upon each irregular applica-

---

[98] These sentiments Mr. Stewart alludes to in his essays, as being at once original, and profound; logical and luminous; giving them his warmest approbation, and supporting them by his sanction; therefore, it may perhaps be some error, (for aught I know), in my judgment, which makes me conceive them as unfounded in fact, and contrary to every principle of correct reasoning. See his Essay on the Philosophy of the Human Mind, vol. 2, chap. 1, sec. 3, p. 68, also Essays, note G [Shepherd refers to Stewart, *Elements* Vol. 2, chapter 1, section 3 (p. 68) and to Stewart, *Philosophical Essays*, pp. 553–61.]

[99] [Shepherd quotes Reid, *Inquiry* 5.5 (p. 63).]

tion to some *sorts* of *beings,* or *qualities,* or *ideas,* which it may call the organs of sense if it *please,* that they regularly reply to that application, justly concludes them to exist when unnoticed, in order to be capable of this readiness to reply. Those objects, also, which do thus reply, yield to the sense of motion from point to point, an idea of resistance and extension in particular; and so are regarded as body; that is, as essences different from the mind, or the powers of sensation in general; but continually existing objects, or qualities, which yield ideas of extension, are not *ideas,* but *continued* existences called bodies.

Thus the organs of sense, are those independent continuous existences, with whose ideas the mind associates the sensible qualities their action excites in the mind; and which are observed to have their share in performing the changes, as well as to detect[100] the presence of objects, which are themselves, neither the organs of sense, nor yet the mind itself.

The foundation of the whole reasoning concerning the independency both of the organs of sense, as well as of other objects, arises from the axiom, '*that no idea, or quality, can* BEGIN *its* own existence'. For we perceive that the *sensation as* of the use of any organ of sense, *does not alter the mind always* in the same way; therefore, the mind and the organs of sense being the same upon any occasion as on a former one, when no other object than themselves were present, a third object is required to occasion the interruption of its present state, which object is to be seen, or heard, or felt, &c.[101] But again, when there is the mind, and any other object known, or supposed present, — if the eye be shut; the hand removed, &c. such object will not appear; therefore, to the observance of any particular object, there is not only required the mind, and the object, but also the organs of sense; those parts of the human frame, (or ideas, or whatsoever else they may be called).

---

[100] See p. 233, 'But again', &c.; also, p. 102, 'It is not sufficient, therefore', &c. [See pp. below on this page, and p. 136 in this volume.]
[101] In this enquiry it ought to be unnecessary to repeat, although I have done it for the sake of clearness, that no object, or *idea,* can begin its own existence, but must appear as a change of those objects already in being, and as requiring corresponding previous interferences, unions, separations, &c.

The organs of sense, therefore, when analysed are *continued existences, which form the media of admixture between other objects and minds*. It is not the consciousness of their use, however, which renders them *a part* of the *whole cause necessary to that end*, because that consciousness is but an *effect*, or sensible quality; they must be considered when they act as causes, as unperceived beings, and so must the minds also, as well as the other objects in relation to them; and it is in the coalescence of these three, that conscious, complex, sensible qualities,[102] must be considered to exist. But to this day the sensible[103] qualities are considered as fastened upon the objects, which are neither organs of sense, nor minds, and to be their own independent qualities on account of the intimate association *between their respective* IDEAS *and* SENSATIONS.[104]

I have already, perhaps, intruded upon the patience of the reader too much, by repeating some things already said, in order to throw light upon this intricate part of the subject; I shall only now add, that the great difficulty and mystery in the affair, is, that in dreams, insanities, &c. the organs of sense are thought to be in use; for there is a sensation, as though they must have been in use, on account of a reference made to them, as the only instruments capable of having let their specific objects into the mind's apprehension. The memory and understanding are then *asleep*, and the mind therefore cannot take notice of all the ideas which would otherwise affect it *and their relations*. The objects, therefore, which appear, are considered as those, which are in relation to the senses, and they are thence expected to be capable of those further qualities which are necessary to their definitions. And, in fact, I perceive not how the proposition can be refuted, that although there may be truth in the world, yet the discovery of *an absolute criterion of* an understanding capable of detecting it, does not seem to be the lot of human nature. Thus the sensible quality *termed the use of the senses*, appears to the mind in dreams, whilst yet the mind

---

102 See 6th Essay, that sensible qualities cannot be causes. [See pp. 82–6 in this volume.]

103 The doctrine of Aristotle is the same as this, which I have found since writing the above.

104 See p. 142, 'Now objects', &c. [See p. 151 in this volume.]

cannot discover that it is but dreaming; it must therefore awake, and be in a state to find that such senses as these, do not fulfil their definitions, that their organs do not *continue* to exist, and cannot exert any unperceived action, ere it is able to discover the delusion.

The reason why the mind is deluded in dreams, and other fancies, is on account of its being known, first, that similar effects must have similar causes, and secondly, *that these causes are usually found along with other compound objects*, which have *further effects, other qualities when meeting with other objects*; a *habit* of expectation is thus formed which even in a disordered fancy leads the mind to consider *similar sensible qualities*, as *a compound general effect, from such a general cause,*[105] or object, as will *fulfil the remainder of its qualities upon trial.*

In dreams the *sensible qualities* arising from what is termed the use of the senses, is not corrected, by other *sensible qualities*; nor by the *reasoning* which the mind when awake is always *latently* using, when it draws inferences from certain consistencies, or inconsistencies, amidst its ideas; to the power of such reasoning it is restored upon the moment of awaking, by which it is made aware of the place where it has long been; then the mass of appearances before the fancy, immediately takes its flight and the enchantment is dissolved.

Indeed it may be remarked, *that in waking as well as in sleeping hours, when memory is gone, we cannot remember that we forget, nor perceive relations which do not present themselves to deficient powers of reasoning; the want of ideas in those who think they have sufficient, will ever yield a ground of scepticism to men of understanding; lest they should lie under the same predicament, without having any criterion by which to detect the difference. It is when ideas of reason are clearly included in those of sensation, that I assert, they are upon the same footing as to certainty. I conclude nothing from the WANT of them.*

Bishop Berkeley has been, I think, much misunderstood on account of his conceiving that things were created each time of

---

[105] See essay on causation; Mr. Hume is so far from being correct in supposing that *regular conjunction* GENERATES *the idea of causation*, that on the contrary, *it is only itself looked upon as* AN EFFECT *of its own regular cause.*

their appearance; he only meant to say, that the formation of the sensible qualities by the use of the senses, existed in and by their use, and that they could not exist *thus*, (in that manner and fashion), except in a mind perceiving them, and thus far I perfectly agree with him.

Essay 3: That the External Causes Which Determine the Various Perception of Sense, Are Not the Immediate Actions of Deity

As our perceptions themselves are allowed on all hands not to be *immediate actions of Deity*, so their causes may be equally observed to require many processes of nature in order to their production; of this we may very well judge by that *comparison of ideas* in which all reasoning consists. For sensation in general being but a simple power, its particular varieties can be no other than measures, tests, or examples of that variety which must necessarily exist in those things which are not included in sensation, that is, in those things which are *excluded* from it, and are therefore in qualities exterior to it, but which meeting with the internal sense, alters it accordingly: thus we may very well know that vast preparations go on of unperceived beings, and of such whose *essences* are unknown, in order to accomplish the formation of an universe, or the growth of the harvest; the creation of man, or the flight of a butterfly; the development of the least, equally with the most magnificent of nature's works, which requires the *progress* arising from successive changes. For it is manifest, that the external causes of our sensations must exist among themselves in the same proportions as do the internal varieties of sensation, their effects; and this notion may be expressed after the same manner in which any usual proportion is stated; thus, *as* is the variety of different simple or compound sensations, *so* is the variety of their causes. Therefore by examining aright the proportions and relations of our ideas, by perceiving that some afford evidence that they are created by living beings; 'beings like ourselves (plus or minus their varieties)', and that others afford evidence that they are created by beings devoid of life; still by beings like ourselves, ('plus or minus the varieties'), we may arrive at the knowledge of external sentiency and insentiency; and thus that *all* which is external cannot be of one kind, i.e. *mind* or *sentiency*; nor yet the conscious actions of a sentient mind. But if it be said that though they are not the conscious actions of mind, yet they are actions which are the effects of a conscious mind, but themselves not conscious; then they are not *immediate* acts of Deity, but *mediate* acts of Deity, whose varieties meeting with the human senses, create our ideas.

And this is the very doctrine for which I contend, and the elucidation of which is not unimportant, now that there exists a disposition among some, to revive a rigid Berkeleian philosophy; admitting no existence in the universe, excepting that of the Deity, and the individual who is *reasoning*. I divide therefore with Berkeley, by applying the argument he himself uses in behalf of the proof that there are other minds than his own in the universe, to the proof of existences which may be other than mind.

Thus there becomes a real distinction between the nature of some existences and that of others, as far as their relative variety and proportion goes. And this difference may be known by the nature of the effects in their varieties: the one kind of existence may very properly be termed *matter,* and the other *mind.* And thus the definition of matter becomes *the capacity of exhibiting upon a sentient nature, the sense of solid* EXTENSION in general; and that of mind, *a capacity fitted to be excited to any sensation in particular.*

Therefore as the capacity for exhibiting extension, appears not itself to be essentially sentient, and in all cases fitted to be excited to sensation; so by thus differing in its enumeration of qualities, it cannot be *mind,* or the sentient actions of Deity.

But although the *proportional varieties* of external objects may be known thus far, nevertheless I consider it never can be too much insisted on, (in order to maintain an *exact* philosophy), that the *positive* nature and essence of unperceived beings *cannot* be known; feeling, thought, sensation under its varieties, is the only essence of which we have absolute *consciousness.* Other essences we know, must exist by reasoning; but the reasoning is here the consciousness, not the other essences. We have the knowledge there must necessarily be such beings; but it is the knowledge of which we are conscious, not the beings themselves. We have proof by the comparison of our ideas, that there are unperceived natures; but it is the proof whose essence we know, not the nature proved. We believe in those things, of the existence of which there are unequivocal signs; but the signs are not the existences.

The real essences of matter and mind we know not; we only know our sensations, *as real beings, very essences*: these are the very things themselves. We know of other things which must 'needs exist' by our sensations, but cannot conceive the nature of any essence not in our experience.

I trust such ideas will not be thought tending to a dangerous scepticism. So different does their tendency appear to my own mind, that I consider them as leading to the most solid belief and conviction, in the existence of every variety of being which alters the conscious sense, and which reason upholds as exterior to it, and independent of it; whether as a perpetual series of changes flowing from the only origin of all things; or as that mysterious being himself, either concealed behind those *mediate* acts which screen his glory from mortal man, or *manifesting* himself in many ways, better suited to our comprehension, and better fitted by the qualities contemplated, to be compared to ourselves in their variety; and to create trust, esteem, and hope, in their decided superiority.

Essay 4: Upon the Philosophy of Mr. Dugald Stewart and Dr. Reid, As It Regards the Union of Colour With Extension; and the Perception of the External Primary Qualities of Matter

Mr. D. Stewart has the following passage in the first volume of the Philosophy of the Human Mind.[106] 'I formerly had occasion to mention several instances of very intimate association formed between two ideas, which have no necessary connexion with each other; one of the most remarkable is that which exists in every person's mind between the notions of colour and of extension. The former of these words expresses a *sensation of the mind*, the latter denotes *a quality of an external object*. So that there is, in fact, no more connexion between the *two notions* than between those of pain and solidity.'

---

[106] Part 2, ch. 5, p. 1. [Shepherd quotes Dugald Stewart, *Elements of the Philosophy of the Human Mind*, Vol. 1, 5th ed. (London: T. Cadell and W. Davies, 1814), chapter 5, part 2, section 1 (p. 349). Hereafter cited as *Elements* Vol. 1.]

Now, I consider, this passage as containing, in a few lines, a complete example of the errors in modern metaphysics, as to the nature and manner of *external perception*. There is here said to be, an intimate association between two *notions*, viz. those of *extension* and *colour*; whilst yet the word extension is said to express 'the *quality* of an external object', instead of a *notion*; and as such must be incapable of associating as an '*idea*', with the '*idea* of colour', which is also said to be '*a sensation of the mind*'. The whole sentence to those who will examine it accurately, must appear to involve a contradiction.

Mr. Stewart,[107] by later publications than this, shows himself the avowed admirer and supporter of Dr. Reid's philosophy, which, although he observes, that it may require some improvement in the way of addition, he conceives to be incontrovertible as far as it goes, and as not involving obvious inconsistencies, and contradictions. It is the philosophy of these authors, that the primary qualities of bodies are objects immediately perceived to be *exterior* to the mind, whose essences also may distinctly be *conceived* of, in their external state; that the *conception* of the *nature* of these essences is *suggested* by means of the *sensations* these qualities excite in the mind, through their action on the senses, but that the *conception* itself is not a sensation. These *exterior* qualities are, therefore, *perceived* NOT *to be sensible qualities*, but to be totally *unlike* them. Along with this perception of the exteriority, and *conception* of the *nature* of external primary qualities, *instinct* affords an aid to the senses; by which power it is, the mind becomes acquainted with the *fact, that these exterior qualities* CONTINUE *to exist when* UNPERCEIVED *by the senses, and independent of any of its* CONCEPTIONS.[108] Thus, the *perceptions* of extension, figure, solidity,

---

[107] 'Essays', and 'Elements of the Philosophy of the Human Mind, vol. 3, addenda', ref. to p. 92, 1st edit. p. 93, 6th edit. [Shepherd has just been quoting from the fifth (1814) edition of Stewart's *Elements* Vol. 1; *Essays* was first published before that, in 1810, but perhaps she means that it was a 'later publication' because *Elements* Vol. 1 was originally published in 1792. The Addenda to the *Elements* was published in 1816.]

[108] This is called the doctrine according to common sense. See Reid's Essay on the intellectual powers; also Reid's Inquiry into the Human Mind, c. 5, sec. 3 to 7, pp. 73 to 88, duod. [Shepherd refers to *Inquiry* 5.3–7 (pp. 58–72).]

motion, hardness, and softness, &c. *are* NOT *sensations of mind*; and there is no occasion for any ideas of *reason*, or other means than an arbitrary impulsion by which to apprehend their situation, as external to it; we have also a clear *conception* of their positive *nature*, as they exist when *exterior* to the mind; yet this clear *conception* of *positive natures*, is not an idea in the mind, nor does it *'suggest any thing which without the grossest abuse of language, can be called a sensation'*.[109]

Visible figure is also supposed by Dr. Reid, to be *'immediately perceived*, as the *position of parts in relation to the eye,* external to it, and distant from it'.[110] Thus *visible figure,* i.e. *vision;* i.e. the *conscious* sight of an object, involves *'no sensation of mind'*, but simply there is 'the *perception* of parts, *external to the eye'*; 'so that if *no appearance of colour* existed in the mind, the external position of an object might be perceived without its intervention'.[111]

When such thoughts as these are still held as the doctrines of *common sense,* how shall there be future improvement in any department of philosophy?

To return to Mr. Stewart, I would take his own view of the subject without any needless cavil at a mere expression. 'The *sensation* of colour is associated with an *external* quality, which

---

Stewart's Essays, Note G. [Shepherd refers to Stewart, *Philosophical Essays,* pp. 553–61.]

109 [Shepherd paraphrases Reid's claim that a perceived figure 'is altogether external; and therefore cannot be called an impression upon the mind, without the grossest abuse of language' at *Inquiry* 6.8 (pp. 100–101).]

110 [Shepherd paraphrases and combines passages from Reid, *Inquiry* 6.7 and 6.8: that 'figure and extension... are the immediate objects of sight' (p. 102), that 'visible figure consists in the position of its several parts with regard to the eye' (p. 96), and that 'the visible figure of bodies is a real and external object to the eye' (p. 101).]

111 That visible figure is perceived altogether external to the eye involves to my mind the statement of a complete contradiction. It is the result, and sum of our present philosophy, and lays the foundation of many a further error. See Reid's Inquiry of the Human Mind, c. 6, sec. 8. pp. 132 and 133. [Shepherd refers to Reid, *Inquiry* 6.8 (pp. 98–103); the quotation above is evidently her paraphrase of Reid's claim that 'it plainly appears to be possible, that our eyes had been so framed, as to suggest to us the position of the object, without suggesting colour' (p. 100).]

is *not a sensation of mind.'*[112] If so the *sensation* of colour is *there where the extension is;* which involves the absurdity of sensation *residing without* the mind; and is an opinion, which (however much modern philosophers may pride themselves upon the discovery of its absurdity) is yet truly included in the whole doctrine of the *immediate perception by sense,* of EXTERIOR PRIMARY *qualities,* of whose *nature there is a clear conception.*

But should it be retorted,[113] that by this phrase is meant that the *notion* or perception of extension is united to the *notion* or *sensation* of *colour;* and that the *association of these thoughts* is IN *the mind,* although the *quality of extension* be EXTERNAL to it: to such a vindication I would answer, that then the *notion,* or *perception of extension,* is allowed to be *in* the mind, notwithstanding the many battles Dr. Reid has fought to keep it thence. Coloured extension is at last, therefore, obliged to be admitted as a COMPOUND NOTION which exists IN the perceiving mind; — Upon which result arising, I will not be unfair enough, in my turn again, to retort with the question, which is tauntingly asked of the idealists: — Is this NOTION of extension, a *square,* or a *round* notion? how broad, or how long is it? because such a question is *not very consistent from those, who admitting every variety of the appearance of colour, or of other secondary qualities of matter to be a sensation of mind, (not possible to exist unperceived),* never consider it necessary to ask, whether any *particular appearance* be a scarlet, or green sensation; a blue, or yellow thought? If an *idea* be sweet, or sour; loud, or soft? &c.

Now, a philosophy which should explain the circumstance of colour being still seen as exterior to, and distant from the mind and body, after so much has been done to prove it to be a mere affection of the mind, would go far by its natural reunion with every abstract and practical science, to put the method of our knowledge of an external universe upon a better footing than it has hitherto appeared.

I have attempted some ideas of this kind, which I fear will hardly be accepted; and I am aware the abstruseness of their

---

[112] [Shepherd paraphrases the passage she earlier quoted from Stewart, *Elements* Vol. 1, chapter 5, part 2, section 1 (p. 349).]

[113] I think, however, Mr. D. Stewart could hardly use such an argument with fairness.

nature, involves me in the danger of being thought inconsistent. The notion of perceiving *primary qualities immediately by the organs of sense*, and that they possess exteriority, and of being able to *conceive* them by suggestion from sensation, *such as they positively exist*, is contradicted by the circumstance of EXTENSION, RESISTANCE, SOLIDITY, FIGURE, DISTANCE, MOTION, being perceived as *immediately*, and as *vividly*, as to every *circumstance* the same, in dreams, insanities, and hallucinations, as in a waking and sane state of mind. Individual appearances will be in every point alike; thus all *conscious qualities*, however deemed primary, and conceptions *unlike* sensations, are proved to exist as mental sensations, or perceptions. They are thus all and equally *effects*; changes upon the principle of sentiency; *various powers of sensation*. It is difficult indeed, to find a phrase at which philosophers will not cavil; but *perceptions* must necessarily be *conscious*, therefore, they are affections of an animated nature. For in whatsoever primary and secondary qualities may differ, yet there must be one quality in which they all agree, namely, as being sentient affections, or consciousnesses. Primary qualities shall be *perceptions* if they please, and secondary ones be only sensations; but, as far as perceptions are *conscious*, they are sentient. The perception, as perception of external qualities, must be conscious, therefore, *perception of extension*, must be a conscious sensation.

I have founded my theory alluded to, upon the observation and analysis of certain facts: — For, first, I perceive there is no difference in a delirium, &c. and sane state of mind, between the DELUSION *and the* REALITY, *as far as all notice of* SENSIBLE QUALITIES *is concerned*. Again it is a notorious fact, according to the laws of light, that were the sun blotted from the heavens, it would still continue to be seen eight minutes after such an event.

Now, according to Mr. Stewart, and Dr. Reid, its figure is *immediately* perceived altogether *external* to mind and body; for whilst its extension consists in an exterior, known, positive quality, suggested to the conception, by a SENSATION OF TOUCH, *unlike* its conception, this *extension* is further associated with the sensation of a brilliant colour, the whole forming a *visible* figure; a relation of parts to the eye far distant from it.

What becomes of such a theory? of so much argument; of so much ridicule of others; of so much *common sense*, in support of a doctrine entirely inconsistent with other discoveries much better supported?

I have endeavoured to enquire into the mystery of the knowledge of external nature, and I own it is wonderful; I am as much persuaded as any, that the objects in relation to the senses, form an independent and external universe; that motion is requisite in order to overcome distance, &c. Yet the argument is demonstrative that sensible qualities, both primary and secondary, are *conscious* exhibited *effects*; *sensations* formed by the *excitement of unknown causes*, on the sentient powers; that motion in this respect is also a sensation; distance likewise; every consciousness, every perception, every notice, is mental.

What, then, is nature? What, then, is the universe? What are our friends and children? I answer, *a whole set of corresponding, but unknown, unperceived qualities*, which have a variety in *that proportion and difference among each other*, which their *perceived varieties possess*, and that the knowledge of such a fact, comes by *reason*, or arises from the perceptions of the *relations of our ideas*.

It is, therefore, because in some cases reason is wanting in its powers of *observation*, and *comparison*; because many results and consequences arising thence, many ideas put in position with others are annihilated in dreams, hallucinations, and insanities; that there is a difference of the most material kind, with respect to our capacity of forming a right judgment as to the causes concerned in the exhibition of sensible qualities. *In delusions the mind cannot take notice that they are not caused as usual, because the sense of place is lost*; and *the notice of the means used in the formation of objects by previous causes, becomes annihilated; which formation* it is that renders *objects truly similar to others*, and not their mere *appearances*. In a sane and waking state of the mind, we can *reason* on *causes*, and can perceive by an act of the understanding immediately coalescing with the senses, all the consistencies, or inconsistencies of the *relations of the ideas of the sensible qualities*. In such a state, we therefore refer sensible qualities to objects permanently, and externally existing; because we take notice they have been *formed in a manner*, and appear under circumstances, which yield the supposition of being similar to those which *will return upon* irregular applications of the organs of *sense*, and so '*must needs continue to exist*'.

In delusion there is *no perception of the understanding*; in sane thoughts there is. In dreams the understanding sleeps, the fancy only is awake: — Yet, however vivacious the images of fancy may be, if the understanding in any particular case should chance to be awake, they are considered by the subject of them as the qualities of a disordered mind; not bodies external to it.

I have heard of a conscious delirium, in which the sensible qualities of extension, resistance, sound, colour, the voice of human beings, and animals, dancing, music, and painting, all, appear as *real*, and *vivacious* as though they had been external and distant, which yet the patient knew did not exist except in his own heated fancy, so long as he retained the sense of the *place* where he lay, and had presence of mind to *reason on that fact*; but when he lost the *recollection of place*, he could not put it in relation with the rest of the ideas or images in his mind; and so referred the sensible qualities to such usual causes as produced such images; i.e. he considered that their causes existed independent of fancy. Thus coloured extension is a *compound sensation*; the sense of motion is another; tangibility and resistance are others; but their unperceived, CONTINUALLY *existing causes*, are independent of *sensation*, unperceived, and unknown; and whilst their positive nature is unknown, yet their relative value, among themselves, is known to be *equal* to the relative variety of the 'ideas and sensations'; i.e. the effects they determine on the mind. But lest in this short exposition I should only by giving a hasty sketch, mislead the reader, I refer to the larger essay for these ideas in their fuller detail. Suffice it to keep to the point in question, and it follows, that *conscious, coloured extension*, is as a *picture* in the mind, and must be associated there with ideas of position, and distance, and direction, in relation to *motion*. The understanding knows these sensible perceptions of motion and distance, have corresponding exterior qualities which can appear to other minds, and which would exist were no consciousness present. Now it is unperceived motion which is in relation to unperceived distance, and unperceived contact; (whatever such qualities may be when unperceived); therefore, when the soul perceives the *picture* in which the coloured atmosphere appears, as well as the objects beyond it; it places them all in proportion to its perception of the motion requisite to attain contact with them; referring all the perceived qualities, which are *effects*, equally to all the unperceived qualities which are their *causes*; and which are in equal mutual relations. *Unperceived motion truly goes forth to unperceived extension*, &c. The perceived qualities are as a *landscape*, sent from an unseen country by which we may know it; as *algebraic signs*, by which we can compute and know the proportions of their qualities; as a *language*, which must be translated, before it can explain the actions of nature. The mind, in this landscape, is taken as an unextended centre, ready to go forth amidst the surrounding scenery; perceives itself amidst the algebraic equations, the simple quantity which never varies; and when it philosophises converts the ideas of its own operations into those analytical forms of expression, to which it is obliged to have recourse when it would adequately comprehend the interactions of the powers of nature.

Visible figure is thus truly nothing more than a conscious line of demarcation between two colours, and so must itself be colour; figure must ever comprehend visible extension; and visible extension does not take place without colour: nor can I conceive of perceiving it externally and immediately without it; for extension without colour is complete darkness.[114]

Now, when the soul goes forth to *that*, which the understanding may be supposed correct in considering a permanently existing object, does it go forth to colour and extension? There is no philosopher of the present day who would not answer, that it does *not* go forth to colour, but that it most certainly goes forth to extension. Now, I say, that in this respect colour and extension must stand or fall together; every argument of Dr. Reid's philosophy applies equally to *both*, for considering them *external*; whilst also every argument in considering *secondary qualities as mere affections of mind, caused* by permanent unlike causes, applies equally to both; therefore, I again ask, Does the soul go forth to colour and extension? I answer, That it does *not* go forth either to *perceived* colour, or to *perceived* extension, but that it does equally go forth to UNPERCEIVED colour, and to UNPERCEIVED extension; for that it attains unto, and forms an immediate junction with those *unperceived permanent causes*, or objects which determine perceived

---

[114] See Reid's Inquiry, c. 6, sec. 8. [Shepherd refers to Reid, *Inquiry* 6.8 (pp. 98–103).]

colour and extension upon the mind; and which unperceived objects, although considered themselves as coloured and extended, are *only* so considered, because incapable of being conceived of, save under the forms of those sensations which are always created by them, and which bear equal varieties of proportions among themselves; and that however every change of step may alter any colour, figure, and perceived extension, yet those permanent exterior existences are considered by the understanding, as they truly are, unvaried in themselves. Thus to endeavour to catch at unperceived relations is a very difficult task for the mind; whilst fit expressions for them are still more so.

The advantages resulting from this doctrine are, that it purports to be an analysis of facts, which, when *synthetically* put together, will again accord with nature.

Secondly, that it admits of examining nature without scepticism; for the *landscape*, the *calculation*, the *language*, are supposed correct in every part, either in respect to the *representation* of the objects, the *computation* of the proportional quantities, or the expression of the *facts*.

Thirdly, a view is here taken which may enable physiologists and physicians, moralists and divines, parents and instructors, better to observe, and more wisely to act than they do, with respect to the health, the opinions, and the practices of those under their care. Sensations are *effects;* the same external causes would yield the same internal sensation to each mind, if the varieties were not in the individuals. Sentient capacities seem also the result of an uniform, permanent power in nature. The varieties by every induction we are capable of making, seem to depend upon variety of organization, either in its arrangement, or its action. The former, whether in men or animals, has its most permanent characters stamped by the Deity. The latter is as multifarious as food, medicine, and climate; the circulation of the blood, the passions, the habits of education, and the notions of individuals, can render it. They are wrong, therefore, who, ignorantly taking no notice of these things, expect the *human will*, to be in all circumstances equal to self-command. Men make excuse for their actions in dreams and insanity, saying, the essences of things are then different; but never consider, that every degree and variety of their state of mind depends upon analogous laws and causes, which wisdom acting in time might alter with advantage, but which afterwards may lie beyond any human power to ameliorate.

I say, that in this doctrine the synthesis is equal to the analysis, because if a sentient being were placed in the midst of various insentient qualities, capable of exciting changes in the sentient being, the sentient being would consciously perceive the changes, would soon reflect on them, would soon perceive the relation of cause and effect, i.e. objects, or *some* changes of mind, *without which others* would not happen, and so would refer its own changes to causes; self, would therefore appear as a general capacity for any sensation, united to a *body*, i.e. a *sphere of certain limited consciousnesses*; and *objects independent of self*, would appear to be the *causes* of specific sensations in particular; *without* which *self in general* might continue to exist.

Thus all things would *justly* be considered as *out* of the mind which were not *in any given state of sensation*; but the objects which existed in relation to the senses would also yield a proof, (by *their regular return on the irregular application of the organs of sense*), that they permanently continued to exist *under certain defined and regular forms*. It is these continuous existences which are called *the objects of nature*. In all this the mind, as I think, from very early infancy, perceives the *true relations of things*, with almost as much ease as it perceives the *sensible qualities of things*. Along with this there would arise an intimate *association* of the sensible qualities with the ideas of their permanent *causes*; an *action of the mind*, which leads to the illusory belief of a corresponding external union. A notion not easily, and which ought not too hastily, to be broken up.

The only reason why pain and pleasure do not seem to exist in the objects capable of yielding them, but to reside within ourselves, is because in those cases there is not a *permanent* association.

Beauty and deformity are (except by some philosophers) considered to exist external to the mind; yet are no more than sensations of satisfaction or disgust, which some unknown, external causes create, and which are transferred upon those causes, and seem at a distance, on the *surface of bodies*, just in the manner in which Mr. Stewart speaks of colour, as seen united to extension at a distance, and which I conceive admits of a similar explanation to that which I have endeavoured to give of that phenomenon. In like manner love, as long as it lasts, considers its rapture to be caused by the merit of its object, but when distaste arrives it is found to reside in a *selfish sensation*; and by a new delusion, the object of its former passion, is now thought equally by its demerit to deserve a contrary emotion.

But the whole of the matter is, I repeat, a mystery; an *'unknown language'* is *not* that in which to think, with much ease and satisfaction. I take the subject in its full amount to be *'one of those secret things which belong to the Lord our God'*.[115] The deep consideration of it is, however, well fitted to afford the conclusion, that apparently like objects may in every sensible quality be similar, and yet they may essentially differ in their remote causes; i.e. in those aggregates or objects which contain their proper effectual causes, and therefore ought to be examined upon their own grounds. There may be no perfect analogy between any complex objects in nature; therefore, to understand them aright there ought to be a complete analysis of every part of them. Whilst it must nevertheless be owned, that an exact examination of objects made by experiment, (or nice observation), is a true source of the demonstration of *similar qualities for the future in like circumstances*. In both these respects modern philosophers err; considering *partial analysis* as affording ground for *analogical conclusions*, which without unwarrantable scepticism, or weak hesitation, are not open to objection:[116] whilst at the same time, *no principle is supposed sufficient* to explain the doctrine, that where there is a complete similitude known, or supposed, in the *formation* of two individuals, *there is any necessity* there should be a complete likeness in their qualities or effects. An association of ideas is thus erected into a fit means for the knowledge of existence; whilst the deductions of reason are considered as inadequate to their discovery.

I have attempted to reverse this order, and to show that *an association of ideas* will never prove any other existence than that of *an association of ideas*, but that *reason* has power to deduce the knowledge of an *universe*, existing independently both of ideas and their associations.

---

[115] [Deut. 29:29].

[116] As in the conclusion *that because* SOME religions *are false*, ALL *are so* — some miracles ill supported, and alleged to have taken place upon frivolous reasons; all are on the same foundation.

[...]

Selection E

(Excerpted from 'Lady Mary Shepherd's Metaphysics', *Fraser's Magazine* [1832], pp. 697–708.)

[...]

[...] Now, the doctrine which I advance simply states, That the ideas of any qualities cannot be like their external causes; that hence the definitions of them ought to be different; and that the confusion between the definitions of those similar names, which usually are applied equally to the causes of ideas and sensations, as to the effects, that is, the ideas and sensations themselves, or to both of these in a mixed state, is the reason of a false philosophy concerning the nature and operation of the mind, in its perception of an extended material universe, external to, and independent of itself.

I define, therefore, the *idea* of extension to be a simple sensation of the mind relative to that external extension which is not an idea, and which is its cause. I define external extension to be an unperceived cause, fitted to create or produce the idea of extension on the mind, and also to be a capacity for the admission of unperceived motion. I define matter to be, unperceived extended impenetrability. Now, as the *idea* of extension will not produce in any other mind the idea of extension, nor will it admit of unperceived motion, so I will not allow that it is capable of possessing qualities not contained in its definition.

As a consequence I deduce, that [the] opposed notion, viz. that the idea of extension is extended, virtually containing the doctrine that the ideas of things resemble the qualities of their causes, is fraught with the most ridiculous corollaries imaginable. For the same argument applies to identify the compound ideas, as much as the simple ones, with the qualities of their elementary causes. In whatever way, therefore, the compound aggregate of the ideas of 'a tall man', for instance, be gained, still the notion is but a compound idea, and must bear in its result the fact, that the whole compound itself is 'a tall man'.

If the simple idea of extension be an extended idea, the compound idea of height (whether acquired by suggestion or association, or by any other supposed means), must be a tall idea: the same of wind, it must be a windy idea; or of wholesome, it must be a wholesome idea: the compound idea of the rough ear of a lap-dog, would itself be the rough ear of a lap-dog. The same reasoning would apply to the idea of sound being noisy; of the idea of smell being sweet or odious; of the ideas of colours being themselves coloured, and of being beautiful or ugly accordingly.

The legitimate consequence of such a doctrine would be, that each mind one met with, might oppose one's progress with its extension, disgust one with its smell, deafen one with its noise, and affright one with its ugliness; or the contrary of all these, according to whichever set of ideas prevailed in it at the time! Yet experience tells me, that whatever pleasure or pain another being may be the means of yielding to me, it does not arise from those ideas within his mind, and which I know nothing of, but from those which he has the art to throw out of his mind, and which are enabled to enter mine by means of the several organs of sense, and to associate themselves there, either with the ideas of the imagination, or with those of the understanding.

[...]

As, therefore, I do not allow that ideas, or mind, possess any capacity by which to admit of unperceived motion round them, through them, or across them, or to offer the resistance of impenetrability to each other, so I will not concede that they are capable of the application of the definitions belonging to extension and to materiality; yet, although the perceptions of pain and pleasure require no more room for their habitation than does the unconsciousness of sleep, yet are they the affections of a universe which offers too many solid helps to the former state of mind, and too much of impenetrable resistance to the latter.

In short, qualities or affections of extension are not necessarily themselves extended, inasmuch as they may not necessarily hold any capacity by which to admit of unperceived motion. Were the mind, or any idea of the mind, truly extended (in my sense of extension) when any idea of broad or round, &c. arose, it would be equal to adding as much more of a capacity for unperceived motion, in order to admit of that successive change of place in relation to it, which, when determined to the perception of the mind, would yield to it the sensation of motion.

Now I believe, that if any definite extension be taken — say, a mile of road — that not one particle more will be added to it, or diminished from it, whether twenty minds enjoy a morning's ride thereon, or the contrary. Thus, ideas, sensations, or mind, may inhere in definite portions of, or the whole of matter, or of infinite space; yet, whilst neither they, nor it, are capable of impenetrability, or of the admission of unperceived motion, neither they, nor it, can bear out the definitions of, nor deserve the names of, extension or of materiality; whilst these inferior qualities, which are expressive of impenetrability and of the admission of unperceived motion, must possess the definitions, and merit the names, either of material extension or of the extension of space.[117] I mean, therefore, still to insist, that a man — that is, his mind — may be in the West Indies, instead of in England; in which latter place I could converse with it better than in the former, although in neither of them would it offer me any resistance. [...]

[...]

The sum of my doctrine on this head is, shortly, That sensation includes perception; that external perception is a contradictory term — all perception, whether of ideas, of bodies, or facts, the passions of others, &c., all are in a mind, which is in a state of feeling at the moment of perception. Yet this hinders not, but that some of the perceptions of our *reason* are those by which we know that our perceptions of *sense* relate unto, and are derived from, external things which themselves are not perceptions; and when we know of these, we habitually associate them under the appearances which are determined to the senses, and name them indifferently as external or internal things — as possessing the qualities of thought only, or as those outward causes of it which are also related to each other: and this, perhaps, in a confused manner, may answer well enough for ordinary life, although it be one so ill-suited to philosophy,

---

117 For the reason why I make a difference between perceived and unperceived motion, see my thirteenth Essay on the Association of Ideas, and the Interaction of Mind and Matter. [Essay 13 is not included in this volume.]

that I despair of ever seeing a correct analysis of the laws of perception; inasmuch as an innovation which should introduce a philosophical language in order to it, would be considered as absurd. But I cannot here enter into a statement of the mode of reasoning which I employ on this subject. Did I do so, it were almost to repeat the essay which I have already published against Bishop Berkeley, where I have put down my ideas in as condensed a form as it was possible for me to do.[118] All I shall at present say, therefore, is, that I conceive ideas of colour, to be from habit immediately associated with those of touch and motion. Contrasting colours yielding us, therefore, by means of their associations, the ideas of distance and of tangible figure, we set ourselves in motion accordingly; not towards perceived visible colours in our minds, but towards their corresponding unperceived causes; that motion having an equal corresponding relation thereunto, and which motion, although it yields to our minds its own peculiar sensation, yet would equally, were it considered as in an unperceived state, be a successive change of relation in respect to the unperceived causes of visual colours.

Our sensations, therefore, of coloured surfaces of different magnitudes, are to be apprehended as such in relation to touch and motion; otherwise they would be mere varieties of feeling, having no more to do with the occupancy of place, than the contrasting passions of joy and sorrow, tranquillity and anger, under the modification of their different intensities;[119] other words, their different degrees or magnitudes.

[...] There is a contrivance of machinery (as it were) in the management of the connexion between sentient and insentient nature, bespeaking in its maker the knowledge of both, beyond most other objects. The problem is difficult to enunciate, from the very circumstance of its apparent simplicity: when it is fully apprehended, the difficulty of its solution is perceived in all its force, and is found to be still greater than that of its enunciation. As, for instance, when we see from our window a beautiful

---

[118] See Essay on the Perception of an External Universe, &c. 'Essays'. 1827. Hatchard.

[119] See Essay on the Union of Colour and Extension, against Mr. Dugald Stewart. 'Essays'. 1827. Hatchard. [See pp. 189–200 in this volume.]

garden, ornamented with flowers of various colours, and determine to walk therein, and to approach the flowers, we set out apparently in the direction of the flowers, and we attain much nearer to them by means of motion. How can this appearance be reconciled to the evidence of reason, which shews that we cannot go forth to the colours in our minds, nor attain in any degree nearer to them by means of the motion we appear to employ? Now it is this seeming contradiction between the perceptions of reason, and the perceptions of sense, which has presented a mysterious appearance to the minds of the wisest men in every age. The difficulty relates analogically to each of the other senses, as much as to that of vision when united to the sense of motion [...] The idea that the motion which we feel, is the *real motion*, or mode of change which gains upon the flowers, is the source of the difficulty in question. Motion should be defined as 'successive change of place'. Our perception that this change is going on, is *not* the change itself. We perceive it because it exists: it does not exist because we perceive it. This being the case, the colours yield the notion of figure and beauty; the sense of which beauty is immediately associated with the desire of change of place. This association is further united to the ideas of tangible figure, to the power of producing motions by the influence of the will, and to the notion of some resistance to the will by the reaction of the body, &c.; whilst the whole of this union of ideas is so rapid, that it may be considered as forming (what truly it is in fact) but one compound idea. The impulse, the mysterious impulse of the mind upon the body, succeeds this union of ideas, and its *unperceived* motion, or successive change of place, results in consequence; whilst a corresponding series of successive changes is observed by the perceiving mind. Thus the changes which are produced are not all on the mind. Of the influence of the will, indeed, we have immediate consciousness. We feel that it is the cause for the beginning of the change called motion. But the body is only a compound idea when perceived by the mind; the cause or object of it is external. But it is upon the object, not upon the idea of it, that a change of place is first made, and the perception of this change is the after effect on the mind. The colours, therefore, being at the same time in our minds, during the perceived motion of our bodies, they will ever be compared together, under the perception of a change of relative distance.

Yet all this time the flowers external to the mind are only those continually existing causes of the colours, not themselves the colours, to which the person perceiving is moving, or, rather, would be changing his place in regard to them, whether he were perceiving that change with respect to them or not. [...]

It will thus appear, that when from my window I see a parterre of flowers, and determine to walk therein, and set out apparently in the direction of the colours, and by means of motion seem to gain upon them, that the whole of this scene goes on inwardly. What is perceived, are changes of sensations and ideas—are effects; the correspondent causes which determine them are all external, except one, and that is, the *beginning* of the change from the state of rest in which are those external things, by the impulse with which the will effects the first change of their relative places, and keeps up a succession of similar changes, by the continuance of a similar will.[120] The mind in this scene is as the reflecting mirror in a *camera obscura*,[121] were it imagined to be *consciously* observing its shifting images, knowing them to be changed by the influence of corresponding, though unlike, objects from without; and directing the succession of its changes, by its power of varying the position of the intervening instruments which connect the exterior changing objects with their responding changing representatives.

From what has been said, it follows, generally, that all reaction in consequence of any idea in the mind does not move any others of one's ideas; the external objects are the things which are moved—which truly change their relative places; the ideas which are the result of this change, are nothing more than the signs, or what may be termed the symptoms of it, on

---

[120] See Essay on the Association of Ideas. [Not included in this volume.]

[121] [A camera obscura was originally a darkened room with a small opening in one wall, whereby an object or scene from outside the room could be projected (upside down) into the interior. In Europe, this was first developed in the thirteenth century for observing the sun without damaging the eyes. Later versions were portable boxes, sometimes designed to look like books when closed, using mirrors and lenses to invert and sharpen the image; these were often used by artists. For a detailed history, see John H. Hammond, *The Camera Obscura: A Chronicle* (Bristol: Adam Hilger, Ltd., 1981).]

account of their forming one set of its effects—one set of its partial qualities. But I have said enough on this part of the subject, and shall quit it by observing, that the above arguments elicit the reason why I have defined extension to be the capacity for receiving unperceived motion, *i.e.* for admitting any object to change its place with respect to it; along it, or across it, or through it. That change of ideas which takes place when we say, 'we walk', 'we ride', 'we dance', &c. is not itself motion; it is only its effect, its partial quality and sign. Of all notions, this latter is the most difficult to inspire another with; and is, I repeat, an almost insurmountable barrier against any explanation of the mysterious connexion between the mind and the external universe proving satisfactory [...] But lest the allusion which I have made to algebraic signs should itself appear to contain some obscurity, I would here briefly offer something in explanation of it.[122] I observe, then, that the signs must not be defined as though they were themselves the same objects as the things signified by them; for the things signified must be defined not only by their powers of determining their respective signs, but also by their powers of affecting each other; and which farther powers can afterwards be made known by the farther signs which they are capable of determining.

But the signs must only be defined by analysing their compounds, (when they are signs of compounds), and when they are simple, by appealing to consciousness concerning their appearances.

Now, the causes of our ideas may be considered as simple algebraic quantities, marked thus:—c for colour, s for smell, s^d for sound, t for taste, e for extension, m for motion, &c.

When these causes determine their effects on the mind, the effects may, to all intents and purposes, be considered as their *squares*: for each is again involved into another power equal to itself, viz. that of each respective organ of sense which exists in relation to it. c is thus, as it were, the root which determines c^2; as when, for instance, by means of the eye, the sentient mind is affected by the corresponding variety that organ has the power of producing,—after its action has become affected by the

---

[122] See Essay on the Knowledge of an External Universe.

exterior object in nature which is relative to it, and which modifies every part of it. The same notion will equally serve to explain the influence of the rest of the senses over their respective roots, or causes. Now c will bear out a different definition from that which will apply to c^2, just as much as the number 2 must be subject to a different definition from that of the number 4; because, when it is placed in various relations unto, and variously combined with those other numbers, 3, 4, 5, 10, 100, &c., it will be the means of determining very different results from those which would arise from the combinations with the number 4. The causes, therefore, of the ideas of sense, which determine their effects, viz. the ideas of sense upon the mind, must never be considered as holding similar definitions with those ideas of sense; nor yet must those causes be considered as fully defined, when their power of determining ideas of sense is the only quality predicated of them: for those causes can externally intermix, and in different ways mutually affect each other, whilst the results of such mixtures can again farther determine themselves upon the mind, in consequence of new applications of the organs of sense in relation to them. The capacities, therefore, which they possess of superinducing[123] such mixtures, must enter into their definitions.

As a short illustration of what I have here imagined, let the observation of a ship upon the ocean — bound, for instance, from Falmouth to Antigua — whose sails are but beginning to be spread before the wind, be supposed as expressed by the following simple formula: $(s^2 + o^2) - (w\,m^2) = f^2$; the first powers, or causes of these squares, previously to their determining any notice of their existences, or of their relative positions on the mind, might be considered as bearing out the equation $(s + o) - (w\,m) = f$. Now these roots, or first powers, viz. s, o, w, m, must be considered as possessing such relative values as render them capable, by means of their mutual affections and involutions, of determining further equations; for $(s + o) + (w\,m)$, i.e. the continued influence of the motion of the wind during each successive moment, in relation to the ship and to the ocean, would eventually determine the equation $(s + o) + (w\,m) = a$. In consequence of which, when the notion corresponding to that

---

[123] superinducing] inducing.

result should be determined to the mind, by various organs of sense, the compound idea would necessarily arise, viz., $(s^2 + o^2) + (w\ m^2) = a^2$; and thus the observation of the determination of this new equation would indicate what changes had been taking place amidst the simple powers, previously to their possessing the capacity of superinducing this altered idea. Should this illustration not appear sufficiently plain,[124] let the ideas be applied to simple arithmetical numbers. It may be observed, that 1, 2, 3, 4, 5, &c. are possessed of a relative value towards each other, and which influences the results of their combinations, accordingly as they may be involved together in a vast variety of different proportions; whilst these relative values, and the results of their combinations, will be very different from those of their respective squares. When, therefore, any new involution of these simple powers takes place, then the square of that result may be determined to the mind; whilst by the quantity determined in that square, it may be known what was the quantity of its root, as also what combination of other simple quantities had concurred to produce it. If, for instance, the number 100 be given as a square number, it would be known that its root was 10; and that $(2 + 3) \times 2$ would form a combination equal to that root.

I consider, therefore, that the successions of ideas which arise in the mind, are as such successions of square numbers whose roots we extract, and the combinations of which we analyse, by an habitually rapid mode of reasoning: the process of it, however, is simple, and is that which enables us to predicate of the future by experience of the past. When the objects to which this operation relates are usual and simple, children and

---

[124] It is not my intention to state the notion with all the strictness and propriety which really exist in an algebraic formula, but merely to shew, generally, that there exist two sets of objects as forming the media of connexion between sentient and insentient nature; viz. external causes and internal effects: which latter qualities being the result of the former, cannot bear out the same definitions with them, whose names, therefore, should possess some variety accordingly; and which clearer language would enable us better to understand the relations of the objects which it would indicate, in a manner somewhat similar to that by which algebraic signs express the relations of the quantities which they represent with perfect exactness, and fitted for easy apprehension.

peasants make use of it equally with others; but in proportion as the quantities determined on the mind become unusual and complicated, it demands each variety of intellect to evolve the roots, and afterwards analyse their component parts, in order to know what further results are capable of existence. Should it be said that children and peasants cannot thus reason, — let any ordinary affair of life be selected as an example, and it may be perceived, that with respect to the circumstances belonging to it, their minds will undergo a mode of consideration analogous to that which I have been describing, and one where there is no difference between them and the philosopher, until he philosophizes too deeply. When, for instance, they perceive a fire in their chamber, they know that the cause of this perception possesses also the capacity of setting fire to the house, but none of setting fire to the idea of a house; they consequently place a guard against the action of that cause, but none over their thoughts of it. In like manner, when they perceive the idea of their house, they know that the object or cause which yields them this agreeable view, also possesses the capacity of being burned to the ground by the fire, but none of its undergoing that alteration from any notion of fire within themselves; accordingly, they insure their houses, without thinking it necessary to obtain any security for their ideas.

Now, from this simple exposition it may be deduced, that the capacity to produce combustion must enter into the definitions of fire and wood, as objects capable of mutually interacting with each other, independently of the observation of the mind; but this capacity must not enter into the definitions of the partial qualities, *i.e.* into the definitions of the successive appearances of fire and wood, and which successive ideas cannot, by any possible combination, be made to produce combustion.

It is hence manifest, that the philosophical difficulty concerning the connexion between the mind and the external universe, arises from not considering that the interaction of objects, as physical causes, necessarily takes place exterior to the mind; whilst the combination of ideas in a mind can never give birth to any other effects than the ideas of memory, imagination, and reasoning.

The difficulty is generated by the operation of the association of ideas from early infancy, by which any name which stands as the name of an external object, becomes, not only the name of the external causes of our sensations, but includes the notion that these causes are archetypes—similitudes of those sensations. Thus a child, by the word fire at first means an object which warms him; afterwards, when he says the fire will burn the house, he unites with the notion of the external and permanent object which exists as fire, the notion of its warmth, and conceives that that whole is concerned in the burning of the house.

Ideologists, in separating the notions of external causes from their internal effects (their partial qualities), and considering that the names of objects merely belong to ideas, and that these ideas are the only physical causes with which they are acquainted, betray a still greater want of philosophy than do the vulgar; for, in a mixed state at least, objects contain the properties by which they are causes; but in a separated state, when the partial effects of some sensible qualities or ideas are only considered as such, no properties which can act as causes are retained. Each of these errors equally arises from a deficiency in the use of the faculty of abstraction, although the absurdities which the philosopher runs into are of the greater magnitude. It appears to me, for instance, to be language equally ignorant, and more absurd than that which a peasant uses, when Berkeley says, distinctly, 'that we eat, and drink, and are clothed with ideas', 'with the ideas of sensible quali-ties'; for at most the vulgar conceive that these qualities coexist with their causes, and, therefore, that they continue their exist-ence along with them, when not perceived.[125] Berkeley, there-fore, and his adherents, do not abstract the notion of a definite external cause, acting differently upon various senses and various objects in the universe; and hence they place some partial effects of things, viz. the ideas of some sensible qualities, as true causes of other sensible qualities, and other effects in nature: but it is impossible that ideas should have it in their power so to act; for they could not, after having been once in the mind as ideas, stand out thence again, to be eaten or

---

[125] See Essay VI, p. 300, where this passage of Bishop Berkeley is exactly quoted and noticed. [The quotation is from Berkeley, *Principles* 38 (pp. 96–7).]

drunken, or to set fire to a house, &c. The vulgar, on the other hand, do not abstract the ideas of the partial effects of things, from the notion of their exterior and permanent causes; the consequence is, that they generally conceive the external causes and the sensible effects to be existing externally and permanently together.

Which of these notions, then, is most absurd, that all is in the mind, or that all is out of it? I conceive the former to be so. Whenever, therefore, [...] c^2 and e^2 are spoken of, as though they were c and e, the most ridiculous confusion must necessarily take place in every attempt at a philosophical analysis of the powers of the human mind, or of the objects of human knowledge.

A like observation may be applied to the notions of some other modern ideologists, to whom I have already alluded, who profess to be ignorant of the fact that such powers as c and e must necessarily exist. They boast of their superior knowledge, in having discovered that the only fact with which they are acquainted, is that of a succession of ideas; insomuch, that when the succession becomes altered to their observation, they need not be under any anxiety to assign the reason of this change. Two different sets of sequences of ideas have been determined to their notice; this is all which they are capable of discovering, and this is all which can be known. The confusion of intellect resulting from such notions as these is so great, that it is impossible to understand where to begin to set it in order, or whether it be possible to introduce into it any arrangement whatever.

[...]

But, to conclude, I trust that I have succeeded in shewing, in these pages, that there is no inconsistency in extension holding inextended qualities of a higher nature than itself. Mysterious this subject must ever be, for two reasons; the one is, that from the very stretch of the fancy towards infinite qualities of a like kind to those which are finite, the mind is overpowered by its own exertion, although there be no inconsistency in its endeavour; and the other is, that the mind strives, if possible, to find the very essences of things from the bare comparison of the relations of its ideas: for, although we be philosophers enough to know it is impossible to do so, we are for ever endeavouring to catch at, and yet for ever disappointed at not meeting with, those essences.

[...] [My doctrine] pretends no more than to find the one essence, viz. consciousness—to observe the mutual relations included in its varieties—to define and name them accordingly —to be content that, by careful observation, I can know so much more than what at first sight I might seem capable of— and, finally, to be resigned to whatever degree of ignorance my very nature renders inevitable. Of one thing I am certain, that if by an attempt to be consistent and clear, I felt that I was running the risk of lessening the sublimity of that beautiful and mysterious truth, that there is an ever-present existing Deity, I would not venture upon the discussion of the subject, even if I conceived that a full explanation of it were within the scope of my intellectual powers.

Three

Mathematical and Physical Induction

Selection F

(Excerpted from *Essays on the Perception of an External Universe* [1827], pp. 278–95.)

Essay 5: That Mathematical Demonstration, and Physical Induction, Are Founded Upon Similar Principles of Evidence

[...]

[Certain passages from *An Essay upon the Relation of Cause and Effect*[1]] are intended to show, first, *that the science of mathematics is truly but one branch of physics*: for that all the conclusions its method of induction demonstrates, depend for their truth upon the implied proposition, 'That like cause must have like effect'; a proposition which being the only foundation for the truths of physical science, and which gives validity to the result of any experiment whatever, ranks mathematics as a *species* under the same *genus*; where the same proposition is the basis, there is truly but one science, however subdivided afterwards.

Secondly, That, *when objects are formed the same upon one occasion as another, their qualities, properties, and effects, will be similar.* It is this proposition on which mathematical demonstration, and physical induction equally, and only, rest for their truth. There is no difference; objects are what their formations

---

[1]   [See pp. 52, 78–9, and 43 in this volume.]

render them, whether in the shape of mathematical diagrams, or other aggregates in nature. Thus they are intended to show, that the laws of causation form the *base* on which mathematical certainty is built; and that the reason why some other branches of science are less secure in their conclusions, is merely because of the difficulty there is in *tracing the original* FORMATIONS *of the objects*,[2] without impugning in the smallest degree, the universality and necessity of the axiom, that if cause in any instance be like, the effect must also be like.

Thirdly, They are furthermore intended to point out the fact, that as we know nothing of objects but the *enumeration of qualities*, so the reasoning which concerns the qualities contained in physical objects, must fundamentally be of the same kind, as that concerning the quality termed quantity, whether it be expressed by abstract numbers, or by mathematical diagrams.[3]

[…][4]

Thus it may be seen, that in the study of mathematical science, the scholar is supposed to know the general axioms, '*that qualities cannot* BEGIN *their own existences*', and *that the* FORMATION *of things being* SUPPOSED *equal, the properties are nothing else but those results, included in their formation, and, therefore, cannot at the same time both be* SAME *and* DIFFERENT; AND THEREFORE, THE DOCTRINE OF CAUSATION IS UNDERSTOOD BY THE SCHOLAR AS THE BASE ON WHICH THE TRUTH OF EVERY THEOREM IS SURELY BUILT. In this point of view, the demonstration, by means of reasoning on a

---

2   Or in finding a criterion whereby to *detect* an unobserved 'secret power' creeping in amidst the most unequivocal determination of similar 'sensible qualities'.

3   This I believe is the old Pythagorean doctrine, and which I am sorry Mr. Stewart considers but '*a dream*'. Pythagoras used to say, 'Leave but ONE quality out of the definition of a pear, and the object is not a pear.' [It is unclear why Shepherd ascribes this quotation to Pythagoras. Stewart refers to the 'dreams of the Pythagoreans' in *Elements of the Philosophy of the Human Mind*, Vol. 2, 2nd ed. (Edinburgh: Archibald Constable and Co., 1816), 4.1 (p. 330) (hereafter cited as *Elements* Vol. 2, followed by chapter and section number, with page numbers). However, the phrase occurs in a discussion of harmonies between the physical universe and numbers, not of definitions and natural kinds.]

4   Shepherd here quotes from her 1824 essay; see pp. 52, 78–9, and 43 in this volume.

diagram, is but the '*one simple and judicious experiment*', which proves the relations of every other formed after a similar fashion in every different time and place. Could these maxims of causation be altered; could qualities begin of themselves; could (therefore) like cause produce other than like effect; all the axioms, diagrams, and demonstrations might stand as they do in the books of Euclid, without any avail as to their application to other diagrams of a similar kind and their properties; and for this plain reason, because, although the objects were formed similar to others, their qualities might differ *of themselves*. We might have the radii of circles, for instance, *forming themselves* unequally, although it were granted their boundary line was made a true circle by its usual mode of formation. Thus the doctrine of *necessary connection* is the result of perceiving that two or more individual objects, or quantities, which are like each other, are to all intents and purposes with respect to any relations which may arise respecting them, *identically the same*, and may be always considered as the *same individual objects or quantities* repeated as many times: instead of as many *various* although *similar* objects. It is such a perception as this, in which consists the essential power of abstraction: an abstraction which Bacon, Newton, Berkeley, all must have allowed, or there could have been no science; and did virtually, and truly allow, notwithstanding some cavils on that head.

The relations of the simple impressions which influence the minds of children, or peasants, nay, even of brutes, enable them to perceive, that *like* things are equal to the *same things repeated*, and that they have no relation to *time*. The past, therefore, governs the *future*, because no *interval of time* can prevent the same thing from being the same. Inferior understandings, indeed, and perhaps all men, consider things to be *like*, or the same kind of object, upon too partial an observation of their qualities or methods of formation; still they expect like causes to have like effects, or like objects to have similar qualities in future, when they do consider them as *like*, only because no interval of TIME can make any difference in respect to them; *and there is no other difference supposed or observed*.

In the mathematics, diagrams are formed by ourselves, and we may therefore be always *sure* of our future and universal conclusions; because we frame an *hypothesis*, and examine by one experiment, (i.e. one experience), the relations which arise;

and the same data being given to all future ages, there is nothing supposed which can make any difference amidst these relations; for all particular instances are included in the first experience made. The notion of *time* is left out of consideration, for it is observed to have nothing to do with the circumstance of one example being capable of proving the relations of all that are like it in every time and place; as each may be considered to be identically the same.

[…]

God no doubt may vary the laws of nature, &c. that is, create, arrange, alter the capacities of objects, by means adapted to those ends. But to understand God aright, he cannot work a contradiction; he cannot occasion the same objects without any alteration amidst them supposed to produce dissimilar effects.

It is, therefore, no more an invasion of the attributes of Deity, to assert that he cannot alter an effect arising from an equal physical cause, than that he cannot render a triangle, at the same time that it remains a triangle, to be without the properties of a triangle. The same kind of object is the same kind of object, and its effects are but qualities the result of its formation, which being *the same* cannot *be different*; and *that*, whether the quality resulting from its formation be a *colour* or a *proportion*.

Mathematical science, therefore, and those physical actions, which are termed laws of nature, *equally depend* upon the one only law,[5] '*Like cause must exhibit like effect*'; and this axiom depends on the principle, that '*No quality can begin its own existence*'. For when the enquiry concerning causation is pushed back as far as it may, it will readily be perceived, *first*, that *if any particular quality were supposed to begin of itself*, the following

---

[5]   Mr. Stewart considers the word *law* to be only a metaphorical expression, E.P.H. Mind, vol. 2, p. 220. [Shepherd refers to Stewart, *Elements* Vol. 2, 2.4, part 2 (pp. 221–5).] I can only give it a rational meaning, by converting it into quality, property, or relation, in which senses, when general, it forms a general efficient cause, and when we *detect* by an exact experiment a similarity of qualities, we cannot but expect similar effects, because we must expect same things will be same, independently of time and place. It may be called a *physical law of thought* thus to believe, but I must believe as much of any data in physics, and cannot believe more in mathematics.

contradiction would arise, viz. that the beginning of existence, which is a quality of being, could belong to a being not yet in existence;[6] secondly, that in this respect all qualities are upon the same footing, and that no variety of accident can make any difference in the universality of that truth.

The faculty of abstraction, is truly the origin of all science. By abstraction, is meant the consideration of any quality apart from others with which it may be usually united, in order to notice what inferences may be drawn from its nature.

Taking that quality apart, therefore, viz. *the commencement of existence,* we perceive that every imaginable being is on the same footing with respect to it, namely, that it is a contradiction to suppose it the quality of a being not yet in existence: — *'That existences cannot* BEGIN *of themselves'*, is thus an *universal* perception, and which ought to govern every deduction of philosophy.

[...]

In short, causation is necessary not arbitrary; and though the nature of any *particular* effect requires to be *ascertained by experience,* yet it is *reason* must show its *necessary* connection with its *cause,* as opposed to its *arbitrary* or accidental connection with it; its *immediate inherence* in its *cause,* as opposed to its mere *subsequency* to it; and the knowledge of its *invariability of connection for the future,* as opposed to the mere *experience of its conjunction in past time.* Thus although *experience* is required to show, 'that blue and yellow mixed in their particles, will form the colour termed green: yet *that experience* must be reasoned on before it can show, *that by, in,* and *with* the mixtures of particles, there exists *immediately* green as a new quality in nature';[7] or such a set of altered particles as shall determine green when meeting with the eye and mind. The aid of *reason* is also equally needful, yet sufficient to show, that the connection between the mixture of such particles, is necessary and invariable. In like manner, one experience shows that ten taken ten times over, yields one hundred; but it is reason which proves that this result coalesces

---

6   See essay on the relation of cause and effect, p. 34, 'Let the object, &c.' [See pp. 32–3 in this volume.]

7   [Shepherd alludes to an example she gives in *Essay Upon the Relation of Cause and Effect* (p. 101n; p. 63 n39 in this volume).]

in and with its cause, and *that* in every step of its progress: and that if it once coalesces it must necessarily and invariably do so always.[8]

---

[8]   *'Things are what their enumeration of qualities make them'; in the abstract sciences, we can limit these ourselves, and therefore can predicate the properties of any given subject in them* UNIVERSALLY, *but physical objects of experiment cannot be* DETECTED *with equal certainty. This is the whole difference; for in any case where we cannot show the reason of any regular appearance in the sciences respecting quantity, a strictly demonstrative proposition cannot be enunciated concerning it, and an* UNIVERSAL INDUCTION *of a constant fact could not thence result.*

Four

Miracles

Selection G

(Excerpted from *Essays on the Perception of External Universe* [1827], pp. 325–45.)

Essay 8: That Human Testimony Is of Sufficient Force to Establish the Credibility of Miracles

Mr. Hume says,[1] 'I flatter myself I have discovered an argument which, if just, will with the wise and learned be an everlasting check to all kinds of superstition and delusion; for so long as the world endures will the accounts of miracles be found in all history, sacred and profane.' Now this argument which Mr. Hume flatters himself he has discovered, is contained in the opinion he has formed on the nature and reason of our belief in causation.

In his sections on the subject of the necessary connection of cause and effect, he has endeavoured to prove that *custom* is the only ground of our belief in *cause* as a 'productive principle'; or of the necessary connection between effects and their causes.

[...]

Now it is a natural consequence resulting from the experience we have of the *value of truth amidst the transactions of life*, that *mankind will speak the truth* in *all* cases, when it appears useful and accords with their interest to do so; as well as that in all other cases where the contrary consequences appear, men will

---

[1]   See Hume's Essay on Miracles, 1st paragraph. [Shepherd paraphrases David Hume, *An Enquiry Concerning Human Understanding*, ed. Tom L. Beauchamp (Oxford: Oxford University Press, 2000), section 10, paragraph 2 (p. 169); hereafter cited as *Enquiry*, followed by section and paragraph number, with page number.]

be strongly tempted to falsehood; being only prevented from using it by observing that a superior value is contained in observing a general rule prescribing truth indifferently, whether for or against their interest. It thence follows as an axiom, that we place *dependence* on the veracity of men, in all cases where we cannot distinctly perceive any motive to false-hood; and in like manner that we proportion our jealousy of the truth of their assertions, according as we may suppose them influenced by any circumstance of self-interest. This being the case when they relate '*marvellous events*', we must enquire if there be any motive to self-interest likely to tempt them in any particular given case to falsify; to invent as fables what they detail as facts; remembering always that nature is so far from keeping up any constant analogy in her works, that the very aversion to believe in excepted cases to those of experience, arises from that puerile adherence to a customary association of thought, which made 'the Indian Prince' a child rather than a philosopher, 'who reasoned *justly*' (according to Mr. Hume's argument) when he *refused* to 'believe the first relation con-cerning frost'.[2]

There is, no doubt, a necessary connection between *similar* qualities in union, but not unless there be similar qualities *present* in order to unite; there can be no necessary connection if circumstances be *dissimilar*. All laws of nature are compre-hended in one universal law, that similar qualities being in union, there will arise similar results; a miracle, therefore, is ill defined by Mr. Hume, when he would express it as 'a *violation* of the laws of nature', because there is always understood to be a power in some superior influence in nature, in the presiding energy of an essential God, acting as an additional *cause*, equal to the alleged variety of effects.

This observation enables me further to comment on the next important sentiment of Mr. Hume's on this head; and which indeed, contains the sum of his doctrine upon it.

'Let us suppose that the fact affirmed instead of being only marvellous, is really miraculous'; ('for a miracle is a violation of the laws of nature'); 'then it follows, that as a firm and unalter-able experience has established the laws of nature, the proof

---

2   [Shepherd quotes Hume, *Enquiry* 10.10 (p. 172).]

against a miracle from the nature of the fact is as entire, as any argument from experience can possibly be imagined.'[3]

Now let us examine this statement with nicety, and with the greatest care observe to what this famous doctrine amounts, which had sufficient attraction in it to draw the opinion of many from the belief of Christianity.

First, This statement contains a false assertion; an assertion contradicted by '*the slightest philosophy*'.[4] Our experience never established, nor can ever be the measure of the laws of nature; if by such laws he meant the original inherent qualities of the 'secret powers' and capacities of bodies and minds; the mysterious influences of distinct masses of things, antecedent to their operation upon our senses. Our experience neither created nor arranged them, such as they are when external to us; and, therefore, never can be the measure of what *alteration* might take place under certain altered circumstances exterior to the senses. Nor can our *past* experience ever acquaint us, what latent influences, what new unseen events, what 'secret powers' might be drawn from the mysterious storehouse of unperceived nature to alter our experience in future.

There may be no perfect analogy in nature, unless it be that there arise exceptions to hitherto universal experience in all classes of things, with which we are acquainted.

The tale of the Indian Prince, who refused to believe a natural occurrence which passed the limits of his own experience, may be told of our ourselves;—we deem some limited observation we make, the measure of an universal fact;—we draw general conclusions from particular premises; until extended knowledge acquaints us with exceptions, and sometimes with single and most important exceptions to otherwise universal facts. It therefore betrays a want of profundity in reflection, as well as of acquaintance with the sacred writings, to define a miracle otherwise than as an exception to the *apparent* course of nature,—than as a marvellous, because an extraordinary occurrence.

[...]

---

[3]   [Shepherd quotes Hume, *Enquiry* 10.11–12 (pp. 172–3).]
[4]   [Shepherd draws this phrase from Hume, *Enquiry* 12.9 (p. 201).]

The definition, therefore, of a miracle is '*an exception to nature's apparent course*'.[5]

Whether the testimony to prove an event alleged, be credible or not; and if it be credible, in what manner the event *proves* a *doctrine*, are two questions beside the main point of enquiry, which is, '*Whether an interruption to nature's apparent course can take place?*' which confusion of three questions involved in one, is the reason that an unsatisfactory answer is generally made. This view of the subject did not occur to Mr. Hume, if we may judge from his incomplete analysis of it.

Therefore, there are really three questions involved.

First, Whether the apparent course of nature can be altered?

Secondly, Whether the evidence produced to prove such an alteration be credible?

Thirdly, If it be credible, in what manner the miracle itself becomes evidence of any particular doctrine, &c.?

Now, first, that the apparent course of nature may be altered; that a singular exception to hitherto universal experience may take place, has been proved by means of the doctrine of efficient cause, not only here, but more at large in a former essay; and it may be added, that when men are not jealous on account of consequences, they are not in the least indisposed to admit evidence to the truth of such 'marvellous' and singular occurrences.

The possibility of an interruption to nature's undeviating method, places therefore a religious miracle as far as its *possibility* goes, precisely upon the same footing as any other *singular* event for which an adequate cause is supposed, although it be undiscoverable, and renders the miracle equally fit to be an object of investigation as to the fact of its existence, with any singular event.

Secondly, If the testimony to marvellous events be made under such circumstances, that no sufficient motive can be imagined to tempt the witnesses to falsehood; if the events be such as would rather induce a cowardice of assertion

---

[5]   The word miracle, in its derivation, signifies only a wonderful thing; that is, something at which we wonder, because contrary to our usual experience, or in other words, an interruption to that we conceive the course of nature.

concerning them than the contrary, then the evidence should be considered as worthy of confidence, and the facts honestly related.

Thirdly, The manner in which marvellous events prove a doctrine is as follows: The events in question being alleged to occur by the operation of a *cause* known to be inadequate to the effect; the mind is thence forced to refer to an *adequate* cause, and rests in the notion of superior power being present, and in action.

The command of *apparently* a human voice bids the dead arise, and they do so. The spectators thence *infer* that necessarily *'one greater than Moses'*,[6] or any human legislator is present, in order to be acquainted with the possibility of the action, and the powers to enforce its accomplishment. Hence it follows, that such events are needed in order to give authority to certain doctrines, and under such circumstances, however marvellous they may be, as exceptions to nature's course in fact, they are nevertheless *probable events*; because as *means* necessary to an *end*, they obey that analogy of nature, which consists, in using necessary means towards every event that is brought about; they are, therefore, to be regarded as exceptions *probable* to take place, and the evidence of them is therefore to be received and examined, by the rules of evidence upon ordinary cases.

When a doctrine is either a wicked or foolish doctrine, such events are so *improbable* to occur as connected with it, that the same evidence will not answer, and I will venture to add, has never been offered.

Therefore it is, that the nonsensical differences in the Church of Rome, cannot be supposed as worthy of being settled by miracles; none, also, who allege miracles to have been wrought on account of such trifling disputes, or other matters equally insignificant, lived the lives, died the deaths, or preached the doctrines of a Paul, Peter, or John.

The testimony of those who assert miracles to have taken place in order to establish some favourite dogma of their own, without the sacrifice of any interest in consequence, is liable to

---

6   [Heb. 3:3].

the strongest suspicion of being the result of self-interest and fraud.

To prove a revelation it is necessary, first, That there should be miracles which testimony alone can be the means of recording. Secondly, That they should be such in which the senses cannot be mistaken. Thirdly, That there should be some notable overt acts of the witnesses, of sufficient self-denial in their sacrifices, in order to prove they believe in their own assertions.

It is in respect of the two latter particulars in which all spurious miracles are found to fail. They are either matters in which the senses of men might be imposed upon by the artful, or such asserted facts, whose truth never cost the blood-shedding of those who professed to have been their eye witnesses.

Such distinctions as these if better analysed and arranged than I can pretend to, would sink into utter disgrace Hume's childish comparison of the miracles of the New Testament with those of the Abbé Paris, and others of a similar description.

It was my original purpose in this Essay only to attempt a refutation of the argument, which Mr. Hume built upon his doctrine of causation; but as there are two objections frequently made to a supposed method of reasoning, in relation to the miracles, which may be thought to bear upon some of my observations, I may be permitted to notice them also.[7]

First, It is objected, '*That to say, the doctrine proves the miracles, and that the miracles prove the doctrine, is to argue in* A CIRCLE.'

To this objection I would simply reply, that it possesses no force, when the questions to which it relates, are properly distinguished in their conception, and separated in their statements. The questions therefore which are proposed ought *not* to be,

1st. Whether the doctrine be true? to which an answer in the affirmative may be supposed as returned, — *because the miracles alleged to be worked in its favour prove it;* — and,

2ndly. *Whether the miracles alleged to be wrought in its behalf be true?* — to which also an affirmative is given; and that, *Because the excellence of the doctrine proves them so.* But

---

7   See pp. 339, 340. [In this volume, see p. 223 and this page, above.]

1st. Whether the doctrine be such as would justify the inter-ference of Deity, IF such interference could be proved? and

2ndly. Whether there be sufficient evidence to prove the fact of alleged miracles, in order to sanction a doctrine which when *independently* considered appears to be worthy of a divine author?

When these two latter questions are answered in the affirmative, no illogical answer in a *circle* is given to them, as any one may plainly perceive, however little skilled in the technical rules of reasoning. No doctrine indeed can *prove* the existence of miracles, but it can be of sufficient use and importance to render itself *worthy* of being authorized by their interference, thereby placing the *probability* of such a fact taking place, *and the evidence required in consequence*, precisely upon the same footing as that of *any event in nature, where means are necessary to be used in order to the attainment of any given end.* The excellence of a doctrine therefore, merely proves, that it *might* be of God, but miracles are wanted to prove that it *is* of God; when therefore miracles are proved by the evidence of the human senses, or by veracious testimony, they establish the authority of the doctrine, which however wise, important, or useful, would not otherwise *be binding* on the consciences of men.

The second objection is, '*That as martyrs have believed false religions, therefore the sufferings of other martyrs cannot afford the proof of a true revelation.*'

This objection arises from an erroneous view of the nature of the circumstance proved by martyrdom. It is *not* the TRUTH of a revelation, but it is the *sincere* belief of the martyr in his own profession; the circumstance of martyrdom affords a proof against *hypocrisy*, not against enthusiasm, or delusion. Now to have a proof that a man *is not an impostor*, is a great point gained; for if he deliver a doctrine, of consequence, it obliges every honest mind to open his books and examine it with impartiality; and to consider seriously, whether with respect to those events which he professes to have witnessed, his senses, and his understanding could have been deceived as to their real occurrence.

To me it appears impossible that the first Christian preachers could be impostors, when I read of their sufferings; or that they could be deluded when I read the history (for instance) of the raising of Lazarus; and if but one miracle be overwhelming in its evidence, the rest which are associated with it in the same cause, are included in that evidence, and yield the same additional force in their testimony to the senses, and to the judgments of those that witnessed them, (and by parity of reasoning, to those who hear of them afterwards), as do the *frequent return* of the external objects of sense, support the belief of that *independent* existence, of which the first vivacious impulse on the senses had originally created the impression.[8]

In short, if the Gospel be a mystery, yet that it should be untrue would be a greater;—however, what I have said with respect to martyrdom as applicable in the way of forming an argument, is only needful for succeeding generations. It is necessary for us who live at this day, that the Apostles should have suffered, and have sealed their books with their blood.

---

[8]   See 1st Essay, C. 3rd, 'on the *Independency* of E. Objects', p. 78, 'Thirdly', &c. comparing that sentence with C. 1st, 'on *Continuous* Existence', p. 13, 'For the mind', &c. [See pp. 128 and 100 in this volume.]

Five

God

Selection H

(Excerpted from *Essays on the Perception of an External Universe* [1827], pp. 151-2.)

Chapter 7: Application of the Doctrine Contained in the Preceding Essay to the Evidence of our Belief in Several Opinions

Section 1

The foundation of our belief in God.

[...]

1. As to the existence of God, let it be remembered that all our *belief* concerning every proposition, is the result of what we conceive to be the consistent relations of ideas present in the mind. Now I have shown, that these relations force our minds to believe in continuous existences unperceived. It is upon similar premises that we build the foundation of our belief in Deity. For after some contemplation upon the phenomena of nature, we conclude, that in order to account for the facts we perceive, 'there must needs be' one continuous existence, one uninterrupted essentially existing cause, one intelligent being, 'ever ready to appear' as the renovating power for all the dependent effects, all the secondary causes beneath our view. To devout minds, this notion becomes familiar and clear; and being mixed with the *sensible impressions* of goodness, wisdom, and power, begets those habitual sentiments of fear, trust, and love, which it is reasonable to perceive and to enjoy. Our constantly familiar friend, whose presence we speak of, and whose qualities we love and admire, affords us no further proof for his existence

and his qualities, than the reasoning adduced in this book: — He must needs be another being than ourselves, having qualities which are not our own, but *his,* that are sufficient to engage our sympathy, or the relations of our thoughts would be rendered inconsistent with each other.

Selection I

(Excerpted from *Essays on the Perception of an External Universe* [1827], pp. 346–71.)

Essay 9: On the Objection Made to Final Causes as Ends, On Account of the Existence of Physical Efficient Means

Those who conclude that a final cause is not wanted for the phenomena of the universe, because there are physical causes in action, efficient to the production of each object, draw their conclusion wider than the premises will warrant. They forget that in doing so, they overlook ONE EFFECT which they have to account for, namely, the *appearance* of contrivance in the universe — this being beyond a chance coincidence of effects, arising out of a *determination of motion* that had *no end in view.* There is therefore, an original direction of motion given to separate portions of different kinds of matter, coalescing to one APPARENT *end;* the cause of which direction *they never arrive at by ever so many steps backwards from motion caused by previous motion;* — nay, could they even come at the original direction in each case, and could they even perceive that a material motion prevening, acted as the first *sensible* propellant, it would not follow that *mind* were not truly the final, i.e. the only efficient cause in that case; — for, mark what it is to be a final cause when it acts in ourselves; — it is to be that perception of future qualities, and that intention to create them, *which forms the efficient cause of the direction of motion upon those qualities which are already in existence:* — To be a final cause is to perceive a future possible quality, capable of being gained by that means in our power, called the direction of motion. But to *perceive* is a mental quality; yet is it a quality which whilst it is not to be descried by any sense or instrument, chemical, or mechanical, in our power, nevertheless intimately unites in and with the action of the brain, which action might be discerned, and would, therefore, be considered by incomplete reasoners as the true prevening motion which alone determined the next in order, towards the supposed end. Yet PERCEPTION *of happiness, or utility,* and the chosen direction of the eye, the ear, or the arm, in consequence, is not the mere action of the brain, the nerves, and the muscles.

According to the language of some modern writers, we might, after beholding a well constructed ship in full sail upon the waters, and examining each part in relation to the wind, and the waves, and the point at which it appeared destined to arrive; consider these aptitudes as *accidental* and undesigned, in order to prove which, each motion might be traced backwards as resulting from the necessary physical, mechanical actions of matter, until we arrived at the original materials from which the vessel was framed, along with those other actions of matter, viz. of the muscles, the nerves, and the brains of the human beings concerned in the arrangement. But we know by experience, this will not explain *the whole* objects which have been in action on the one hand; nor on the other, could we descry, by the nicest instruments we possess, the power of sentiency as a physical cause, changing all the various material beings concerned in the formation of the magnificent object before us;—going on its way in its grand and easy motion. It is not possible *a priori,* therefore, *among our own contrivances,* to discover by *physical examination* when it is that reflection, determination of reason, or passion, have interfered to alter the things we see; the powers of mind are one with THE VISIBLE AFFECTIONS of matter, they inhere as one physical cause along with them; the one power may be discerned by the senses, but the other cannot; and is only to be known by experience of what passes within ourselves. To know whether the action of mind in any case be the director of motion upon the things already in existence, we must examine some given state of their being; and comparing them with such things as we know to be governed, arranged, and adopted by mental qualities, judge with discretion and impartiality, whether they be of *a like kind.* We must judge of the probability whether they be designed aptitudes, where perception of possible qualities had directed the motions of matter towards their accomplishment, or whether such appearances were the mere accidental results of the necessary efficient causes of undesigned interactions of material qualities.

In human affairs to judge properly in many cases, whether intellect has been at work or not, requires extraordinary powers of understanding,—higher faculties of mind than the abstract sciences stand in need of. The knowledge of human nature, 'which though no science, fairly worth the seven',[1] is nothing but the penetration which enables us to discover the intentions that govern the motions of ourselves and others. In many cases it may be difficult to say, whether *any design whatever* has been in action, and in many more of what number and kind were the ends designed; certain it is, that in productions of the highest order, or in very involved operations, *design* is not apparent to some meaner capacities. The master pieces, for instance, of music, sculpture, or painting; the delicate workmanship of a time-piece; the simple positions of the parts of a telescope; the wonders of the steam-engine;—might any or all of them upon being presented to an Esquimeaux Indian, merely occasion him to stare with an undefined astonishment; or if closer examination and reflection suggested that they were productions of more accomplished beings than himself, upon the friendly, or unfriendly exercise of whose powers, his well-being might depend, his anxiety might endeavour to hide itself under some such words as these: 'Ces merveilles meritent bien sans doute l'admiration de *nos esprits reflechies*: mais elles sont toutes dans les faits; on peut les celebrer avec toute la magnificence de notre langue; mais gardons nous bien d'admettre dans les causes rien d'étranger aux conditions necessaires de chaque existence.' 'Nulle part sans doute les moyens employés ne paraissent si clairement relatifs a la fin; cependant ce qu'il y a de sur, c'est que si les moyens n'avaient ici resulté necessairement *des lois generales, ces creatures* n'existeraient pas.'[2]

---

[1]   [Shepherd quotes Alexander Pope's 1731 poem 'Epistle to the Right Honourable Richard Earl of Burlington'.]

[2]   ['These marvels are undoubtedly well worth the admiration of our thoughtful minds; but they are, in fact; one can celebrate them with all the magnificence of our language; but let's guard well against admitting among their causes anything outside the necessary conditions of each existence.' 'Without a doubt, the means employed appear nowhere so clearly related to the end; however, what is certain is that if the means had not resulted necessarily from general laws, these creatures would not exist.' Shepherd paraphrases the work of the materialist

If in any case we mean to exercise an unbiased judgment, whether a mental foresight and design have been in action, we must begin *a posteriori* to consider the object, and examining some pieces of *apparent* workmanship, ask, if they are instruments and organs fitted and *designed* to ends or not? and if they do *seem* to be such, we ought to judge they are so; and *if* they are, no mechanical, or physical actions of mere matter will account for the mental quality of design. There must, no doubt, in every step of progress be efficient material causes for each various state; but amidst those material actions *somewhere* there must have been perception of possible qualities, and direction of motion in consequence.

Amidst the apparent contrivances which mortal beings have had no hand in arranging, it appears impossible to descry, or detect, the point where mind *perceived possible qualities*, and directed the aptitudes of various motions, but that mind must be the cause of that which the understanding concludes to be contrivance, is an argument, though short of demonstration, yet of the highest analogical proof; and one which determines our conduct in human affairs invariably, and irresistibly. The original intention, *with its effect*, the immediate direction of motion, may have commenced in the eternal mind at the beginning of this universe, or it may have existed through eternity, coeval with and essential to the Deity: As to which of these, we have no possibility of preferable conjecture; but the eye, and the heart, and the brain in animals; the sun, the earth, and the moon, amidst what is termed inanimate existence, and all things of a like kind must all have been matters of contrivance.

If any man looking at these, and the like objects with me, denies this, I need not compare my ideas with him. — Now all the efficient causes in the world put together, will not account for a mental result. We must have *the efficient cause* for the disposal of existences which are instruments and means to

---

philosopher Pierre J.G. Cabanis (*Rapports du physique et du moral de l'homme*, 2nd ed., vol. 2 [Paris: Imprimerie de Crapelet, 1805], pp. 531 and 516).]

ends. We must have intention of such, perception of qualities, direction of motion.

I consider, therefore, first, the appearance of design, that is to say, that which *reason* after examination admits to be the appearance of design, as the only proof of design; it is the only proof of it in human contrivances; and, secondly, that the argument is futile which would attempt to show, 'That the physical actions of matter being sufficient to account for the mere physical results which accompany such apparently designed results, the efficiency of INTENTION *in the direction of motion on matter*, is not needed.'[3] Because admitting for the sake of argument, there is no design, then the physical actions of matter must be allowed to account for, or be deemed the whole cause of the apparent contrivance; yet, on the other hand, admitting for the sake of argument, that there is design, still all the physical actions of matter *must be* same, and yet could not be deemed the whole cause of this apparent contrivance, for by the terms of the proposition, design is admitted as one. The efficiency, therefore, of physical cause is evidence neither for nor against design, but leaves it open to proof by analogy or otherwise.

Thus the examination of the actions of matter *a priori*, can never in any case form a criterion, whether design, mental perception, has been in action or not. Therefore, whether a circumstance be designed or not, must always be examined *a posteriori* and be judged of by a sound mind, observing its analogies, its tendencies, its bearings upon others, &c. If these favour the notion of design, we must conclude that *the mental perception*, which is the only efficient cause equal to that beginning and direction of motion which can accomplish contrivance, has been in action. *Detected, or detectable,* physical efficients *prove neither one side of the question nor the other;* because *in both cases* they are *equally* wanted towards *the mere physical* results taken notice of: the only difference is, that in *the one case* there must have been a

---

[3]   [I have been unable to locate a source for this passage. Given Shepherd's propensity for paraphrasing, it seems likely that this is not a direct quotation. She may have in mind the views of Baron d'Holbach in his 1770 *Système de la Nature* or his 1772 *Le bon sens ou idées naturelles opposes aux idées surnaturelles.*]

point where some mental perception directed the motions of matter: (an event not detectable amidst those motions); on the other, motion of matter must have directed the motion of matter through all eternity,—leaving its beginning and direction to have existed without any reason or intention whatever, although wherever we turn our eyes, different and independent kinds of matter coalesce to useful and important results.

Lord Bacon has been quoted as authority for rejecting the doctrine of final causes, as though he supposed it unnecessary to explain the motions of nature, and as fitted only to deceive the mind from physical enquiries. All that Bacon meant to say, or indeed did say, was, that it was equally ignorant and vulgar, idly to give design as the only reason for the physical properties beneath our view; for the interaction of different kinds of matter; and thus prevent *the analysis by experiment* of their physical properties, in different situations with respect to each other, as well as in relation to our senses.

Lord Bacon was a severe theist, and never imagined for a moment, but that a God had designed and arranged to given ends the whole of what we see around us. Lord Bacon, for instance, would have thought it ignorant, idle, and vulgar, were the physical *causes of* HEAT enquired into, to have it answered, that it arose from the spark *intentionally* communicated to a heap of wood. Nevertheless he could not deny in such a case that the intention to create a partial fire, and the means used towards it, were the one its final cause, the other, its efficient causes. Bacon admitted the mental ruler of motion in the immense ends contemplated in the universe, and the wise and efficient means which must have been used towards them.

But to say the truth, I much doubt if Bacon, or Newton, or any philosopher, has sufficiently considered the manner by which a final cause truly becomes an efficiently physical cause for the beginning and direction of motion. No doubt it is an answer 'barren' of every idea capable of yielding a notion that the question is properly understood, when the *reason* for the voluntary compounding of any aggregate of materials is given as a satisfactory answer to an enquiry into the nature, and the number of the materials used for such an aggregate; or, if the ends to which any parts have a tendency as means, be assigned as the given, physical efficient for each step of the means towards that end. On the other hand, all things in a strictly philosophical sense, form ONE NATURE, and it is impossible to see the *operations of nature* in a clear point of view, unless the manner be clearly perceived, by which final causes become identical with those which are efficient.

A final cause properly signifies the mental perception of an attainable end; the contemplation of a certain number of qualities, the determination of whose existence is known to be in the power of the efficient agent, by his voluntary direction of the motion of those already present with him. Thus *a final cause is the efficient cause that determines the will; and* WHICH WILL, *is the efficient cause that determines the direction of motion upon matter in any given case.*

In this sense, the whole forms one compound PHYSICAL *efficient cause, without which* EVERY ENDEAVOUR *to explain the different directions of motion which we perceive in the world would be* NUGATORY. We might, for instance, in vain lay out to observation every *material* motion, which could be detected by the senses, or by the nicest experiments, and all the general laws as they are called of physical attributes, whether mechanical or chemical, in order to account for the powers by which a bird at first exerts herself, and for the path in which she directs her flight; if her perception of the intention to build her nest, and of the place where the materials lay; if the inherent nature she possesses of a capacity capable of perception; if the interfering causes capable of exciting it, were omitted in the examination of the *physical causes* for the beginning and direction of her motions. In this sense *final* is nothing more than *a name* for a compound set of PHYSICAL EFFICIENT CAUSES, undetectable by the organs of sense, but known of by experience of their very *essence* and *primeval nature in themselves*, and by *reason* and *analogy* to be exercised in other similar beings, as alone capable of yielding those appearances of contrivance and design of which we take notice, and of forming the conception of those wise ends we every where perceive around us, and which appear to be gained by appropriate, various, complicate, and elective means.[4]

---

4   See Recapitulation. [See pp. 158–68 in this volume.]

If we direct our views from the contemplation of the ends attained by animated nature, and look abroad upon the material motions, and the effects which they determine in the inanimate universe, we also every where perceive appearances of designed ends to have been held in view, and of means of accomplishment to have been used towards them, incomparably more numerous, more difficult of arrangement, and of a larger comprehension than these.

It is in vain therefore, to invent the word *attraction*, as though it were *alone* sufficient to express the whole of the physical causes known for the beginning and direction of the motions we see. It is a word as well suited as any other to express the *effect*, the direction of the motion of *bodies towards each other*, according to those laws of velocity which given densities observe; but to imagine there is a certain given physical quality in all matter, which makes it endeavour to *draw* other *matter* at a distance towards it, which in its turn possesses *the physical quality to be drawn* in that direction, is to invest matter by the deceptious use of a metaphor with a mental quality, while yet *no consciousness* is supposed. It is in this sense a mere hypothesis; no organ of sense ever detected it; no experiment ever found it; no reasoning ever deduced it from admitted premises; the laboratory of the chymist never elicited it from any convincing trial; — on the contrary, so far as the conception of the mind can frame such an one, let it be done. — Let two balls be supposed, of the relative sizes and densities of the sun and moon; — and to be placed at the same relative distance in a state of *complete rest* in an exhausted receiver, with *empty space* alone between them; is it imagined for a moment they would ever begin to move, and direct their motions towards each other after any *law of attraction* whatever? They could not, — for the causes being efficient to *rest*, they could not be also efficient to motion. And if it be said the bodies were not or could not be *at rest*, then they were in motion — but motion is not *attraction*, and the motion supposed, still lies in need of being accounted for, both in its beginning and direction.

It may be thought bold to venture any objection to the Newtonian theory; let it, however, be remembered, that I am speaking of Bacon's method of philosophizing. He wished to introduce observation of, and experiments upon nature, before he assigned physical and proximate causes for any given fact, instead of hypothetical occult modes of action; or the ends, instead of the means. I therefore say, that the Newtonian doctrine of attraction is contrary to Bacon's mode of philosophizing; I am aware the Newtonians shift their ground when it is said, '*the principle stated for the motions of the universe is but an hypothesis*'; they retort, 'the word is merely used as standing for *the effect*, for the motions we see, and the laws they observe'; to which sense I am willing the word should be applied;—but in the original Newtonian meaning, it signifies a *quality, an attribute of all matter as matter*, by which it *begins* and *directs* the motions of bodies according to their densities, at a distance from each other; and that they can do this with empty space alone between them. To which doctrine I would oppose, that the existence of such a quality is a mere hypothesis, not to be detected by observation of the senses, or by the experiments of the laboratory, or imagined by a mental conception of possibilities.

The beginning and direction of motion among what we term *inanimate bodies* has still therefore to be accounted for; and I much doubt whether any notice of the senses, any trial of the receiver, the retort, or the cylinder, any mental conception of a possible experiment, will yield to us the true knowledge, of the causes for the beginning, the direction, and the continuance of the magnificent operations we have it in our power to contemplate, rather than to understand.

The most that I would contend for on the subject is this, that we should reason with impartiality from what we know, to what we know not. To consider things as probable to be like, which appear so; to refer such like effects to like proximate causes, however such proximate causes may be united with different aggregates of qualities;—with *beings* not in relation to our senses or *experimental* observations.

Keeping to so simple a mode of reasoning as this, the ends, and apparent contrivances we perceive in nature must have had their final causes; must have been effected by reason of the mental perceptions which yielded to some mind those results of the understanding, and that determination of will, which were necessary to discover and to direct all the efficient motions towards the phenomena in the universe.

When so much of intention must have had its share of physical impulse in some time and place, whilst the nature of matter in general, and different kinds of it in particular, is for ever hidden from our scrutiny, and on which such intention must have operated; how is it possible that we should ever arrive in this world by the few inlets of knowledge we possess, at the true causes for the whole physical phenomena in the motions we perceive in any given case. *Attraction* is a word fitted to keep the Deity forever out of view; and I freely confess it often suggests to my mind an idea as ludicrous, as the supposed quality to which it is applied appears to be futile. It suggests qualities in matter which are only consistent with a capacity for sensation; and when it is used with respect to inanimate objects is but of metaphorical application. Its direct meaning expresses a mental perception, a determination of the will, governed by the approbation of qualities belonging to the object of attraction.

To transpose therefore, the word which is expressive of this kind of *drawing* towards each other, to the motions of matter, as though the conversion of a term could suggest any defined idea of the true nature of governing causes, is merely to hide an unproved hypothesis by means of a metaphorical allusion. — The assignation of this occult quality, as forming a component part of the very essence of matter, has afforded to atheism its most powerful refuge. When other arguments have failed, the attractions and *repulsions*[5] of matter, elective attractions, &c. are assumed as *efficient causes* in each step of the progress which forms an animal, or that governs the motions of a planetary system, and no other is supposed requisite to account for those grand and beautiful designs.[6] When such an *experimentum crucis* shall be made, as that parcels of matter of different bulks, shall at a distance from each other, with empty space alone between them, and being forcibly placed at rest for a moment, be afterwards left at perfect liberty, without any foreign impulse on either towards motion, *and without their being affected by the*

---

[5] When bodies start off from one another, then attraction as a quality of matter as a component part of its essence, is obliged to be given up; and the *repulsion* of particles (its very contrary) is assigned as the *efficient cause* of the *particular motions* of matter so affected. In what sense then is it possible that attraction can be called a general quality or law?

[6] I allude here to a well known French author. [Shepherd may mean Baron d'Holbach, author of the 1770 *Système de la nature*.]

motions of the earth, of which they are forming a part; when in such a case, they shall bound *towards* each other, then shall I believe in an inherent quality as capable of such a propulsion, but till then, I feel it to be impossible:—I say *forcibly* held to rest, because, if attraction be the quality described, all things would ever be running towards each other, and eventually form but one being, unless there were opposing forces, which must in their turn have an extraneous cause. Also if the *inherent* capacities of matter are equal to motion, they cannot likewise ALONE *be equal to rest*. And if equal to rest, they cannot ALONE *be equal to motion*; because I trust, that I have proved, that every *various effect* must have its cause. An *exact experiment*, however, could never be made, because the earth's motion must affect all the bodies on it—and the *forced* rest would only be a relative state. The moment the balls were left at liberty, they must be acted upon in some way, by the swift motion of the greater ball on which they were called forth to exhibit their minor movements.

But it must be *rest* which is the natural state of matter, and it must be motion which requires an extraneous cause:—because rest does not suppose motion, but MOTION implies REST;—for the difference between the times of the respective velocities of any two given bodies, over a given space, is equal to the *rest* of that which has been the slowest, during the time of the differ- ence. Rather, therefore, than refer the beautiful arrangements of the heavens and the earth to the occult, unproved qualities of attraction and gravitation, I would chuse to attribute the beginning and direction of their motions to causes analogous to those with which I am acquainted. Then it is that a grand feeling bursts upon the mind.—A cause in action like in kind to that which I know of, but different in degree, and which may account for the origin of all the motions in the universe, and all their directions towards the designed ends, which in every various manner take place in the infinite and eternal universe— such an adequate and efficient cause as this suggests a con- ception commensurate with the Deity it demonstrates, and compels an unlimited worship of his unbounded essence.

Six

Mind and Body

Selection J

(Excerpted from *Essays on the Perception of an External Universe* [1827], pp. 152–9.)

Chapter 7: Application of the Doctrine Contained in the Preceding Essay to the Evidence of Our Belief in Several Opinions

Section 2

The knowledge of our own independent existence – how gained.

Again, the idea of our own independent existence is generated by observing, that the compound mass we term SELF can exist when we do not observe it; and we have thus the *idea* of our own existence, in that it needs must CONTINUE to exist when *unperceived*, as well as during the *sensation* of it when perceived. Besides, on this subject, as every other, it is to the *causes* for the *constant* effects, (the objects whose union shall bear out similar results), to which there is a tacit reference as the *true* and *continued existences in nature*: –

Now the *causes* for the general powers of sensation cannot be the same as those for any particular sensation, and so must be independent of each;[1] and indeed each sensation is always *felt* as an effect, as '*beginning to be*'; therefore what we allude to as *self*, is a continued existing capacity in nature, (unknown, unperceived), fitted to revive when suspended in sleep, or otherwise, and to keep up during the periods of watchfulness the powers of life and consciousness, especially those which

---

[1] See p. 83, 84, 'It is such a perception', &c. [See p. 130 in this volume.]

determine the union of memory with sense. For as sensation is interrupted, and is an *effect*; the original cause must be uninterrupted; and such an uninterrupted cause as is equal to keep up the life of the body, or mass deemed our own body, and to unite it under that form with the powers of memory and sense: Identity, therefore, has nothing to do with *sameness of particles*, but only has relation to those powers in nature (flowing from that continuous Being the God of Nature) which are capable of giving birth to that constant effect, the *sense of continuous existence*; which sense, when analysed, is the union of the *ideas of memory*, with the *impressions of present sense*. Should it be objected that the causes for such an union might be interrupted; then as these would '*begin their existences*', and would *only be effects*, the mind would go backwards till it reposed in some *uninterrupted* cause, and would consider such, and such only, as an independent capacity in nature, fitted to excite the union of memory with present sense, and as the complicate being *self*; which when conscious, could take notice of its existence, and when unconscious (as in sound sleep) could exist *independently of its own observation*.

Section 3

Observations on the essential difference between body and mind.

Hence also may be seen all the *essential difference* between *body* and *mind*;—BODY is the *continually exciting cause*, for the exhibition of the perception of *extension* and *solidity* on the mind in particular; and MIND is the CAPACITY or CAUSE, for *sensation in general*. And these two must be different in 'their proportions among themselves', (in their unperceived state), as well as in their '*positive values*' in their perceived state.[2] Now whether these *causes* or capacities can exist separate from each other, is the question which is always asked, and still remains unanswered in philosophy. Abstractedly there seems no hindrance for such separate existence. *Practically*, sensation in *general is never known, but in company with that* which excites the *sensation of extension in particular*, and which seems so much *a part* of the *whole* causes *necessary* for sensation in general, that

---

2   See p. 38. [See p. 111 in this volume.]

under the form and action of the brain, it only seems capable of being elicited. Still we know not whether in many other beings, sensations may not go on without brain, and whether, where ideas have once been generated through its means, some other causes in nature may not be equal to keeping them up — analogous to the power there is in this state of being, by which we recollect the images of colours, and sounds; of beings, or virtues, &c. &c. without the use of those organs of sense, which were at first necessary to the formation of such notions. [...]

I confess I think the further we extend our views into the regions of metaphysics, the more possible and probable does the resurrection from the dead appear; or at least an existence analogous to it. For it is evident, more is wanted for the capacity for sensation in general, than that exterior cause which is necessary or the exhibition of *extension in particular*; which extension in many varieties appears *insentient*. Various effects must have *proportional* causes, and therefore there must be some extraneous reason for sentiency, beyond what is absolutely necessary for mere insentient extension; — Yet it has been said, extension seems to form a *part* at least of that combination of powers which elicits sentiency. Now if the causes for sentiency, *minus* the brain, find in the great womb of nature, any other cause equal to the brain, a finer body, an ethereal stimulus, or any thing which may *help to unite memory with sense*, then the difficulty attending the notion of the resurrection vanishes.

It would appear therefore equally inconclusive for man to argue against the possibility of a future life on account of the dispersion of the particles of the present gross body by death, as for the worm[3] to suppose it could not again live because its outside crust wholly perishes: — He might resist every notion (however prompted by his instinct or his wishes) of an exist-ence beyond the range of his present experience, beyond the extent of the leaf on which he is born to die; yet the time would equally arrive, when as a winged insect he would roam through boundless space in comparison of the circumscribed spot to which his former existence was confined, and chase the brilliant image of himself, through a live-long summer's day, amidst the sweets of a thousand flowers.

---

3   worm] caterpillar.

Man in his present state, feels occasional aspirations towards another, prompted by the craving want of some unknown unimaginable good, of which he has no intimation but from the consciousness of an unsatisfied capacity: — Let him not then too easily reject the belief that this capacity has a corresponding object, that his nature is capable of a nobler modification, a higher flight in more exalted regions than this, and enlarged as to every power of action, thought, and enjoyment.

Selection K

(Excerpted from *Essays on the Perception of an External Universe* [1827], pp. 372–92.)

Essay 10: The Reason Why We Cannot Conceive of Sensation as Existing Necessarily, and Continuously by Itself

Section 1

The general power of sensation contrasted with that which is particular: — its connection with immortality.

It is difficult to perceive the ground of our belief in the continuous existence of something, the subject matter of all changing sensations, and why that something must be other than continuous sensation itself. I believe this opinion is not owing to any unreasonable or accidental association of ideas; but to have its ground in those simple modes of the under-standing which are only of difficulty in the detection, because they are too simple to be capable of much analysis, and have from the most early habits of thought, become so much a part of our very being, that they do not admit of the recollection of their commencement. Nevertheless I consider the fact as indisputable, namely, that we cannot conceive of sensation existing in, and by itself, and therefore, that there must be a cause for this opinion.[4] Let us endeavour to find what it is, and whether when found, it can be substantiated by reason, or,

---

4   Mr. Reid and Mr. D. Stewart regard this idea as an ultimate fact, or instinctive belief.

whether it must be rejected as some fallacy, generated rather by an association, than concluded from a comparison of ideas.

The first and original reason for this opinion, is justly founded in that notion which forms the primeval law of the understanding, '*that no quality can begin* its own existence'.

Had there been but one simple quality in existence, and that at rest, no other could ever have been deduced from it: for there could have been no interference, no producing cause, whereby another might have been created. Now, although we do in our experience know of a stream of conscious sensation kept up at intervals for many hours, and therefore it might be supposed that we could imagine such in a superior nature, to be continued without sleep; and thus sensation, simple sensation, exist in and by itself without interruption;—yet let it be remembered, that during any state of continued conscious sensation, the whole is compounded of parts of different kinds: there exists a succession of different sensations, (simple or compound), each of which in its turn vanishes; therefore as each vanishes, all vanish, and sensation could have no reason for its existence, unless a continuous being existed, indifferent to sensation, capable of being excited when interfered with, by appropriate qualities fitted to produce it.—Such a being is the subject of successive sensation,—such is a capacity for sensation,—such is mind. The interfering beings may be called organs or any thing else; but the continuous capacity for sensation alone is mind. Its nature we cannot tell. Its essence cannot be *matter*, or the quality of solid extension simply, because *all* matter does not *feel* with the same *interferences*. If a stone be thrown from a height, it does not suffer pain; but if there be a quality so far inhering as a dormant capacity in all matter, that being placed under certain supposed conditions, and fitly interfered with, it will feel; still that continuous capacity to sensation is a being properly termed mind;—If on the contrary, it be a quality which has its own appropriate extension as ready to be interfered with by fit organs, much more does it seem to merit that appellation, as one used in contradistinction to every other kind of extension whatever:—In either case, *the organs* or qualities which excite a *variety* of sensations, are no more the one continuous being which feels, than the hands of a watch that mark the hour, form the essence of time, or than the instruments which serve to keep alive a partial flame, are of the nature of eternal heat.

It is here that the materialists err, — they can make no distinction between the nature and use of those organs which are necessary towards the eliciting each sensation in particular, from the *continuous* power which must exist as a totally different being, as a complete variety of essence from that of the solidity, the extension, and the action of such interfering organs. — These may be wanted either as *interferers*, or as instruments fitted to generate some peculiar quality of matter in a more appropriate relation to the capacity of sensation than themselves, but they are not the mysterious eternal power of feeling, which has been conveyed to each animal as its inheritance from the commencement of its species; and which as a continuous existence must be an eternal power in nature, and as immortal for the future, as it must have been without beginning in the past.

It may be modified by methods of infinite interferences — but its essence is one, and for ever. Memory of sensations in the rounds of time may be obliterated or retained, according to the mysterious and occult laws which govern the interferences; — but the capacity, the being, which can respond to joy or sorrow; can be lofty or degraded; can be wise or foolish; can be '*the first-born of all things*',[5] or the crawling insect; can 'understand' *the imaginary motions* of 'fluxions',[6] — or being fastened to the rock, possess no powers of motion, even of the simplest kind, whereby to resist or escape the influence of the surrounding wave; — this subject matter for each variety of sentient perception, or action, must for ever exist: it may, for aught *we can demonstrate*, retain its individual consciousness of personality, communicated to it by particular interferences as in man, or be lost in the eternal ocean of mind: it may, under such modification, be improved and go on in a state of moral amelioration from the smallest touches of instinctive affection towards the first of its own kind which it acknowledged, to the perception of all the charities of friendship, and kindred, as preliminary to the consummation of angelic love hereafter; or be absorbed

---

5   [Col. 1:15.]
6   fluxion] In Newton's calculus, the rate of change of a varying quantity.

amidst the properties only subservient to animal existences. — Still the invisible, but demonstrated existence, must live for ever; it may be interfered with more or less, — it may be modified more or less, by all kinds of organs and their powers; — but its essence is one, and for ever.

The proper question, therefore, concerning the immortality of the soul, is not whether it can survive the body as a continuous existence — for it must be eternally independent of any particular set of organs in past, as in future time. — But the enquiry should be, whether when the organs which are in relation to any individual capacity, undergo the change called DEATH, if the *continuing mental* capacity become simple in its aptitudes again, or, whether it remain so far in an altered state by what it has gone through in the present life, that it continues as the result of that modification? Whether from any other interfering powers than those of the visible body, memory and sense shall be elicited; or whether a total variety from any memory shall be the result and consequence of its former state, — analogous to the powers of knowledge which fetal consciousness yields to infancy, and infancy to manhood, without conscious *memory occurring* as an intervening cause? — Whether as a dormant capacity it remain unexcited and unconscious of existence during eternity, or, whether amidst the infinite changes of duration it shall start into life, under the modification of appropriate interfering qualities?

The *latter* supposition is a resurrection from the dead, is the life of the same mind anew excited; whilst the *previous* suppositions imply those states of mental existence so much discussed by the different sects of philosophers: for almost all men and nations have perceived with more or less distinctness, that the *subject matter* of their changing sensations *could never die.*

That a total obliteration of feeling should take place when there is a capacity for it, is contradicted by the analogy of nature, though we may not be able to demonstrate the contrary; — powers of change amongst organs perpetual motions in nature fitted to act as interferers, are around and about us visibly, and invisibly.

Also, by the laws of the same analogy every thing is progressive; every thing, (whether designedly so or not, is not now the question), is a means to an end. That moral capacities and improvements; superior benevolent feelings of some above others; the higher acquirements of intelligence; the completion of virtuous habits, &c. should have no connexion with that portion of the eternal mind which has been allotted to the species called man in the ages of futurity, seems contradicted by that analogy.

This argument appears to me to be as far as philosophy is capable of going. It demonstrates the essential eternity of all mind; it renders probable any given state of it, as connected with any after state in the relation of cause and effect; whether with or without the revival of memory, and thus must to every candid enquiring mind offer a very strong presumption in favour of the testimonies of tradition, (to call revealed religion by no higher name, for the present). If any one should conceive the analogy of nature not to be maintained by the supposition of the possible extinction of memory in after life, let it be recollected that the infant remembers not its state before birth, nor the young child the state of infancy, nor the full grown man that of the very young child; yet that each of these mental states improves by what it has learnt in knowledge, (*if not in virtue*), from that which immediately preceded it:—All the ideas of simple, sensible qualities; of colour, figure, sound, and taste; of heat and cold, hardness and softness, smoothness and roughness; of rest and motion;—all axioms termed *'mental laws of belief'*, as well as many which are the foundations of science; such as, 'There must be existence in order to feel'; 'Things do not make themselves'; 'We ourselves and the causes of our feelings are not the same beings'; 'The whole is greater than its part'; 'Equals added to equals the wholes are equal',—with the converse of that proposition; the original feelings and all the principal associated emotions of self-love; the chief features of the grammar of a language, with names assigned to most of the objects of sense, and many *abstract* ideas; in short the foundations of all knowledge, and the ability to express it, are acquired at a time, which does not by any method transfer the memory of the impressions by which the knowledge gained was acquired; although its result, the memory of these ideas, be united to every new impression which then arises.

Therefore, in like manner as the child must assuredly be born though the fetus know it not, and man be in possession of ideas whose source is hidden from him, so may there in succeeding ages arise from the ashes of this, another universe connected with it as its natural effect and consequence: — Then every sentient power it may elicit, every single thought each various being may possess; every capacity which shall then be demonstrated, may be the results of the present universe of thought, will, passion, suffering, or joy; ignorance or knowledge, virtue or vice, faith or profaneness; and that perhaps without any acquaintance being imparted to it of the former state on which its then destination shall hang. On the other hand, we are all aware of the analogies in favour of conscious memory hereafter, from the conscious memory of man through youth and manhood, of transactions during those periods.

Under the balance of these analogies the testimony of scripture in favour of the renewal of conscious memory is as a casting die, which to any man who reasons as a philosopher, must affect his judgment.

I am convinced there are many whose understandings take this view of the subject, notwithstanding they may permit themselves considerable latitude in their reflection on it. As for myself, though I think that, independent of the inference from scripture, the reunion of memory to future consciousness presents no philosophical difficulty, yet I could be well content in the trust that, the enquiry for truth should be rewarded by the finding it, whether the present labour in its search be remembered or not; that the charity which sympathizes in witnessing pain, should be enlarged only to promote or to delight in the perception of pleasure, whether former misery be obliterated from the fancy, or not; — that an instinctive devotion towards God should meet with higher demonstrations of his presence than our faint conceptions here are able to embrace, though the satisfaction arising from the comparison should be then denied; and that the conflict here with doubt, difficulty, suffering, temptation, and the observation of evil, should terminate as well as the memory of it, in the personal consciousness, and the notice of surrounding happiness; in a secure and perpetual possession of truth; in the love and the enjoyment of the practice of every noble and kindly virtue.

Essay 11: On the Immateriality of Mind

Sensation as a simple quality contrasted with that of solid exten-sion. – Its power to begin and direct motion. – Application to Deity.

But there is still another reason for considering sensation as a simple quality incapable of existing *in itself* and *by itself*; which is, that though it does not occupy space as solid extension, yet it has a necessary relation to space, by requiring space in which to exist. In this light each particular sensation must be the unextended quality of some kind of extension, whether con-sidered as empty space, or as solid matter; or as some form of extended being not detectable by any organ of sense. If for argument's sake, there should be supposed to exist one hundred square feet of empty space, and ten sensations at any moment within that boundary,—those ten sensations would appear as a component part, or affection of that space during such time, and they would together form one being. If again during each succeeding moment for an hour, ten sensations of a different kind from the ten preceding ones, should successively arise, that space would as the substratum, or continuous exist-ence of which the sensations were the varieties, be the subject matter of which they were the changes. Now instead of empty space, of *nothing*, which never could be rendered a *something* fraught with every changing sentient quality by any inter-ference whatever,—let there be that mysterious *something* capable of feeling, offering no solidity to touch, no impenetra-bility to resistance, no colour, nor sound, nor taste, smell, or other quality to the observation of any sense;—let it be equally as extended as empty space, as little of matter as that unresisting, equally diffused medium would be in any given place—but let the *capacity* to feel exist in its own extraordinary essence; let such be within the given compass of any individual organization, and this substance would exist as the capacity of an individual mind. Its power may be perfectly simple, or it may possess fit aptitudes to retain the impressions once made on it, independently of the organs; but certain it is that its *simple perceptions* of happiness or utility direct the motions of matter, and that the union of sentient and insentient qualities is so intimate as to coalesce, and together to form the physical efficient cause of the beginning and direction of motion amidst the powers of nature; and that in a manner which is not capable of being discovered by any sense, or instruments in our power: — so perfectly *one*[7] is it, indeed, with the powers of matter, with whose mechanical actions it *interferes*, that were it not for their own experience, our modern atheists might deny its perception of ends, and its direction of means, as final and efficient causes amidst the motions they witness.[8]

Let not any one think from what I have advanced that the mind and consciousness of Deity are put in doubt by this reasoning; so far from it, the ideas really contain a demonstration of his essence, and the steps towards it are few, and short, — since we perceive instruments in existence which are means to ends, there must be the director of motion, the *perceiver of ends*, the former of instruments in the universe; — perception of ends and direction of means, are mental qualities; are the properties of the continued existence, called mind; mind therefore must have been at the fountain head of these contrivances; but not a mind whose existence is more invisible than that of our own minds to each other; although experience informs us, that the great, the universal mind which must have executed these works is not united to any small defined body with which we can become acquainted by our senses; therefore it is a hidden mind, although we know of its existence, by means of REASON. As mind, its eternal continuous capacity is demonstrable by the same argument as that of all minds. The capacities for being must be eternal; — changes may vary, but *the subject* for changes is eternal, and can have derived its original essence from no previous change.

The universal mind, the infinite space for his residence, the amalgamation of all possible qualities in nature in One Being necessarily existing, — the capacity of perceiving all ideas executed in his own mind by the eternal, necessary, and essential union of such qualities as are fitted to the consciousness of all future knowledge, the circumference, towards which is propelled every direction of motion which forms the

---

7   See note, p. 312. [See p. 86 n70 in this volume.]
8   See preceding Essay, p. 360, also, the following Essay, pp. 404 and 405. [See p. 234 in this volume. Essay 12 is not included in this volume.]

creatures,[9]—this is God, as far as our natures can contemplate such an awful, infinite, and invisible being.

Let it not be retorted, that it is easier to conceive of all the little changing beings we know of, as existing without a creator than of such a being; for I answer, it is *not* easier so to think; the one side of the dilemma involves a contradiction, the other does not; the one is to imagine the existence of a series of dependent effects without a continuous being of which they are the qualities, and is equal to the supposition of the possibility of every thing springing up as we see it, from an absolute blank and nonentity of existence; the other is the result of referring like effects to like causes. The one is to regard each little being we know of, as the strange appearance of contrivance without design, and of being at once a series of changes in relation to no end, though apparently directed to it; the other is to believe in the infinite universe of mind, matter, space, and motion, eternally and necessarily existing: generating the creation of all minor existences in every form and kind that is possible, through the rounds of ceaseless time.[10]

The author hopes it will be understood that the object of these latter essays is to answer certain atheistical opinions to be found in various writers; and not to arrange a system of theological philosophy, or to attempt an improvement of those stronger arguments in favour of Deity, which have been advanced by abler hands.

Selection L

(Excerpted from *An Essay Upon the Relation of Cause and Effect* [1824], pp. 162–73.)

---

9   See Paley's Theo., pp. 301, 302. [Shepherd likely refers to Chapter 24 of William Paley, *Natural Theology: Or, Evidences of the Existence and Attributes of the Deity, Collected from the Appearances of Nature* (London: R. Faulder, 1802).]

10 See note on matter, p. 401. [Not included in this volume.]

Chapter the Fifth: Observation on Mr. Lawrence's Lectures[11]

[...]

Section the Fourth

Now as the muscle and nerve can and do exist as organized beings, without irritability and sentiency when under death, so when as substances, they are placed under that condition called *life*, and are then only capable of putting on these qualities of irritability and sentiency, it must be by a *truly necessary connexion*, between life and these qualities. Irritability and sentiency are verily new powers and beings *created* by efficient, *creating* circumstances. *Sensation* and all its variety, is not an effect without a cause; and *life* is that object without which it will not exist in the *nerve*; and therefore according to the doctrine laid down in this Essay, is a true cause for it: being *one* of the objects *absolutely necessary* and efficient to *that* result in *certain circumstances*; — although what the WHOLE of those conditions may be, the *combination* of which is needful, may possibly ever remain beyond the scrutiny of man. Should Mr. Lawrence retort, that the phrase 'the living nerve', stands *merely* as a *sign* of enumerated *qualities* and properties found together, in the way that I have said *gold* may stand as a *sign* for those that lie under that term; that it is in this sense he compares the two propositions concerning them; and in this sense, he alleges there is no difference in the evidence for the *only kind* of necessary connexion there exists between an *object* and its properties?

I answer the very statement of the proposition 'the *living nerve* is *sentient*', *assigns a cause* and *producing principle* for sensation; for by placing an adjective before a noun, it becomes a *qualified noun*. And the qualities beneath the whole term are a mass of *altered* qualities, which alteration, is alleged to be *efficient* to the production of a new mode of existence; viz. that of sensation.

---

[11]   [Shepherd refers to William Lawrence, *Lectures on Physiology, Zoology, and the Natural History of Man, Delivered at the Royal College of Surgeons* (London: Printed for J. Callow, 1819). Hereafter cited as *Lectures*.]

Thus (to use a familiar illustration) the saying a *bilious* man is *choleric*, assigns bile as the *cause* of anger, and it would be puerile after such a proposition, to add, that 'however strong the feeling may be, that there is the close bond of Cause and Effect between these objects, yet it is a mistake to suppose it.'[12] This would but be a subsequent denial of *what the statement previously asserted.*

Whereas *gold*, or any other noun, when it stands as a sign for any collection of qualities, and properties; is neither a cause nor an object; it is a word, a *name* merely, and when thus placed as the subject of a proposition, of which the qualities stand as the predicate, signifies, that, by such a name, shall such masses, being found together and set apart from other collections, be signified.[13]

This distinction between a *qualified*, and *unqualified* noun, on account of the different *nature* of the *connexion* of the predicate of the proposition, with its subject, Mr. Lawrence did not take notice of; or he would not have thought 'there was not the faintest shade of difference'[14] between the two propositions he states, in this respect.

[...]

Section the Fifth

[...]

[...] there must be causes for every thing, and sometimes *a vast multitude of objects are wanted*, before their *mutual bearings* and *mixtures* with each other operate so as to *produce* any peculiar existence. The highest, and the greatest we know of is, *sensation, and its varieties*; and although we know that life is *wanted* as a *cause* without which it cannot exist in *this world in*

---

12 [Shepherd paraphrases Lawrence, *Lectures*, p. 70.]
13 See Locke's Essay in several places, especially Book 3, Chap. 8, Sec. 2. compared with Chap. 9, Sec. 12, 13, and 17, and Chap. 10, Sec. 20, 21, and 22. [Shepherd refers to John Locke, *An Essay Concerning Human Understanding*, ed. Peter H. Nidditch (Oxford: Clarendon Press, 1975), 3.8.2 (pp. 474–5); 3.9.12–13 and 3.9.17 (pp. 482–3 and 485–6); and 3.10.20–22 (pp. 501–4). Hereafter cited as *Essay*, followed by book, chapter, and section numbers, with page numbers.]
14 [Shepherd quotes Lawrence, *Lectures*, p. 70.]

the nervous system; yet we have no notion of *all* the objects that may be necessary to its creation.

[...]

Now the truth is, that nature affords not experiment, or data enough to show, what are the *whole* causes necessary; i.e. *all* the objects required, whose *junction* is necessary to *sentiency as the result*. — For as the words *life*, and *nerve*, stand only for a few sensible qualities, whereby they affect us; so does it appear there is no existing definition of them, no possible experiment which can be made on their nature, sufficient to afford premises wide enough to admit the conclusion, that sentiency shall result from their conjunction only, and shall not be able to exist without them.

Section the Seventh[15]

If indeed the powers of matter in general, (whatever matter may be), were sufficient to elicit sentiency when placed under *arrangement* and mixed with life, then the true causes for it are assigned, and found. But we cannot *prove* this. If on the contrary, the essential qualities of matter arranged and in motion be not thought sufficient to account for so extraordinary a difference as that between conscious and unconscious being, then there must be a *particular* cause for it: which cause must be considered an immaterial cause, that is, a *principle, power, being,* an unknown quality *denied* to exist in matter. — This must have a name, and may be called *soul,* or *spirit*. And this statement, really contains the whole argument either way. It is on this point, that not only *here*, but in an after Lecture ('on the functions of the brain'[16]) Mr. Lawrence betrays a want of philosophical precision, by denying that any cause beyond the brain is necessary to thought, on account of the impossibility of assigning the *time* of its union with the body; whereas a Cause must have originally been necessary, upon the creation of man, for the phenomenon in question; and the capacity of sensation may, as a component part of the whole animal mass, be always generated with it, yet retain its individuality, after having once

---

15   [This section is misnumbered; it is in fact the sixth section in Chapter 5.]
16   [Shepherd refers to a section in Lawrence's fourth lecture (*Lectures*, pp. 90–100).]

been formed with each being;—analogous to the whole plan of nature, in other respects;—analogous to the physical individuality of all the millions of mankind, each of which was formed of the general clay;—analogous to the separate, and particular properties, which wait upon the differences of vegetable life, where every various plant is expanded from similar juices.

But I must be true to my own doctrine in all its bearings; and as I have said, that in order to form the *proximate cause* of any event, *a junction or mutual mixture of all* the objects *necessary to it must take place;* so I conceive it to be impossible, but that a *distinct* and *different* action of the brain (without which organ there is no sensation in man, and all thought is but a mode of it) must be *synchronous* with whatever other powers are also necessary for that result; viz. sensation and thought with their varieties. I say, the junction must be *synchronous*—for sensation is an *effect*, and must require the union of those objects whose mixed qualities elicit it.

Now those causes *not* contained in matter, may be called mind, or soul. I have said also, that a different action of brain is wanted for *each variety of thought and sensation;* and so it must, because there must be a *separate* or different cause, for every *separate or diverse* Effect in nature, as before discussed. And thus the brain becomes the *exponent of the soul;* or is *in the same proportion in its actions,* as the actions of mind: and thus what is termed *association of ideas,* must have *corresponding unions,* in the actions of the brain.

Now Mr. Lawrence contradicts at once his own arguments for materialism, as well as nature, and fact; when he says (tauntingly) 'thus we come to diseases of an immaterial being! for which suitably enough *moral* treatment has been recommended',[17] inferring thereby the *absurdity of mental treatment,* to a *material mind.*

Now moral treatment, according to his *own notion* of *only a material* capacity for thought, might still be proper, as it would still act on that *material capacity for thought,*—and though 'arguments, syllogisms, and sermons',[18] might not reach it, of

---

17   [Shepherd quotes Lawrence, *Lectures*, p. 97.]

18   [Shepherd quotes Lawrence, *Lectures*, p. 99.]

an *ordinary* kind; yet, the persuasions of friendship; the influence of beauty, and of love; the pleasures of social intercourse; the calm discussions of reason; scenes that please the imagination, or enchant the sense, will reach it, and do. Nevertheless all this is *'moral treatment'*, and which yet requires the brain and nervous system. In short, to address the mind is to address the body, which *instantly* acts along and with it, not *after* it. And to address the body is to address the mind—for *every sensation*, however popularly called *bodily*; requires *mind*, equally with thought as a cause for it, and is not merely to be considered as a simple being, or feeling, beginning and ending in itself; but as intimately *associating with those of a* LIKE KIND, *which certain* THOUGHTS *are capable of exciting, and as having, therefore, a most material agency, when first in order, by suggesting such specific thoughts.*—This mode of thinking on the subject I know not that any have sufficiently heeded, much less cultivated.

[...]

Chapter the Sixth

[...]

Section the Third

[...] Without life in the parents, the organs could not have been formed; and without life they cannot act in their juxtaposition, upon the surrounding *elements*, either before or after birth, in order to their growth and support. Yet when life is once *given*, the *use of the organs is absolutely necessary to keep it up.*

Thus combustible matters may be heaped upon each other, yet neither warmth nor light succeed; but let an *'extra cause'* kindle the pile, then the flame may be kept alive for ever, by the constant addition of such substances.—In like manner life as we find it, as a perpetual flame, must be kept up and transmitted, whilst the proper objects for its support are administered; but for its original *Cause*, we must go back, until some extraneous power is referred to as its first parent. It is an *Effect*; it begins to be in all we know and have known, yet it is wanted in its own turn as a cause, and as a quality already in being, to mix and unite with the gross elements of brute matter, for the formation and continuance of all animated nature.

We are told that '*God breathed into man the breath of life*',[19] and here philosophy supports Scripture, for the organs must origin-ally have been kindled into life by a power, equal to giving them that internal vigour and motion, capable of enabling them to act afterwards for themselves, upon the objects which surrounded them. Then the living lungs could play upon the air, the living stomach be hungry and assimilate its food, the living heart beat, and the living blood circulate through every vein, and become capable of transmitting *the principle* communicated to it, to similar natures, without any assignable termination.

[...]

---

[19]   [Gen. 2:7.]

Seven

Vision

Selection M

(Excerpted from *Essays on the Perception of an External Universe* [1827], pp. 408–16.)

Essay 14: On the Reason Why Objects Appear Single Although Painted on Two Retinas, and Why They Appear Erect Although the Images Be Inverted on Them

It has long been a matter of great surprise to me, that so much obscurity should hang over all attempts to explain the fact of our seeing objects single when there are two pictures of an object, one on each retina: for upon examination of the only reason why we distinguish one object from another in any case, it may be plainly perceived, that it entirely arises on account of a colour *different* from that of the object itself *forming a line of demarcation around its edges*; and that therefore, it would be impossible in the nature of things, but that two or twenty, or any number of objects painted upon as many retinas could be seen other than single, provided *the same line of demarcation alone is painted on them*. For what is it makes the visual figure of an object, but a line of demarcation between it and some surrounding object of another colour?

Now, when the sense of colour is precisely the same, however often repeated, (if the repetition be but at one and the same moment of time), there can be *but the sense of that colour alone*; for there is *no line of demarcation presented* which can give the notion of two objects.

If there be more than one object painted upon each retina, as many will be perceived by the mind, because there will be a line of *demarcation painted between them*, but there cannot be duplicates of these perceived; because although upon each retina there is painted a line of demarcation between two or more objects, and so the same is presented to the mind; yet *there is no line of demarcation presented between the duplicates*, which could possibly render four or more objects to the mind.

If that circumstance which alone forms a *sense* of the distinction of figure, is *not* presented upon *either retina*, how shall there be any means of its perception because there exists two retinas?

The puzzle arises from our conceiving in the imagination of the space between the eyes, existing between the images of the two objects; but this space and the figure of it does not present itself upon the retina. The two objects on the retinas, can only then have the nature of a superposition of figure; the feeling to the mind is one, and the line of demarcation which shows figure can be but one.

On the other hand, when a different mass of colouring is painted upon the two retinas, objects may be seen as two or more though single; *because there will necessarily appear to the mind some extra colouring between edges of the figures*, which is the only circumstance as has been said, that gives the idea of two figures of a similar kind. Dr. Reid has employed a great deal of reasoning to show *first*, that where objects are painted upon what he terms *corresponding points of the retina*, there is single vision; and when upon points which do not correspond there is double vision;—and secondly, to resolve the connection of these facts into '*an original law of our constitution*'. Now it is evident from what I have said, that when objects are painted upon corresponding points,—that is, a similar point of colouring taken as a centre in each retina;—it is a *law*, (as it is called), i.e. it is in the very nature of things, not of our constitution, that they must appear to be single—because the circumstance which can at any time present two similar figures does not take place, namely, the presentation of *extra colouring* between the edges of the two figures. If for instance, in any ordinary case, without reflecting upon the retinas, and the painting of images on them, two black spots are seen, they will appear thus (••), that is an interval of a different colouring will appear between the two spots; but if 500 spots are painted of the same colour, upon as many retinas, without such an interval of different colour between them, upon *any* of the retinas, there can only be seen one spot, for then the *effect,* the sense of two spots cannot take place, because the *cause,* i.e. the different colouring between them, does not take place.

A similar mistake as to the simplicity of the phenomena takes place when the mystery is presented of objects being painted inverted on the retina, and yet seen as erect; there appears a contradiction in nature, that on the one hand, the painting on the retina should be the cause of vision, and represent the relative position of external objects as they exist to the touch, and yet the printing of these objects be a variety from that relative position. Now the real fact is, the painting of objects, though they be inverted, does not alter the painting of their *relative* positions; the *whole* colouring of *all* within the sphere of vision, maintains precisely the same position of things towards each other: but it is the appearance of an *opposite* position of things, i.e. an opposition of the relative colouring of things, which only can yield the idea of inversion of images: — Thus a candle would appear to be *topsy turvey* upon a table, if the flame appeared to touch the table, and the bottom of the candlestick pointed upwards towards the ceiling; but if the bottom of the candlestick maintains its relative position to the table, and the flame the same relative position to the heavens, and the table the same to the earth, and the earth the same to the table; then the *whole,* — from the earth to the heavens, being painted in an inverted position upon the retina, cannot possibly occasion any sense of inversion of images; — because the sense of the soul must be to perceive the whole relative position of objects, precisely in that relation of parts they appear to have to touch and motion.

Dr. Reid says, 'When I hold my walking-stick in my hand and *look* at it, I take it for granted, that I *see* and *handle* the same individual object; when I say that I *feel* it erect, my meaning is, that I feel the head directed from the horizon, and the point directed towards it; and when I say that I *see* it erect, I mean that I *see* it with the head directed from the horizon, and the point directed towards it. I conceive the horizon as a *fixed* object both of sight and touch, *with relation to which* objects are said to be high or low, erect or inverted, and when the question is asked, Why I see the object erect and not inverted? it is the same as to ask, Why I see it in that position it really hath? or, why the eye shows the real position of objects, and doth not show them in an inverted position?' The whole answer is too long to quote, it may be seen, sec. 12, chap. 6, of 'Inquiry into the Human Mind'.[1]

Suffice it to say, that it is an ingenious labour to account for a *fact* not appearing as a contradiction to nature, which fact never takes place—namely, '*that the (visible) horizon is taken as a fixed place in relation to which objects are erect or inverted*'; for when the whole is within the sphere of vision, then the horizon is equally turned upon the retina; and the stick maintains on it the same relative position;—whilst the soul can only have the sense of one piece, (or canvass), of relative colouring, which upon motion, or touch being applied to the corresponding external varieties, will reply to those actions in the same relative proportions.

Selection N

('On the Causes of Single and Erect Vision', *The Philosophical Magazine and Annals of Philosophy* [1828], pp. 406–16.)

In order to understand aright the reason of single and erect vision, it is necessary first of all to perceive the truth of certain metaphysical positions in relation to vision, without the establishment of which, confused ideas, hypothetical assumptions, and inconclusive reasonings on optical experiments and facts are presented to the mind, and tend to embarrass the simplicity of that truth which might otherwise be immediately revealed.

First,—Vision is a consciousness in the mind, and its next proximate cause must be a power equal to its production, and which unites it to the material world.

Secondly,—Vision of *one colour only* can never yield the vision of figure, because the proximate cause of the vision of figure is a line of demarcation formed by the sensation of the junction of *two colours*.

---

1   [Shepherd refers to Thomas Reid, *An Inquiry Into the Human Mind on the Principles of Common Sense*, ed. Derek R. Brookes (University Park: Pennsylvania State University Press, 1997), hereafter cited as *Inquiry*, followed by chapter and section number, with page number. The passage she quotes (with minor alterations) is from Reid, *Inquiry* 6.11 (p. 119).]

Thirdly,—The physical impulse producing such conscious-ness of colouring, is an equal proportional variety upon the retina of an eye; one eye alone being first supposed, as it is truly efficient to yield the idea of figure.

Fourthly,—An object cannot be in two places at the same time.

Fifthly,—An object cannot exist and put forth its action *where it is not.*

These premises being supposed to be granted, let the question be asked, Why with two eyes given, two objects are not seen, although there be but one object given externally?

The answer (when supported by the foregoing premises, and conjoined with certain optical facts with which all, who are conversant with the subject, are acquainted) will be, *because there is not presented to the mind that variety of colouring which is necessary and alone efficient as the next proximate cause of vision; that is, there are not two lines of separate demarcation between two objects, but one line of demarcation only is presented, as in* ONE *eye supposed.* Should it be asked, whence is it that such a pro-portional variety is not presented to the mind? The answer which the premises and optical experiments equally support, is, *because the impulse upon each eye (when the axes of both are directed to the same point or object), being precisely alike, there is no variety of colouring painted upon either eye, equal to the production of that variety of perception, necessary to yield the ideas of two objects separated from each other, between their interior and horizontal edges.*

Let the letter A, for instance, be painted upon *one* eye, and the perception of its figure arises in the mind, from the points of distinction between the black letter and the white around it: there is a sense of difference created. Place it on similar points of two retinae, and each point of the figure painted on each retina will yield to the mind but *one* point of conscious black against *one* point of conscious white; and not *two* points of black against *two* points of white, because there is no intervening white painted on either retina, which can yield a consciousness of the separation of the two A's to a distance from each other, thus A—A.

The white space between the two A's is not painted on either retina. How then can any idea of it arise in the mind?

If, in order to render these ideas more intelligible, we analyse with still greater nicety the question, why we see duplicates of similar figures with *one* eye only supposed, it will at once appear obvious why we can perceive but *duplicates* of such figures, instead of *quadruplicates,* when *two* eyes are used.

Now if *one* eye should see but one colour only, it is supposed to be granted that there could be no sense of any defined figure whatever: one impulse therefore yields not figure.

If one and the same colour should be seen by two eyes, it must still be acknowledged there would be no figure: two *similar* impulses therefore cannot give the sense of figure to the mind. Now upon *one colour* (say a purple ground) painted upon one retina, mark a scarlet circle O; a sense of one figure will immediately arise from two varieties of colour being carried to the mind, viz. a line of demarcation to the purple ground by the scarlet circle: *two* impulses, or *two* varieties of colouring, are therefore necessary to the perception of *one* figure. Again, if with *one* eye given, I wish to see *two* scarlet circles upon the purple ground, what must I do? Will *four* impulses yield *two* similar figures? I answer, No. There must be *five* impulses in order to convey to the mind the sense of *two* figures: there must be $\begin{smallmatrix} & 2 & & 4 \\ ① & & ⑤ & ③ \\ & 5 & \end{smallmatrix}$; that is, the impression of the purple ground must be

repeated in *two* different parts of the sentient retina; *two* scarlet lines must be thence impelled, and these made obvious by *the intervening horizontal impulse between the circles;* for could the intervening space be absorbed, and each point of scarlet coalesce with each point of scarlet, and purple with purple, there would then be but *four* impulses of colouring, but *four* varieties, which would be inefficient to the observation of *two* figures. A coalescence of similar points of colour may perhaps produce a superposition or increment of colour, so as to create a superior brilliancy in the appearance of the object; but a *coalescence of points* cannot give a sense of *the separation of points.* Therefore for the mind to have a sense of *one* figure, there must be two consciousnesses of colour; and to have a sense of *two* figures, there must be *five* distinguishable consciousnesses of colour. However often *one* colour only be repeated, there will be no figure; however often *two* similar colours be repeated, (no intervening one being supposed), but *one* figure will arise; whilst to entertain a sense of *two* figures, *five* impulses are necessary. I hold it therefore as an axiom in the laws of vision, *that the repetition of similar impulsions of colour will not yield a number of figures equal to the number of such impulsions; but that the number of figures perceived, arises from those proportional intervals of the impulsions of colour, which must vary in a certain ratio to the number of figures impelled.*

However, therefore, the number of eyes may be multiplied, the mind can have no consciousness of any additional number of figures, whilst only similar impulsions of colour are yielded to it.

Let us enter into some further detail. If *one* scarlet circle on the purple ground be painted on the corresponding points of *two* retinae, and thence impelled to the mind, there can still only arise the sense of *one* scarlet circle; for there have existed but *four* physical varieties on the retinae, and but *four* varieties have been impelled to the mind: and it has been proved that *five* physical varieties are necessary to exist upon a retina, or upon retinae however numerous, in order to impel corresponding consciousnesses to the mind, and which would be necessary for the mental apprehension of *two* figures. Let the figures without an intervening horizontal colour be supposed to be marked thus, $\overset{2}{\underset{①}{}}\ \overset{}{\underset{0}{0}}\ \overset{4}{\underset{③}{}}$. The intervening horizontal colouring necessary to

separate the painting of *two* figures on the retinae, is not painted on either retina; *it does not exist;* and therefore no conscious separation of *two* figures can possibly arise to the mind. There exists indeed a certain space between the two eyes outwardly on the face, but the colouring of this intervening space is not painted on either retina, and therefore cannot be noticed by the mind; nor is there any intervening horizontal purple presented to the mind: Each point of scarlet does but coalesce with each point of scarlet, and each point of purple on *one* retina, with each point of the similar purple on the *other* retina; there is no surplus intervening purple on either retina, and it has been shown that 'repetitions of similar impressions of colour do not yield to the mind the sense of an equal number of figures'.

But should the scarlet circle be painted on points of the retinae which do *not* correspond, then there will necessarily arise the sense of *two* figures; because in that case dissimilar impulsions of colour are carried forward to the mind, and yield that proportional variety which determines the observation of conscious duplicates: for the pictures are then immediately painted upon different parts of their respective retinae, and the distance between two objects 'will be proportional to the arch of either retina, which lies between the picture on that retina, and the point corresponding to that of the picture on the other retina'.[2] On this intervening arch a surplus quantity of purple would be interiorly and horizontally painted, and would thence separate the two scarlet figures: *five* impulsions would carry *five* conscious colours to the mind, and *two* separated figures would immediately be observed.

An illustration of these ideas, and especially of this last statement of Dr. Reid's, might very easily be imagined, by conceiving two small terrestrial globes to be painted with precisely similar colours: Let them be rectified to the same degree of latitude and longitude, and similar colours only will appear on the visible surfaces of each; turn them both so many degrees to the east or west, still only similar colour will present themselves; but let one of the globes remain at rest, and turn the other any number of degrees of longitude to the west, a new country will arise to the east on the globe so moved, whose *variety* of colouring must necessarily prevent the notice of a *mere uniformity of colouring* on the two globes, and which variety will separate the appearance of any given country on them, '*proportionally to the number of degrees marked on the arch of the horizon*', through which the globe so moved had passed. Inspire the colouring on their surfaces with a simultaneous single sensibility, and it will immediately be perceived, that no consciousness of the existence of any two similar countries could arise, so long as the surfaces were regulated to the same degree of latitude and longitude; but the moment they were separated by an alteration of the longitude of either, or both, the sense of that newly arisen continent, or sea, would divide the sense of the remainder.

The following passage is extracted from the Encyclopedia Britannica, and is a quotation from Dr. Wells's Essay on Single Vision. 'If the question be concerning an object at the concourse of the optic axes, it is seen single; because its two similar

---

2   See Dr. Reid's Inquiry, ch. vi, sec. 13. [Shepherd refers to Reid, *Inquiry* 6.13 (pp. 132–7).]

appearances in regard to shape, size, and colour, coincide with each other through the whole of their extent.'[3]

This opinion thus expressed, comes nearer to my meaning than any other with which I am acquainted; nevertheless Dr. Wells's argument on the subject (and which is too long to insert here) is as fallacious as that of any of his predecessors; inasmuch as it assumes *an hypothetical law of vision,* in order to establish that *coincidence of shape, size, and colour* upon which the perceived single vision did necessarily depend.

This laborious argument of his, is as entirely needless as it is futile; because it proceeds upon the supposition that objects are *seen by the mind, beyond the mind,* at the angle formed by the axes of the eyes, in their direction to the same point of distance.

Now when, on the one hand, colour (conscious visible colour) is admitted to be *in* the mind, and never to proceed again *out* of it, in any line, or at any angle to form an object; and on the other hand, by those demonstrable laws of optics established by Sir I. Newton and others, 'that when the axes of the eyes are directed to a given point or figure, the said figure is painted on corresponding points of the retinae', — then the *coincidence* which Dr. Wells speaks of, must of necessity take place; and such coincidence can only determine a consciousness of single vision to the mind; or in other words, can only determine those similar appearances of colour, on which visible size and figure ultimately and alone depend: for the centres coincide with the centres, and the edges with the edges, of the figures; without any variety, or interval of colouring between the interior and horizontal edges, — the conscious sense of which is absolutely necessary in order to induce a *sense* of *variety* or plurality of figure. When the figure is painted upon points of the retinae which do not correspond, then there must necessarily arise a *sense of two figures;* because the centres *not coinciding* with the centres, nor the edges with the edges, *there exists a surplus colour* in one eye which divides the interior and horizontal edges of the two figures. This surplus colouring is

---

3 [Shepherd refers to 'Optics', *Encyclopedia Britannica,* vol. 15 (1823), pp. 171–295, which at pp. 225–6 quotes from and discusses William Charles Wells, *Two Essays: One Upon Single Vision with Two Eyes; the Other on Dew* (London: Printed for Archibald Constable and Co., 1818).]

determined to the retina by some exterior object, which by the shifting of the axis finds a place on which to paint its rays, 'and is equal to the arch between the picture of the given figure on that retina, and the point corresponding to that of the picture on the other retina'; and which surplus colouring must determine a proportional consciousness to the mind, observing thereby the same rule which determines the 'notice of two similar figures, when one eye only is used; ...*when the apparent distance of two objects seen with one eye is proportional to the arch of the retina which lies between their pictures'*, and on which an interval of colouring is necessarily painted, *but which circumstance Dr. Reid did not consider it material to notice.*[4]

The optical facts to which I have alluded are very shortly and very well expressed in Dr. Reid's 'Inquiry':[5] The passages in the chapter from which I have partially quoted, and which it may be as well to give entire, are the following; and I repose on them as stated facts, not containing either hypothesis, opinion, or reasoning.[6]

'First,—When the axes of both eyes are directed to one point, an object is seen single; and in this case the two pictures which show the objects single, are in the centres of the retinae. Now in this phenomenon it is evident that the two centres of the retinae are on corresponding points.

'Secondly,—Pictures of objects seen double, do not fall upon points of the retinae similarly situate with respect to the centres of the retinae.

'Thirdly,—The apparent distance of two objects seen with one eye, is proportioned to the arch of the retina which lies between their pictures: in like manner the apparent distance of two appearances seen with two eyes, is proportioned to the arch of either retina, which lies between the picture on that retina and the point corresponding to that of the picture on the other retina.'

---

4   See Dr. Reid's Inquiry, ch. vi, sect. 13. [Shepherd refers to Reid, *Inquiry* 6.13 (pp. 132–7). The quotation is from p. 136.]

5   Ibid.

6   [Shepherd condenses three of Reid's list of nine visual phenomena. The first passage Shepherd cites is at Reid, *Inquiry* 6.13 (p. 132); the second, at 6.13 (pp. 133–4); the third, at 6.13 (p. 136).]

These facts are valuable for many reasons; but on no account more so, than because they serve to explain the manner by which nature yields the knowledge of external tangible figure, and the proportional motion which in relation to it, by means of corresponding varieties of colour.

Dr. Reid's *arguments* (although he was in possession of these facts, which might have afforded premises for better reasoning) are altogether inconclusive, not to say puerile; and that on account of his steady adherence to the main object with which he set out upon his 'Inquiry', namely, to show upon the principles of *common sense* whence comes the knowledge we have of the existence of an external universe: Following up these principles, he placed *visible* figure beyond the body, at a distance from the perceiving mind, denying it to consist either in a sensation, impression, or idea, – and as possible to be *seen* without the intervention of colour.[7]

It appears to me strange, when contradiction is stamped upon the very expressions which convey these ideas, that Dr. Reid's notions should seem to be the data for the reasonings of the author of the '*Explanation of Erect and Single Vision*', published in the 'Library of Useful Knowledge'.[8]

I must however, in common honesty, here take notice of an objection which I have known to be made to the views I entertain on this subject: it is, 'that we see objects in different directions by either eye, when the other is alternately opened or closed'. This objection appears to me perfectly nugatory; when it is considered, that both eyes being opened together, they are allowed by the condition of the question to be *directed to one point*; in which case *neither* of them can be directed *to any point beyond that point*; it would be a contradiction in terms to admit it. The axes cannot *cross* each other, and look *at points beyond the*

---

[7]   See Dr. Reid's Inquiry, ch. vi, sect. 12, p. 135. 12mo. [Shepherd refers to Reid, *Inquiry* 6.12 (pp. 120–31).]

[8]   [Shepherd refers to Sir David Brewster, 'Optics', *Library of Useful Knowledge* (London: Baldwin and Cradock, 1827–8), chapter 17, section 2 (p. 42) and section 9 (p. 45). This was a biweekly publication on popular science produced by the Society for the Diffusion of Useful Knowledge. See Rosemary Ashton, 'Society for the Diffusion of Useful Knowledge', *Oxford Dictionary of National Biography* (May 2008), www.oxforddnb. com.]

given point, and that with a separate consciousness in the mind of so doing; for then these would not be merely *one* given point, but *three* given points; and the figure, the cause of whose single vision is in question, would be supposed to be placed, and at the same time supposed *not* to be placed, at the junction of the axes. For instance, when two eyes are directed to A, the left eye cannot be turned to B, look by itself at B, and the right eye at the same time be made to look by itself at C.

Experience shows this to be an impossibility; but when either eye is shut, the other may be moved in any direction we please. However, were I in error in this statement, the argument of my objector would by no means be conclusive against my doctrine of single vision, provided only that A be placed at the junction of the axes; for the utmost which could happen would be, that A plus B, plus C would appear to the mind; but *not* two A's (two B's and two C's), because there would still be only a super-position, or increment, of the colouring of A.

The central point of the colour of A would coincide on each retina; the whole of the rest of the colouring in relation to it would be painted on corresponding points, and coincide on their respective retinae; and there could in no wise arise that proportional variety of colour, painted between the interior horizontal edges of the two A's, which is necessary to yield the ideas of their separate figures.

But to return 'to the explanation of the Cause of Erect and Single Vision, published by the Society for the Diffusion of Useful Knowledge';[9] — it appears to me to be as much at variance with a sound, metaphysical, demonstrable conclusion concerning the nature of the perception of visible figure by the mind, as are the authors to whom I have alluded; and as much so with an acknowledged law, — with a proved physical fact, in respect to the *time* required for the motion of light.

---

9   Optics, part ii. 'Library of Useful Knowledge.' [Shepherd refers to Brewster, 'Optics', pp. 1-68.]

The author of the 'Explanation of the Cause of Erect and Single Vision', says:[10] 'As the lines of *visible direction* cross each other at the *centre* of visible direction, an erect object is the necessary result of an inverted image'; but this is not the same thing with THE PERCEPTION *of an erect object*. If it be said the word *perception* is understood though not expressed, then the mind is supposed to see the very erect object, out of itself, at a distance from itself; that is, the mind feels colour, perceives visible figure (its result), *there, where it is not,* which is impossible.

Again, it is a known fact, that the light emitted from the sun, employs about eight minutes in its journey to the earth. Now let an object be seen at that distance in an erect position, but the moment after its light is effused, let it be obliterated: the mind will still see it erect, eight minutes after its annihilation; how then shall it signify the drawing of any rays back through a centre, towards the place of an obliterated object, which *once* stood there erect? The author's explanation is little more than the very circumstance in question, re-stated by an inversion of words. 'An erect object (at a distance) is the result of an inverted image on the retina by the crossing of rays at a centre'; is merely saying over again, *that an inverted image on the retina is the result of an erect object at a distance,* when rays cross at a centre.

The question still remains untouched and unexplained; namely, why does the mind perceive an erect image, the result of an inverted image, which inverted image is the proximate cause of vision, and not the erect object which might be obliterated without affecting the mental consciousness of it? The only answer appears to me to be that, which I have formerly stated in my 'Essay on Single and Erect Vision'; viz. *'Inversion of figure is merely a* RELATIVE *quality: when all rays from every object within the sphere of vision become inverted on the retina, there truly can be no mental consciousness of any inversion whatever: for there is no relative variety by comparison with any other set of similar images; and they will necessarily bear a given relative proportion to the ideas of motion and tangibility: and which ideas,*

---

10 Ibid. [Shepherd quotes Brewster, 'Optics', chapter 17, section 2 (p. 42).]

taken collectively, include all the ELEMENTS *we have of the knowledge of the position, figure, and colour of objects'.*[11]

No doubt the relations of these in indefinite modifications are perceived by the judgment, as well as innumerable associations of them by the imagination; and thence the large use of vision in the world; thence the warm affections which are approved of by the understanding, or delighted in by the fancy.

But instead of taking this simple and easy mode of viewing the subject, philosophers, when they discuss the reason of erect vision, really suppose (although they may not be willing to allow it in so many words), that mental vision arises from, and is occupied about, *two* sets of objects at the same time; viz. the *external objects in nature*; and the *inverted images of them on the retina*: whereas the external object becomes virtually null and void immediately upon the rays of light being emitted from it.

The idea of inversion is the result of the comparison of the line of demarcation of one object with that of another of a similar kind placed in a contrary direction to it. But as in the picture on the retina, the line of demarcation of each particular image touches the line of demarcation of the rest, in the same manner and after the same proportion as their corresponding objects do in external nature; so no such comparison can take place: for *one* set of images only is painted, and these in precisely the same relative positions to each other as are their counterparts. The mind therefore necessarily perceives the same positions with respect to each other; for no *two* objects of a kind present themselves, by which a comparison can take place.

Philosophers, therefore, when they compare the image on the eye of an ox, for instance, with the object in external nature of which such image is the reflection, forget that both together make but one picture on their own eyes: For any given object forms on the human eye an inverted image, and the mind sees it erect; but the image on the eye of the ox (which is already inverted) makes on the eye of the person who observes it, an image again inverted that is erect, and the mind perceives it *inverted.*

---

[11] See 'Essays on the Perception of an External Universe', &c. by Lady Mary Shepherd. 1827. Essay, xiv. p. 408. [See p. 257 in this volume.]

In this latter case there is a comparison of the line of demarcation of one object with that of another of a similar kind, placed in a contrary direction to it. In the former case, *two* objects do not present themselves, but only *one* of a kind, and that surrounded by each and every line of demarcation, precisely in the same relations to each other as are those of external nature. The same observation holds good when drawings are used with two images on them, placed contrariwise to each other; as an arrow without the retina, and an arrow within the retina. Did the arrow within the retina *feel* along with the surrounding lines of colouring, there could be no *sense* of an inverted arrow; for there would exist no reference to another arrow, which reference is only made by the observer, who is looking on *two* arrows.

Observations analogous to these must be made on the attempted explanation 'of the cause of single vision', by the same author, who says,[12] 'Because the lines of visible direction from similar points of the image (on *one retina*) meet the lines of visible direction from similar points of the other *image* upon the *other retina*, each pair of similar points must be seen as *one* point.' How so, when the mind sees not *out* of itself *at the junction of the points*, and when if the object which sent forth the rays were annihilated, there would still result a *single vision from separated points of colour painted on* SEPARATED RETINAE *at a distance from each other*; such duplicate separate figures on the retinae being the proximate cause of the single vision of the object, and *not the junction of similar points*, when rays are drawn *back* again from the retinae to such points of junction.

The question still recurs, and is still untouched and unexplained; *Why are pairs of points perceived by the mind as single points?* No doubt the determination of rays upon the retinae in such a manner that when drawn back again they will meet at a central point, is a property closely connected with the method of vision; but it is rather *a corollary or consequence of the manner of the entry of the rays at the pupil of the eye* by which equal arches are subtended upon the retina, than the efficient cause of either *single* or *erect* vision. I again ask, Why are *two* objects on the retinae perceived as only *one* object by the mind? For it is *not a*

---

[12] Optics, part ii. 'Library of Useful Knowledge.' [Shepherd quotes Brewster, 'Optics', chapter 17, section 9 (p. 45).]

junction of *external* points which is perceived, but *two* sentient retinae determine two separate images (equally perfect in their form, equally brilliant in their colouring), as but *one* image to the mental capacity of perception. Is not the answer, *Because there are no points of colouring painted on either retina, by which the separation of their forms can be distinguished?*

Press the axis of either eye sufficiently to the right or left, a larger quantity of colouring will immediately be painted upon one retina than upon the other, which will separate their interior and horizontal edges, and *two* images will thence immediately and necessarily arise upon the perception of the mind.

I feel convinced that the more these ideas are contemplated, and the more clearly they are apprehended, the better will they serve to elicit the reason of several other phenomena concerning vision, which it has hitherto been considered difficult to explain; and what is of still greater importance, they may throw some light upon those which belong to every analogous operation of the human senses and intellect.

Index